Study Guide
Volume 1, Chapters 1–12

for use with

Fundamental Accounting Principles

Eighteenth Edition

Volume 1

John J. Wild
University of Wisconsin-Madison

Kermit D. Larson
University of Texas-Austin

Barbara Chiappetta
Nassau Community College

Prepared by
Barbara Chiappetta
Nassau Community College

 **McGraw-Hill Irwin**

*Boston   Burr Ridge, IL   Dubuque, IA   Madison, WI   New York   San Francisco   St. Louis
Bangkok   Bogotá   Caracas   Kuala Lumpur   Lisbon   London   Madrid   Mexico City
Milan   Montreal   New Delhi   Santiago   Seoul   Singapore   Sydney   Taipei   Toronto*

**McGraw-Hill
Irwin**

Study Guide, Volume 1, Chapters 1–12 for use with
FUNDAMENTAL ACCOUNTING PRINCIPLES
John J. Wild, Kermit D. Larson, and Barbara Chiappetta

Published by McGraw-Hill/Irwin, an imprint of The McGraw-Hill Companies, Inc., 1221 Avenue of the
Americas, New York, NY 10020. Copyright © 2007 by The McGraw-Hill Companies, Inc. All rights reserved.

1 2 3 4 5 6 7 8 9 0 QPD/QPD 0 9 8 7

ISBN-13: 978-0-07-326643-5
ISBN-10: 0-07-326643-4

www.mhhe.com

The *McGraw-Hill* Companies

TO THE STUDENT

This study guide is provided as a learning tool for your study of *Fundamental Accounting Principles* by John J. Wild, Kermit D. Larson, and Barbara Chiappetta. You should understand that the material provided is not intended to substitute for your textbook. Instead, the objectives of this guide are as follows:

1. To summarize important information that is explained in the text. For example, the **chapter outline** of each chapter identifies important topics in the chapter. In reading the outline, you should ask yourself whether or not you understand each of the topics listed. If not, you should return to the appropriate chapter in *Fundamental Accounting Principles* and read carefully the portions that explain the specific outlined topics about which you are unclear.

2. To provide you with copies of **visuals** that your instructor may use in class to introduce selected topics. Even if not used in class, these visuals serve as useful study tools.

3. To provide you with a quick means of testing your knowledge of the chapter. If you are unable to correctly answer the **problems** that follow the chapter outline, you should again return to the appropriate chapter in *Fundamental Accounting Principles* and review the sections about which you are unclear.

Your best approach to the use of this booklet out of class is:

- **First,** read the learning objectives and the related summary paragraphs. Then, ask whether your understanding of the chapter seems adequate for you to accomplish the objectives.

- **Second,** review the chapter outline, taking time to think through (describing to your self) the explanations that would be required to expand the outline. Use the notes column to indicate your questions or weaknesses. Return to *Fundamental Accounting Principles* to answer questions and cover areas of weakness.

- **Third**, review visuals if provided in the chapter. These will reinforce major concepts of the chapter.

- **Fourth,** answer the requirements of the problems that follow the chapter outline. Then, check your answers against the solutions that are provided after the problems.

- **Fifth,** return to *Fundamental Accounting Principles* for further study of any material you have not fully mastered.

You may also find it helpful to **bring outlines and visuals to class**. In class you can use a highlighter to mark areas your instructor emphasizes. Use the note section for additional notes and/or to indicate the numbers of relevant quick studies or exercises from the text that were worked in a notebook or on working papers during class. You can then refer back to these when studying with the outline later.

The next page is provided to recommend an **overall approach to succeeding** in an accounting course.

HOW TO SUCCEED IN YOUR ACCOUNTING COURSE

A.   Stay Up-To-Date

Accounting is a unique discipline in that learning takes place in "building blocks." The best analogy is that it is almost impossible to learn to read without learning the sounds of the letters in the alphabet. It is almost impossible for you to learn topics in accounting without having a level of understanding of the previously addressed topic. Accounting is the language of business, and like any language, it is learned through a developmental process.

Staying up-to-date includes completing all assignments on a timely basis. This allows you to take full advantage of classroom assignment check. The best insurance for staying up-to-date is to use good time management skills. This means plan a regular study schedule for the week—and stick to it! Staying up-to-date will give you the foundations to learn and *succeed!*

B.   Know How to Use Your Textbook

1.   Overview the chapter

a.   Preview the learning objectives and mark those that the instructor has listed in the course outline or mentioned in class.

b.   Read title page which provide a very brief look at chapter contents, as well as a look back and ahead. This allows you to see the links or building blocks you will put in place.

c.   Read the Summary of Learning Objectives found at the end of the chapter as well as in this study guide. This first pass on summaries is just to get a broad perspective of the contents. Do not expect to understand all that you read at this point.

2.   Read the chapter

a.   Using a highlighter as you read will keep you mentally alert. Writing is a proven vehicle for learning. Use the wide text margins to note key concepts as well as your questions. This will clarify your thoughts as you read.

b.   Use Quick Checks. These are brief questions interspersed throughout the chapter. Use them to check whether you are grasping essential concepts. Guidance answers are found at the end of the chapter.

c.   Reread the Summary of Learning Objectives. Make sure you thoroughly understand those specified by the instructor.

3.   Use the demonstration problems

Don't miss these! Students find these most helpful in learning how to solve accounting problems. They address all major topics of the chapter. An approach to planning the solution is offered. Complete solutions are also provided.

C.   Get Involved

1.   The more actively involved you are in the learning process, the more you will understand and retain. Ask questions that arose while you were reading the chapter. Fully participate in all classroom activities.

2.   Form a study group or a learning team. Meet regularly outside class. Support each other's learning. Teaching others is proven to be the most effective way of reinforcing your learning and increasing your retention. All students benefit from collaborating in the learning process.

TABLE OF CONTENTS

Learning Objective C1:

Explain the purpose and importance of accounting in the information age.

Summary

Accounting is an information and measurement system that aims to identify, record, and communicate relevant, reliable, and comparable information about business activities. It helps assess opportunities, products, investments, and social and community responsibilities.

Learning Objective C2:

Identify users and uses of accounting.

Summary

Users of accounting are both internal and external. Some users and uses of accounting include: (a) management for controlling, monitoring, and planning; (b) lenders for measuring the risk and return of loans; (c) shareholders for assessing the return and risk of stock; (d) directors for overseeing management; and (e) employees for judging employment opportunities.

Learning Objective C3:

Identify opportunities in accounting and related fields.

Summary

Opportunities in accounting include financial, managerial, and tax accounting. They also include accounting-related fields such as lending, consulting, managing, and planning.

Learning Objective C4:

Explain why ethics are crucial to accounting.

Summary

The goal of accounting is to provide useful information for decision making. For information to be useful, it must be trusted. This demands ethics behavior in accounting.

Learning Objective C5:

Explain the meaning of generally accepted accounting principles and define and apply several key accounting principles.

Summary

Generally accepted accounting principles are a common set of standards applied by accountants. Accounting principles aid in producing relevant, reliable and comparable information. The business entity principle means that a business is accounted for separately from other business entities including its owner(s). The objectivity principle means independent, objective evidence supports the information. The cost principle means financial statements are based on actual costs incurred. The monetary unit principle assumes transactions can be reflected in money terms. The going-concern principle means financial statements assume the business will continue. The revenue recognition principle means revenue is recognized when earned.

Learning Objective C6^B (Appendix B):

Identify and describe the three major activities in organizations.

Summary

Organizations carry out three major activities: financing, investing, and operating. Financing is the means used to pay for resources such as land, buildings, and machines. Investing refers to the buying and selling of resources used in acquiring and selling products and services. Operating activities are those necessary for carrying out of the organization's plans.

Learning Objective A1:

Define and interpret the accounting equation and each of its components.

Summary

The accounting equation is Assets = Liabilities + Equity. Assets are resources owned by a company. Liabilities are creditors' claims on assets. Equity is the owner's claim on assets *(the residual)*. The expanded accounting equation is Assets = Liabilities + [Owner Capital – Owner Withdrawals + Revenues – Expenses].

Learning Objective A2:

Analyze business transactions using the accounting equation.

Summary

A *transaction* is an exchange of economic consideration between two parties. Examples include products, services, money and rights to collect money. Transactions always have at least two effects on one or more components of the accounting equation. The equation is always in balance.

Learning Objective A3:

Compute and interpret return on assets.

Summary

Return on assets, also called return on investment is computed as net income divided by the average assets. For example, if we have an average balance of $100 in our savings account and it earns interest of $5 for the year, then our return on assets is $5/$100 or 5%.

Learning Objective A4^A (Appendix A):

Explain the relation between return and risk.

Summary

Return refers to income, and *risk* is the uncertainty about the return we hope to make. All investments involve risk. The lower the risk of an investment, the lower is its expected return. Higher risk implies higher, but riskier, expected return.

Learning Objective P1:

Identify and prepare basic financial statements and explain how they interrelate.

Summary

Four basic financial statements report on an organization's activities: balance sheet, income statement, statement of owner's equity, and statement of cash flows.

I. **Importance of Accounting**—it provides information about what businesses own, what they owe, and how they perform. Information is essential for decision makers.

   A. Accounting Activities
   Accounting is an information and measurement system that identifies, records and communicates relevant, reliable, and comparable information about an organizations business activities.

   B. Users of Accounting Information
   1. External Information Users—those not directly involved with running the company. Examples: shareholders (investors), lenders, customers, suppliers, regulators, lawyers, brokers, the press etc.
      a. Financial Accounting—area of accounting aimed at serving external users by providing them with *general-purpose financial statements*.
      b. General-Purpose Financial Statement—statements that have broad range of purposes which external users rely on.
   2. Internal Information Users—those directly involved in managing and operating an organization.
      a. Managerial Accounting—is the area of accounting that serves the decision-making needs of internal users.
      b. Internal Reports—not subject to same rules as external reports. They are designed with special needs of external users in mind.
   3. Internal Controls—procedures set up to protect company property and equipment, ensure reliable accounting reports, promote efficiency, and encourage adherence to company policies.

   C. Opportunities in Accounting
   Four broad areas of opportunities are financial, managerial, taxation, and accounting related.
   1. Private accounting offers the most opportunities.
   2. Public accounting offers the next largest number of opportunities
   3. Government (and not-for-profit) agencies, including business regulation and investigation of law violations also offer opportunities.

II. **Fundamentals of Accounting**—accounting is guided by principles, standards, concepts, and assumptions.

   A. Ethics—a key concept. Ethics are beliefs that distinguish right from wrong.

B. Generally Accepted Accounting Principles (GAAP)—concepts and rules that govern financial accounting. Purpose of GAAP is to make information in accounting statements relevant, reliable and comparable.

1. Setting Accounting Principles

   a. In U.S. major rule-setting bodies are the Securities and Exchange Commission (SEC) and the Financial Accounting Standards Board (FASB).

   b. The International Accounting Standards Board (IASB) issues standards that identifies preferred accounting practices in the global economy and hopes to create harmony among accounting practices in different countries.

2. Principles of Accounting—two types are *general* (concepts and guidelines for preparing financial statements) and *specific* (detailed rules used in reporting transactions). The principles discussed in this chapter are:

   a. *Objectivity principle*—financial statement information is supported by unbiased evidence not someone's opinion.

   b. *Cost principle*—financial statements are based on actual costs incurred in business transactions. Cost is measured on a cash or equal-to-cash basis.

   c. *Going-concern principle*—financial statements are to reflect the assumption that the business will continue operating instead of being closed or sold.

   d. *Monetary Unit*—transactions and events are expressed in monetary, or money, units. Generally this is the currency of the country in which it operates but today some companies express reports in more than one monetary unit.

   e. *Revenue Recognition*—revenue is recognized (recorded) when earned.

   f. *Business entity principle*—a business is accounted for separately from other business entities, including its owner.

3. Business Entity Forms

   a. *Sole proprietorship* is a business owned by one person that has unlimited liability. The business is not subject to an income tax but the owner is responsible for personal income tax on the net income of entity.

   b. *Partnership* is a business owned by two or more people, called partners, who are subject to unlimited liability. The business is not subject to an income tax, but the owners are responsible for personal income tax on their individual share of the net income of entity.

      c.   Three special partnership forms that limit liability

          i.   Limited partnership (LP)—has a general partner(s) with unlimited liability and a limited partner(s) with limited liability restricted to the amount invested.

          ii. Limited liability partnership (LLP)—restricts partner's liabilities to their own acts and the acts of individuals under their control.

          iii. Limited liability company (LLC)—offers the limited liability of a corporation and the tax treatment of a partnership.

      d. *Corporation* is a business that is a separate legal entity whose owners are called shareholders or stockholders. These owners have limited liability. The entity is responsible for a business income tax and the owners are responsible for personal income tax on profits that are distributed to them in the form of dividends.

    4. Sarbanes-Oxley—Law passed by congress that requires public companies to apply both accounting oversight and stringent internal controls to achieve more transparency, accountability and truthfulness in reporting.

III.   **Transactions Analysis and the Accounting Equation**

    A. Accounting equation (Assets = Liabilities + Equity)—elements of the equation include:

      1. Assets—resources owned or controlled by a company. (i.e. cash, supplies, equipment and land)

      2. Liabilities—creditors' claims on assets. These claims reflect obligations to transfer assets or provide products or services to others.

      3. Equity—owner's claim on assets. Also called *net assets* or *residual equity.*

    B. Changes in Equity—result from investments, revenues, withdrawals, expenses.

      1. Investments—assets an owner puts into the company results in increase in an equity. Recorded under the title *Owner, Capital.*

      2. Revenues—gross increases in equity resulting from a company's earning activities.

      3. Owner's withdrawals—assets an owner takes from the company for personal use (results in decrease in equity).

      4. Expenses—cost of assets or services used to earn revenues (results in decrease in equity).

    C. Expanded Accounting Equation:

      Assets = Liabilities + Owner's Capital – Owner's Withdrawal + Revenues – Expenses

    D. Transaction Analysis—each transaction and event always leaves the equation in balance. (Assets = Liabilities + Equity)

        1. Investment by owner =
+Asset (Cash) = + Owner's Equity (Owner's Name, Capital)
reason: investment
Increase on both sides of equation keeps equation in balance

        2. Purchased supplies for cash =
+Asset (Supplies) = – Asset (Cash)
Increase and decrease on one side of the equation keeps the equation in balance.

        3. Purchase equipment for cash =
+ Asset (Equipment) = – Asset (Cash)
Increase and decrease on one side of the equation keeps the equation in balance.

        4. Purchase supplies on credit =
+ Asset (Supplies) = + Liability (Account Payable)
Increase on both sides of equation keeps equation in balance.

        5. Provided services and facilities for cash =
+ Asset (Cash) = + Owner's Equity (reason: revenue earned)
Increase on both sides of equation keeps equation in balance.

        6. Payment of expense in cash (salaries, rent etc.) =
– Asset (Cash) = – Owner's Equity (reason: expense incurred)
Decrease on both sides of equation keeps equation in balance.

        7. Provided services for credit =
+ Asset (Accts Receivable) = + O E (reason: revenue earned)
Increase on both sides of equation keeps equation in balance.

        8. Receipt of cash from account receivable =
+ Asset (Cash) = – Asset (Accounts Receivable)
Increase and decrease on one side of the equation keeps the equation in balance.

        9. Payment of accounts payable =
–Asset (Cash) = – Liability (Accounts Payable)
Decrease on both sides of equation keeps equation in balance.

      10. Withdrawal of cash by owner =
–Asset (Cash) = – Equity (reason: owner's withdrawal)
Decrease on both sides of equation keeps equation in balance.

IV. **Financial Statements**

    A. The four financial statements and their purposes are:

        1. *Income Statement*—describes a company's revenues and expenses along with the resulting net income or loss over a period of time. (Net income occurs when revenues exceed expenses. Net loss occurs when expenses exceed revenues.)

        2. *Statement of Owner's Equity*—explains changes in equity from net income (or loss) and from owner investment and withdrawals over a period of time.

3. *Balance Sheet*—describes a company's financial position (types and amounts of assets, liabilities, and equity) at a point in time.

4. *Statement of Cash Flows*—identifies cash inflows (receipts) and cash outflows (payments) over a period of time.

B. Statement Preparation from Transaction Analysis—prepared in the following order using the *procedure* indicated below.

1. Income Statement—information about revenues and expenses is conveniently taken from the owner's equity column. Total revenues minus total expenses equals net income or loss. Notice that owner's withdrawals and investments are not part of measuring income or loss.

2. Statement of Owner's Equity—the beginning owner' equity is taken from the owner's equity column and any investments of owner are added. The net income, from the income statement is added (or the net loss is subtracted) and finally the owner's withdrawals are subtracted to arrive at the ending capital. Ending capital is carried to the Balance Sheet.

3. Balance Sheet—the ending balance of each asset is listed and the total of this listing equals total assets. The ending balance of each liability is listed and the total of this listing equals total liabilities. The ending capital (note that this is taken from the statement of changes in owner's equity), is listed and added to total liabilities to get total liabilities and owner's equity. This total must agree with total assets to prove the accounting equation. Either the *account form* or the *report form* may be used to prepare the balance sheet.

4. Statement of Cash Flows—the cash column must be carefully analyzed to organize and report cash flows in categories of operating, financing, and investing. The net change in cash is determined by combining the net cash flow in each of the three categories. This change is combined with the beginning cash. The resulting figure should be the ending cash that was shown on the balance sheet.

V. **Decision Analysis—Return on Assets (ROA)**—a profitability measure. Also called Return on Investment (ROI)

A. Useful in evaluating management, analyzing and forecasting profits, and planning activities.

B. The return on assets is: calculated by dividing net income for a period by average total assets. (Average total assets is determined by adding the beginning and ending assets and dividing by 2.)

C. As with all analysis tools, results should be compared to previous business results as well as competitor's results and industry norms.

Chapter Outline

VI. **Risk and Return Analysis—Appendix 1B**

    A. Risk—the uncertainty about the return we will earn on an investment.

    B. The lower the risk, the lower the return.

    C. Higher risk implies higher, but riskier implied returns.

VII. **Business Activities and the Accounting Equation—Appendix 1B**

    A. The accounting equation is derived from business activities.

    B. Three major business activities are:

       1. Financing activities—activities that provide the means organizations use to pay for resources such as land, buildings, and equipment to carry out plans. Two types of financing are:

          a. Owner financing—refers to resources contributed by owner including income left in the organization.

          b. Nonowner (or creditor) financing—refers to resources contributed by creditors (lenders).

       2. Investing activities—are the acquiring and disposing of resources (assets) that an organization uses to acquire and sell its products or services.

       3. Operating activities—involve using resources to research, develop, purchase, produce, distribute, and market products and services.

    C. Investing (assets) is balanced by Financing (liabilities and equity). Operating activities is the results of investing and financing.

WARNING: <u>NO MATTER WHAT HAPPENS</u>
ALWAYS KEEP THIS SCALE
IN BALANCE

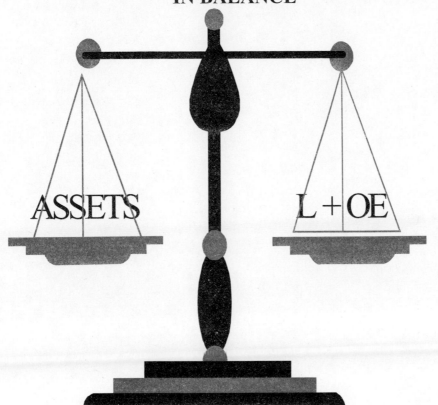

Basic Accounting Equation

ASSETS = LIABILITIES + OWNER'S EQUITY

TRANSACTION ANALYSIS RULES

1) Every transaction affects at least two items.
2) Every transaction must result in a balanced equation.

TRANSACTION ANALYSIS POSSIBILITIES:				
A	=	L	+	OE
(1) +	and		+	
OR(2) -	and		-	
OR(3) + and -	and		No change	
OR(4) No change	and		+ and -	

Problem I

The following statements are either true or false. Place a (T) in the parentheses before each true statement and an (F) before each false statement.

1. ( ) The return on equity ratio is calculated by dividing average owner's equity by net income.

2. ( ) Two businesses with the same owner must have separate accounting records.

3. ( ) Land appraised at $40,000 and worth that much to its purchaser should be recorded at its worth ($40,000), even though it was purchased through hard bargaining for $35,000.

4. ( ) The statement of cash flows shows a company's revenues, expenses, and net income or loss.

5. ( ) Net income + Owner investments - Owner withdrawals = The increase in owner's equity during the year.

Problem II

You are given several words, phrases, or numbers to choose from in completing each of the following statements or in answering the following questions. In each case select the one that best completes the statement, or answers the question, and place its letter in the answer space provided.

_____ 1. Financial statement information about Boom Company is as follows:

December 31, 2007:

Assets	$42,000
Liabilities	17,000

December 31, 2008:

Assets	47,000
Liabilities	14,800

During 2008:

Net income	18,000
Owner investments	?
Owner withdrawals	10,800

The amount of owner investments during 2008 is:

a. $ 7,200.

b. $14,400.

c. $25,000.

d. $ 0.

e. Some other amount.

_____ 2. The board that currently has the primary authority to identify generally accepted accounting principles is the:

a. APB.

b. FASB.

c. FEI.

d. ASB.

e. AICPA.

_____ 3. The business entity principle:

a. States that revenue should be recognized at the time it is earned; the inflow of assets associated with revenue may be in a form other than cash; and the amount of revenue should be measured as the cash plus the cash equivalent value of any noncash assets received from customers in exchange for goods or services.

b. Requires financial statements to reflect the assumption that the business will continue operating instead of being closed or sold, unless evidence shows that it will not continue.

c. States that every business should be accounted for separately and distinctly from its owner or owners.

d. Requires the financial statements to present information based on costs incurred in business transactions; it requires assets and services to be recorded initially at the cash or cash-equivalent amount given in exchange.

e. Is another name for the going-concern principle.

_____ 4. Properties or economic resources owned by a business, or probable future economic benefits obtained or controlled by a particular entity as a result of past transactions or events, are called:

a. Dividends.

b. Assets.

c. Retained earnings.

d. Revenues.

e. Owner's equity.

_____ 5. If on January 16, 2007, Kay Bee Company rendered services for a customer in exchange for $175 cash, what would be the effects on the accounting equation?

a. Assets, $175 increase; Liabilities, no effect; Owner's Equity, $175 increase.

b. Assets, no effect; Liabilities, $175 decrease; Owner's Equity, $175 increase.

c. Assets, $175 increase; Liabilities, $175 increase; Owner's Equity, no effect.

d. Assets, $175 increase; Liabilities, $175 decrease; Owner's Equity, $350 increase.

e. There is no effect on the accounting equation.

Problem III

Many of the important ideas and concepts discussed in Chapter 1 are reflected in the following list of key terms. Test your understanding of these terms by matching the appropriate definitions with the terms. Record the number identifying the most appropriate definition in the blank space next to each term.

_____	Accounting	_____	Liabilities
_____	Accounting equation	_____	Managerial accounting
_____	Assets	_____	Monetary unit principle
_____	Audit	_____	Net income
_____	Balance sheet	_____	Net loss
_____	Bookkeeping	_____	Objectivity principle
_____	Business entity principle	_____	Owner investment
_____	Common stock	_____	Owner withdrawal
_____	Corporation	_____	Partnership
_____	Cost principle	_____	Proprietorship
_____	Equity	_____	Recordkeeping
_____	Ethics	_____	Return
_____	Events	_____	Return on assets
_____	Expanded accounting equation	_____	Revenues
_____	Expenses	_____	Revenue recognition principle
_____	External transactions	_____	Risk
_____	External users	_____	Sarbanes-Oxley Act
		_____	Securities and Exchange Commission (SEC)
_____	Financial accounting		
_____	Financial Accounting Standards Board (FASB)	_____	Shareholders
_____	Generally Accepted Accounting Principles (GAAP)	_____	Shares
_____	Going-concern principle	_____	Sole proprietorship
_____	Income	_____	Statement of cash flows
_____	Income statement	_____	Statement of owner's equity
_____	Internal transactions	_____	Stock
_____	Internal users	_____	Stockholders
_____	International Accounting Standards Board (IASB)	_____	Withdrawals

1. An information and measurement system that identifies, records, and communicates relevant information about a company's business activities.

2. The rules that specify acceptable accounting practice.

3. Persons using accounting information who are not directly involved in running the organization.

4. A business owned by two or more people that is not organized as a corporation.

5. The federal agency created by Congress in 1934 to regulate securities markets, including the flow of information from companies to the public.

6. The recording of financial transactions and events, either manually or electronically (also called bookkeeping).

7. An analysis and report of an organization's accounting systems and records using various tests.

8. A financial statement that lists the types and dollar amounts of assets, liabilities, and equity as of a specific date; also called the *statement of financial position*.

9. Arises when expenses are more than sales.

10. The accounting principle that requires financial statement information to be based on actual costs incurred in business transactions.

11. A principle that assumes transactions and events can be expressed in money units.

12. Codes or conduct by which actions are judged as right or wrong, fair or unfair, honest or dishonest.

13. The owners of a corporation (also called shareholders).

14. A business owned by one individual that is not organized as a corporation (also called a proprietorship).

15. A business that is a separate legal entity under state or federal laws with owners that are called shareholders or stockholders.

16. Accounting principle that provides guidance as to when revenue must be recognized..

17. The principle that requires a business be accounted for separately from its owner(s).

18. A financial statement that lists cash inflows (receipts) and cash outflows (payments) during a period; arranged by operating, investing, and financing activities.

19. Resources expected to produce future benefits.

20. Creditor's claims on an organization's assets.

21. A principle that requires financial statements to reflect the assumption that the business will continue operating; also called the continuing concern principle.

22. The income from an investment.

23. The owner's claims on an organization's assets.

24. The equality where Assets = Liabilities + Owner's Equity.

25. The amount of uncertainty about an expected return.

26. Ownership of a corporation divided into units.

27. The financial statement that subtracts expenses from revenues to yield a net income or loss over a specified period of time.

28. Persons using accounting information who are directly involved in managing and operation an organization; examples include managers and officers.

29. A board that identifies preferred accounting practices and encouraging their worldwide acceptance.

30. A report of changes in equity over a period of time; adjusted for increases (owner investment and net income) and for decreases (withdrawals and net loss).

31. The amount a business earns after subtracting all expenses necessary for its sales (also called profit).

32. The accounting guideline that requires financial statement information be supported by independent, unbiased evidence.

33. A ratio serving as an indicator of operating efficiency; defined as net income divided by average total assets.

34. A payment of cash or other assets from a proprietorship or partnership to its owner or owners.

35. The area of accounting aimed at serving the decision-making needs of internal users.

36. The costs incurred to earn sales.

37. The area of accounting aimed at serving external users.

38. A part of accounting that involves recording transactions and events, either electronically or manually (also called recordkeeping).

39. The amounts earned from selling products or services (also called sales).

Fundamental Accounting Principles, 18/e

40. An independent group of seven full-time members who are currently responsible for setting accounting rules.

41. The owners of a corporation (also called stockholders).

42. Happenings that both affect an organization's financial position and can be reliably measured.

43. Exchanges within an organization that can also affect the accounting equation.

44. Exchanges of economic consideration between one entity and another.

45. Assets = Liabilities + Equity where Equity equals [Owner capital – Owner withdrawals + Revenues – Expenses].

46. Amount earned after subtracting all expenses necessary for and matched with sales for a period; also called *income, profit,* or *earnings*.

47. Assets put into the business by the owner.

48. Passed by congress to help curb financial abuses at companies that issue their stock to the public.

49. The name given to stock when a corporation only issues one class.

50. Assets an owner takes from the company for personal use.

Problem IV

Complete the following by filling in the blanks.

1. The cost principle requires financial statement information to be based on _____ incurred in business transactions. The _____ principle requires financial statements to reflect the assumption that the business will continue operating instead of being closed or sold. The _____ principle requires financial statement information to be supported by evidence other than someone's opinion or imagination.

2. Under the _____ principle every business is to be accounted for as a separate entity separate and distinct from its _____ or _____.

3. Assets created by selling goods and services on credit are called _____.
    Liabilities created by buying goods and services on credit are called _____.

4. Equity on a balance sheet is the difference between a company's _____ and its _____.

5. The statement of changes in owner s equity discloses all changes in equity during the period including _____, _____, and _____.

6. The balance sheet equation is _____ equals _____ plus _____. It is also called the _____ equation.

7. Probable future sacrifices of economic benefits arising from present obligations of a particular entity to transfer assets or provide services to other entities in the future as a result of past transactions or events are called _____.

8. An excess of revenues over expenses for a period results in a _____. An excess of expenses over revenues results in a _____. The financial statement that lists revenues and expenses is the _____.

9. A balance sheet prepared for a business shows its financial position as of a specific _____.
    Financial position is shown by listing the _____ of the business, its _____, and its _____.

10. Expenses are outflows or the _____ of assets as a result of the major or central operations of a business.

11. Individuals or organizations entitled to receive payment from a company are called _____ and those owing money to a business are called _____.

12. The statement of cash flows shows the events that caused _____ to change. It classifies the cash flow into three major categories: _____, _____, and _____ activities.

Problem V

The assets, liabilities, and owner's equity of Linda Cornell's law practice are shown on the first line in the equation in the table on the following page. Below you will find eight transactions completed by Ms. Cornell. Show by additions and subtractions in the spaces provided in the table, the effects of each transaction on the items of the equation. Show new totals after each transaction as in Exhibit 1-9, page 17 in the text.

1. Paid the rent for three months in advance on the law office, $3,000.
2. Paid cash to purchase a new typewriter for the office, $900.
3. Completed legal work for Ray Holland and immediately collected the full payment of $2,500 in cash.
4. Purchased law books on credit, $700.
5. Completed $1,500 of legal work for Julie Landon on credit, and immediately entered in the accounting records both the right to collect and the revenue earned.
6. Paid for the law books purchased in Transaction 4.
7. Received $1,500 from Julie Landon for the legal work in Transaction 5.
8. Paid the weekly salary of the office secretary, $575.

Refer to your completed equation table and fill in the blanks:

a. Did each transaction affect two items of the equation? _____

b. Did the equation remain in balance after the effects of each transaction were entered? _____

c   If the equation had not remained in balance after the effects of each transaction were entered, this would have indicated that _____.

d. Ms. Cornell earned $2,500 of revenue upon the completion of Transaction 3, and the asset that flowed into the business as a result of this transaction was in the form of _____.

e. Ms. Cornell earned $1,500 of revenue upon the completion of Transaction 5, and the asset that flowed into the business upon the completion of this transaction was _____.

f. The right to collect $1,500 from Julie Landon was converted into _____ in Transaction 7. Nevertheless, the revenue was earned upon the completion of the _____ in Transaction 5.

g. The $1,500 collected in Transaction 7 was recognized as revenue in Transaction 5 because of the _____ principle, which states that (1) revenue should be recognized at the time it is _____; (2) the inflow of assets associated with revenue may be in a form other than _____; and (3) the amount of revenue should be measured as the cash plus the cash equivalent value of any _____ received from customers in exchange for goods or services.

Problem V Table

#	Cash	+	Accounts Receivable	+	Prepaid Rent	+	Law Library	+	Office Equipment	=	Accounts Payable	+	L Cornell, Capital	−	L. Cornell, Withdrawals	+	Revenues	−	Expenses
	$4,000						$12,000		$3,250				$19,250						
1																			
2																			
3																			
4																			
5																			
6																			
7																			
8																			

ASSETS   LIABILITIES   EQUITY

Solutions for Chapter 1

Problem I

1. F
2. T
3. F
4. F
5. T

Problem II

1. D
2. B
3. C
4. B
5. A

Problem III

1	Accounting		20	Liabilities
24	Accounting equation		35	Managerial accounting
19	Assets		11	Monetary unit principle
7	Audit		31 or 46	Net income
8	Balance sheet		9	Net loss
38	Bookkeeping		32	Objectivity principle
17	Business entity principle		47	Owner investment
49	Common stock		34	Owner withdrawal
15	Corporation		4	Partnership
10	Cost principle		14	Proprietorship
23	Equity		6	Recordkeeping
12	Ethics		22	Return
42	Events		33	Return on assets
45	Expanded accounting equation		39	Revenues
36	Expenses		16	Revenue recognition principle
44	External transactions		25	Risk
3	External users		48	Sarbanes-Oxley Act
37	Financial accounting		5	Securities and Exchange Commission (SEC)
40	Financial Accounting Standards Board (FASB)		41	Shareholders
2	Generally Accepted Accounting Principles (GAAP)		26	Shares
21	Going-concern principle		14	Sole proprietorship
46 or 31	Income		18	Statement of cash flows
27	Income statement		30	Statement of owner's equity
43	Internal transactions		26	Stock
28	Internal users		13	Stockholders
29	International Accounting Standards Board (IASB)		50	Withdrawals

Problem IV

1. costs; going-concern; continuing concern; objectivity
2. business entity; owner; owners
3. accounts receivable; accounts payable
4. assets; liabilities
5. net income or net loss; new investments by the owner; withdrawals
6. Assets; Liabilities; Owner's Equity; accounting
7. liabilities
8. net income (profit); net loss; income statement
9. date; assets; liabilities; equity
10. using up (consuming)
11. creditors; debtors
12. cash, operating; investing; financing

Problem V

	Cash	+	Accounts Receivable	+	Prepaid Rent	+	Law Library	+	Office Equipment	=	Accounts Payable	–	L. Cornell, Capital	–	L. Cornell, Withdrawals	+	Revenues	–	Expenses
	$4,000						$12,000		$3,250				$19,250						
1.	-3,000				+3,000														
	$1,000				$3,000		$12,000		$3,250				$19,250						
2.	-900								+900										
	$100				$3,000		$12,000		$4,150				$19,250						
3.	+2,500																+$2,500		
	$2,600				$3,000		$12,000		$4150				$19,250				$2,500		
4.							+700				+700								
	$2,600				$3,000		$12,700		$4,150		$700		$19,250				$2,500		
5.			+1,500														1,500		
	$2,600		$1,500		$3,000		$12,700		$4,150		$700		$19,250				$4,000		
6.	-700										-700								
	$1,900		$1,500		$3,000		$12,700		$4,150		$700		$19,250				$4,000		
7.	+1,500		-1,500								$0						$4,000		
	$3,400		$0		$3,000		$12,700		$4,150		$0		$19,250				$4,000		
8.	-575																		575
	$2,825+		$0+		$3,000+		$12,700+		$4,150=		$0+		$19,250–		$0+		$4,000–		$575

a. Yes

b. Yes

c. an error had been made

d. cash

e. an account receivable

f. cash; legal work

g. revenue recognition (or realization); earned; cash; noncash assets

CHAPTER 2
ANALYZING AND RECORDING TRANSACTIONS

Learning Objective C1:

Explain the steps in processing transactions.

Summary

The accounting process identifies business transactions and events, analyzes and records their effects, and summarizes and prepares information useful in making decisions. Transactions and events are the starting points in the accounting process. Source documents help in their analysis. The effects of transactions and events are recorded in journals. Posting along with a trial balance help summarize and classify these effects.

Learning Objective C2:

Describe source documents and their purpose.

Summary

Source documents identify and describe transactions and events. Examples are sales tickets, checks, purchase orders, bills, and bank statements. Source documents provide objective and reliable evidence, making information more useful.

Learning Objective C3:

Describe an account and its use in recording transactions.

Summary

An account is a detailed record of increases and decreases in a specific asset, liability, equity, revenue, or expense. Information from accounts is analyzed, summarized, and presented in reports and financial statements for decision makers.

Learning Objective C4:

Describe a ledger and a chart of accounts.

Summary

A ledger (or general ledger) is a record containing all accounts used by a company and their balances. It is referred to as the *books*. The chart of accounts is a list of all accounts and usually includes an identification number assigned to each account.

Learning Objective C5:

Define *debits* and *credits* and explain their role in double-entry accounting.

Summary

Debit refers to left, and *credit* refers to right. Debits increase assets, withdrawals, and expenses, while credits decrease them. Credits increase liabilities, owner capital and revenues; debits decrease them. Double-entry accounting means each transaction affects at least two accounts and has at least one debit and one credit. The system for recording debits and credits follows from the accounting equation. The left side of an account is the normal balance for assets, withdrawals, and expenses , and the right side is the normal balance for liabilities, capital and revenues.

Learning Objective A1:

Analyze the impact of transactions on accounts and financial statements.

Summary

We analyze transactions using the concepts of double-entry accounting. This analysis is performed by determining a transaction's effects on accounts. These effects are recorded in journals and posted to ledgers.

Learning Objective A2:

Compute the debt ratio and describe its use in analyzing financial condition.

Summary

A company's debt ratio is computed as total liabilities divided by total assets. It reveals how much of the assets are financed by creditor (nonowner) financing. The higher this ratio, the more risk a company faces because liabilities must be repaid at specific dates.

Learning Objective P1:

Record transactions in a journal and post entries to a ledger.

Summary

Transactions are recorded in a journal. Each entry in a journal is posted to the accounts in the ledger. This provides information that is used to produce financial statements. Balance column accounts are widely used and include columns for debits, credits, and the account balance.

Learning Objective P2:

Prepare and explain the use of a trial balance.

Summary

A trial balance is a list of accounts from the ledger showing their debit or credit balances in separate columns. The trial balance is a summary of the ledger's contents and is useful in preparing financial statements and revealing recordkeeping errors.

Learning Objective P3:

Prepare financial statements from business transactions.

Summary

The balance sheet, the statement of owner's equity, the income statement, and the statement of cash flows use data from the trial balance (and other financial statements) for their preparation.

I.   **Analyzing and Recording Process—steps include:**

   A.   Analyzing each transaction and event from *source documents*. *Source documents* are *business papers* that identify and describe economic events and transactions. Examples: sales tickets, checks, purchase orders, bills, and bank statements. Source documents provide objective and reliable evidence about transactions and events.

   B.   Record relevant transactions and events in a *journal*.

   C.   Post journal information to ledger *accounts*.

   D.   Prepare and analyze the *trial balance*.

II.   **The Account and its Analysis**

   A.   An *account* is a record of increases and decreases in a specific asset, liability, equity, revenue, or expense item.

   B.   Accounts are arranged into three basic categories based on the accounting equation. Categories are:

      1.   *Assets*—resources owned or controlled by a company that have future economic benefit. Examples include Cash, Accounts Receivable, Note Receivable, Prepaid Expenses, Prepaid Insurance, Office Supplies, Store Supplies, Equipment, Buildings, and Land.

      2.   *Liabilities*—claims (by creditors) against assets, which means they are obligations to transfer assets or provide products or services to other entities. Examples include Accounts Payable, Note Payable, Unearned Revenues, and Accrued Liabilities.

         a.   Unearned revenue—revenue collected before it is earned; before services or goods are provided.

         b.   Accrued liabilities—amounts owed that are not yet paid.

      3.   *Equity*—owner's claim on company's assets is called *equity* or *owner's equity*. Examples include Owner's Capital, Owner's Withdrawals (decreases in equity), and different kinds of revenue (increases in equity) and expense (decreases in equity) accounts reflecting their own important activities.

III.   **Analyzing and Processing Transactions**

   A.   The *general ledger* or *ledger* (referred to as the *books*) is a record containing all the accounts a company uses.

   B.   The *chart of accounts* is a list of all the accounts in the ledger with their identification numbers.

   C.   A *T-account* represents a ledger account and is a tool used to understand the effects of one or more transactions. Has shape like the letter T with account title on top.

IV.   Debits and Credits

    A. The *left* side of an account is called the *debit* side. A debit is an entry on the left side of an account.

    B. The *right* side of an account is called the *credit* side. A credit is an entry on the right side of an account.

    C. Accounts are *assigned balance sides* based on their classification or type.

    D. To *increase* an account, an amount is placed on the *balance side,* and to *decrease* an account, the amount is placed on the *side opposite its assigned balance side.*

    E. The *account balance* is the difference between the total debits and the total credits recorded in that account. When total debits exceed total credits the account has a debit balance. When total credits exceed total debits the account has a credit balance. When two sides are equal the account has a zero balance.

V.   Double-Entry Accounting—requires that each transaction affect, and be recorded in, at least two accounts. The total debits must equal total credits for each transaction.

    A. The assignment of balance sides (debit or credit) follows the accounting equation.

        1. *Assets* are on the *left side* of the equation; therefore, the left, or *debit,* side is the normal balance for assets.

        2. *Liabilities and equities* are on the *right side;* therefore, the right, or credit, side is the normal balance for liabilities and equity.

        3. *Withdrawals, revenues, and expenses* really are changes in equity, but it is necessary to set up temporary accounts for each of these items to accumulate data for statements. Withdrawals and expense accounts really represent decreases in equity; therefore, they are assigned debit balances. *Revenue* accounts really represent increases in equity; therefore, they are assigned credit balances.

    B. Three important rules for recording transactions in a double-entry accounting system are:

        1. Increases to assets are debits to the asset accounts. Decreases to assets are credits to the asset accounts.

        2. Increases to liabilities are credits to the liability accounts. Decreases to liabilities are debits to the liability accounts.

        3. Increases to equity are credits to the equity accounts. Decreases to equity are debits to the equity accounts.

VI.   Journalizing and Posting Transactions

    A. Four steps in processing transactions are as follows:

    Journalizing--The process of recording each transaction in a journal.

       1. Analyze transaction and source documents.

       2. Apply double-entry accounting. (Determine account to be debited and credited.)

       3. Journalize—record each transaction in a journal. (A journal gives us a complete record of each transaction in one place.)

         a. A *General Journal* is the most flexible type of journal because it can be used to record any type of transaction.

         b. When a transaction is recorded in the General Journal, it is called a *journal entry*. A journal entry that affects more than two accounts is called a compound journal entry.

         c. Each journal entry must contain equal debits and credits.

       4. Posting—transfer (or *post*) each entry from journal to ledger.

         a. Debits are posted as debit, and credits as credits to the accounts identified in the journal entry.

         b. Actual accounting systems use *balance column accounts* rather than T-accounts in the ledger.

         c. A *balance column account* has debit and credit columns for recording entries and a third column for showing the balance of the account after each entry is posted.

Note: To see an illustration of analyzing, journalizing and posting of 16 basic transactions refer to pages 57-61 of the textbook.

VII. Trial Balance

    A. A *trial balance* is a list of accounts and their balances at a point in time.

    B. The purpose of the trial balance is to summarize the ledger accounts to simplify the task of preparing the financial statements. It also tests for the equality of the debit and credit account balances as required by double-entry accounting.

    C. Three steps to prepare a trial balance are as follows:

       1. List each account and its amount (from the ledger).

       2. Compute the total debit balances and the total credit balances.

       3. Verify (prove) total debit balances equal total credit balances.

    D. When a trial balance does not balance (the columns are not equal), an error has occurred in one of the following steps:

       1. Preparing the journal entries.

       2. Posting the journal entries to the ledger.

       3. Calculating account balances.

4. Copying account balances to the trial balance.

5. Totaling the trial balance columns.

(*Note*: Any errors must be located and corrected before preparing the financial statements. Financial Statements prepared from the trial balance are actually *unadjusted* statement. The purpose, content and format for each statement was presented in Chapter 1. The next chapter will address adjustments)

E. Correcting Errors

1. Approach to correcting errors depends on the kind of error and when it is discovered.

2. Correcting entries may be necessary.

F. Presentation Issues

1. Dollar signs are not used in journals and ledgers but do appear in financial statements.

2. Common practice on statements is to put dollar signs before the first number in each column and before any number after a ruled line.

VIII. **Decision Analysis—Debt Ratio:**

A. Companies finance their assets with either liabilities or equity.

B. A company that finances a relatively large portion of its assets with liabilities has a high degree of financial leverage.(greater risk)

C. The debt ratio describes the relationship between a company's liabilities and assets. It is calculated as total liabilities divided by total assets.

D. The debt ratio tells us how much (what percentage) of the assets are financed by creditors (non-owners), or liability financing. The higher this ratio, the more risk a company faces, because liabilities must be repaid and often require regular interest payments.

THREE PARTS OF AN ACCOUNT

(1) ACCOUNT TITLE	
Left Side called (2) DEBIT	Right Side called (3) CREDIT

Rules for using accounts

Accounts are <u>assigned</u> <u>balance</u> sides (Debit or Credit).

To <u>increase</u> any account, use the balance side.

To <u>decrease</u> any account, use the <u>side opposite</u> the balance.

Finding account balances

If total debits = total credits, the account balance is zero.

If total <u>debits are greater</u> than total credits, the account has a <u>debit</u> <u>balance</u> equal to the differencc of the two totals.

If total <u>credits are greater</u> than total debits, the account has a <u>credit balance</u> equal to the difference of the two totals.

<u>REAL ACCOUNTS</u>

<u>ALL</u> ACCOUNTS ARE <u>ASSIGNED</u> BALANCE SIDES

BALANCE SIDES FOR ASSETS, LIABILITIES, AND
EQUITY ACCOUNTS ARE ASSIGNED BASED ON
SIDE OF <u>EQUATION</u> THEY ARE ON.

ASSETS	=	LIABILITIES + EQUITY

are on the
<u>left</u> side of the equation
therefore they are

are on the
<u>right</u> side of the equation
therefore they are

ASSIGNED LEFT SIDE
BALANCE

ASSIGNED RIGHT SIDE
BALANCE

DEBIT BALANCE	CREDIT BALANCE

<u>All Asset Accts</u>
Normal
Debit | Credit
Balance
+ side | - side

<u>All Liability Accts</u>
Normal
Debit | Credit
Balance
- side | + side

<u>All Equity Accts</u>
Normal
Debit | Credit
Balance
- side | + side

*In a sole proprietorship, there is only one equity account, which is called capital. For that reason, the terms equity and capital are often used interchangeably. (When corporations are discussed in detail, you will learn many stockholders' equity accounts.) Equity is an account classification like assets. Owner's Name, Capital, is the account title.

TEMPORARY ACCOUNTS

Temporary accounts are established to facilitate efficient accumulation of data for statements. Temporary accounts are established for withdrawals, <u>each</u> revenue, and <u>each</u> expense. *Temporary accounts are assigned balances <u>based</u> on how they affect equity.*

(Equity Account)

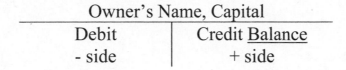

Owner's Name, Capital

Debit	Credit <u>Balance</u>
- side	+ side

Temporary Accounts	Effect on equity? ↑E or ↓E
Owner, Withdrawals*	↓ E = Dr
Revenues	↑ E = Cr
Expenses	↓ E = Dr

<u>All Withdrawal Accts</u>

Normal Debit Balance + side	Credit - side

<u>All Revenue Accts</u>

Debit - side	Normal Credit Balance + side

<u>All Expense Accts</u>

Normal Debit Balance + side	Credit - side

Note:

Transactions <u>during</u> the period always <u>increase</u> the balances of these <u>temporary</u> accounts since the transaction represent <u>additional</u> withdrawals, revenues, and expenses. We will later learn how to move these amounts <u>back</u> to the <u>real</u> account they affect → <u>CAPITAL</u>. At the end of the accounting period, transferring withdrawals, revenues, and expenses back to capital is the main use for the decrease side of the temporary accounts.

*The "Owner's Name, Withdrawals" is the account title and the <u>classification</u> of account is a contra-equity.

USING ACCOUNTS - SUMMARY

Real Accounts

All Asset Accts	All Liability Accts	All Equity Accts
Debit + Balance —	— Credit + Balance	— Credit + Balance

RULE REVIEW

Transaction analysis rules
- Each transaction affects at least 2 accounts.
- Each transaction must have equal debits and credits.

General account use rules
- To increase any account, use balance side.
- To decrease any account, use side opposite the balance

Temporary Accounts

All Withdrawal Accounts

Debit + Balance	—

All Revenue Accounts

—	Credit + Balance

All Expense Accounts

Debit + Balance	—

Problem I

The following statements are either true or false. Place a (T) in the parentheses before each true statement and an (F) before each false statement.

1. ( ) Debits are used to record increases in assets, withdrawals, and expenses.

2. ( ) The process of recording transactions in a journal is called posting.

3. ( ) In double-entry accounting, all errors are avoided by being sure that debits and credit are equal when transactions are recorded.

4. ( ) The cost of renting an office during the current period is an expense; however, the cost of renting an office six periods in advance is an asset.

5. ( ) The debt ratio is used to assess a company's risk of failing to pay its debts when they are due.

Problem II

You are given several words, phrases, or numbers to choose from in completing each of the following statements or in answering the following questions. In each case select the one that best completes the statement or answers the question and place its letter in the answer space provided.

_____ 1. Hans Hammer's company had a capital balance of $12,300 on June 30 and $23,800 on July 31. Net income for the month of July was $14,000. How much did Hammer withdraw from the business during July?

   a. $22,100

   b. $25,500

   c. $2,500

   d. $11,500

   e. $ 0

_____ 2. Which of the following transactions does not affect the equity in a proprietorship?

   a. Investments by the owner.

   b. Withdrawals of cash by the owner.

   c. Cash receipts for revenues.

   d. Cash receipts for unearned revenues.

   e. Cash payments for expenses.

_____ 3. A ledger is:

   a. A book of original entry in which the effects of transactions are first recorded.

   b. The collection of all accounts used by a business.

   c. A book of original entry in which any type of transaction can be recorded.

   d. A book of special journals.

   e. An account with debit and credit columns and a third column for showing the balance of the account.

_____ 4. The following transactions occurred during the month of October:

Paid $1,500 cash for store equipment.

Paid $1,000 in partial payment for supplies purchased 30 days previously.

Paid October's utility bill of $600.

Paid $1,200 to owner of business for his personal use.

Paid $1,400 salary of office employee for October.

What was the total amount of expenses during October?

a. $3,000

b. $4,500

c. $2,000

d. $3,500

e. $5,700

_____ 5. The journal entry to record the completion of legal work for a client on credit and billing the client $1,700 for the services rendered would be:

a. Accounts Receivable 1,700

    Unearned Legal Fees   1,700

b. Legal Fees Earned 1,700

    Accounts Receivable   1,700

c. Accounts Payable 1,700

    Legal Fees Earned   1,700

d. Legal Fees Earned...1,700

    Sales...   1,700

e. Accounts Receivable 1,700

    Legal Fees Earned   1,700

Problem III

Following are the first 10 transactions completed by P. L. Wheeler's new business called Wheeler's Repair Shop:

   a.   Started the business with a cash deposit of $1,800 to a bank account in the name of the business.

   b.   Paid three months' rent in advance on the shop space, $675.

   c.   Purchased repair equipment for cash, $700.

   d.   Completed repair work for customers and collected cash, $1,005.50.

   e.   Purchased additional repair equipment on credit from Comet Company, $415.50.

   f.   Completed repair work on credit for Fred Baca, $175.

   g.   Paid Comet Company $290.50 of the amount owed from transaction (e).

   h.   Paid the local radio station $75 for an announcement of the shop opening.

   i.   Fred Baca paid for the work completed in transaction (f).

   j.   Withdrew $350 cash from the bank for P. L. Wheeler to pay personal expenses.

Required

1.   Record the transactions directly in the T-accounts that follow. Use the transaction letters to identify the amounts in the accounts.

2.   Prepare a trial balance as of the current date using the form that follows.

Cash	Accounts Payable

Accounts Receivable	P. L. Wheeler, Capital

	P. L. Wheeler, Withdrawals

Prepaid Rent	Repair Services Revenue

Repair Equipment	Advertising Expense

WHEELER'S REPAIR SHOP

Trial Balance

_____, 20____

Problem IV

Journalize the following transactions and post to the accounts that follow.

a. On November 5 of the current year, Sherry Dale invested $1,500 in cash, and office equipment having a market value of $950, to start a real estate agency.

b. On November 6, the business purchased office equipment for $425 cash.

GENERAL JOURNAL

DATE	ACCOUNT TITLES AND EXPLANATION	P.R.	DEBIT			CREDIT		

GENERAL LEDGER

Cash   Account No. 101

DATE	EXPLANATION	P.R.	DEBIT	CREDIT	BALANCE

Office Equipment   Account No. 163

DATE	EXPLANATION	P.R.	DEBIT	CREDIT	BALANCE

Sherry Dale, Capital   Account No. 301

DATE	EXPLANATION	P.R.	DEBIT	CREDIT	BALANCE

Problem V

Many of the important ideas and concepts discussed in Chapter 2 are reflected in the following list of key terms. Test your understanding of these terms by matching the appropriate definition with the terms. Record the number identifying the most appropriate definition in the blank space next to each term.

_____ Account
_____ Account balance
_____ Balance column account
_____ Chart of accounts
_____ Compound journal entry
_____ Credit
_____ Creditor
_____ Debit
_____ Debt ratio
_____ Double-entry accounting
_____ General journal

_____ Journal
_____ Journalizing
_____ Ledger
_____ Owner's capital
_____ Posting
_____ Posting reference (PR) column
_____ Source documents
_____ T-account
_____ Trial balance
_____ Unearned revenues

1. Liabilities created by advance cash payments from customers for products or services; revenues are earned when the products or services are delivered in the future.

2. A list of accounts and their balances at a point in time; total debt balances equal total credit balances.

3. An account with debit and credit columns for recording entries and a another column for showing the balance of the account after each entry.

4. Another name for *business papers*; these documents are the source of information for accounting entries and can be in either paper or electronic form.

5. A record where transactions are recorded before they are posted to ledger accounts; also called *book of original entry*.

6. A location within an accounting system where increases and decreases in a specific asset, liability, equity, revenue, or expense are recorded and stored.

7. An account form used as a tool to show the effects of transactions and events on specific accounts.

8. Process of recording transactions in a journal.

9. Recorded on the left side; an entry that increases asset and expense accounts, and decreases liability, equity, and revenue accounts.

10. A column in journals where individual account numbers are entered when entries are posted to ledger accounts.

11. The difference between the increases (including the beginning balance) and decreases in an account.

12. A list of accounts used by a company, includes an identification number for each account.

13. A journal entry that affects at least three accounts.

14. A record of the debits and credits of transactions; can be used to record any transaction.

15. Individuals or organizations entitled to receive payments from a company.

16. A ratio of total liabilities to total assets; used to describe risk associated with a company's debts.

17. Recorded on the right side; an entry that decreases asset and expense accounts, or increases liability, equity, and revenue accounts.

18. Account showing the owner's claim on company assets; equals owner investments plus net income (or less net losses) minus owner withdrawals since the company's inception; also referred to as *equity*.

19. Record containing all accounts of a business.

20. The process of transferring journal entry information to the ledger.

21. An accounting system in which each transaction affects at least two accounts and has at least one debit and one credit.

Problem VI

Complete the following by filling in the blanks.

1. The objectivity principle creates the need for credible _____, such as sales tickets, invoices, checks, bank statements, bills to customers, and employee earnings records.

2. The _____ is known as the book of original entry, while the _____ is known as the book of final entry.

3. The process of recording transactions in a journal is called _____. The process of transferring journal entry information to the ledger is called _____.

4. The _____ creates a link between a journal entry and the ledger accounts by providing a cross-reference for tracing the entry from one record to the other.

5. Notes receivable and prepaid insurance are examples of a(n) _____ account. Unearned revenues and interest payable are examples of a(n) _____ account.

6. Balances of _____ and _____ accounts flow into the income statement. Then, net income from the income statement and balances from _____ and _____ accounts flow into the statement of changes in equity.

7. a. The normal balance of an asset account is a _____.

    b. The normal balance of a liability account is a _____.

    c. The normal balance of the capital account is a _____.

    d. The normal balance of the withdrawals account is _____.

    e. The normal balance of a revenue account is a _____.

    f. The normal balance of an expense account is a _____.

8. When an account has the opposite of a normal balance, this abnormal balance can be indicated by _____.

9. The steps in preparing a trial balance are:

    _____.

    _____.

    _____.

    _____.

    _____.

10. A trial balance that fails to balance is proof that _____ either in journalizing, in posting, or in preparing the trial balance.

11. A trial balance that balances is not absolute proof that no errors were made because _____.

12. One frequent error that is made is called a _____, which occurs when two digits within a number are switched. This type of error probably has occurred if the difference between the two trial balance columns is evenly divisible by _____.

Solutions for Chapter 2

Problem I

1. T
2. F
3. F
4. T
5. T

Problem II

1. C
2. D
3. B
4. C
5. E

Problem III

Cash		
(a)	1,800.00	(b)	675.00
(d)	1,005.50	(c)	700.00
(f)	175.00	(g)	290.50
		(h)	75.00
		(j)	350.00

Repair Equipment	
(c)	700.00
(e)	415.50

P.L. Wheeler, Withdrawals	
(j)	350.00

Accounts Receivable		
(f)	175.00	(i)	175.00

Accounts Payable		
(g)	290.50	(e)	415.50

Repair Services Revenue		
	(d)	1,005.50
	(f)	175.00

Prepaid Rent	
(b)	675.00

P.L. Wheeler, Capital		
	(a)	1,800.00

Advertising Expense	
(h)	75.00

WHEELER'S REPAIR SHOP
Trial Balance
(Current Date)

Cash	$ 890.00	
Prepaid rent	675.00	
Repair equipment	1,115.50	
Accounts payable		$ 125.00
P.L. Wheeler, capital		1,800.00
P.L. Wheeler, withdrawals	350.00	
Repair services revenue		1,180.50
Advertising expense	75.00	
Totals	$3,105.50	$3,105.50

Problem IV

GENERAL JOURNAL

DATE	ACCOUNT TITLES AND EXPLANATION	P.R.	DEBIT			CREDIT		
20— Nov. 5	Cash	101	1 5 0 0	00				
	Office Equipment	163	9 5 0	00				
	Sherry Dale, Capital	301				2 4 5 0	00	
	Owner's initial investment.							
6	Office Equipment	163	4 2 5	00				
	Cash	101				4 2 5	00	
	Purchased office equipment							

GENERAL LEDGER

Cash   Account No. 101

DATE	EXPLANATION	P.R.	DEBIT		CREDIT		BALANCE	
20— Nov. 5		G-1	1 5 0 0	00			1 5 0 0	00
6		G-1			4 2 5	00	1 0 7 5	00

Office Equipment   Account No. 163

DATE	EXPLANATION	P.R.	DEBIT		CREDIT		BALANCE	
20— Nov. 5		G-1	9 5 0	00			9 5 0	00
6		G-1	4 2 5	00			1 3 7 5	00

Sherry Dale, Capital   Account No. 301

DATE	EXPLANATION	P.R.	DEBIT		CREDIT		BALANCE	
20— Nov. 5		G-1			2 4 5 0	00	2 4 5 0	00

Problem V

6	Account	5	Journal
11	Account balance	8	Journalizing
3	Balance column account	19	Ledger
12	Chart of accounts	18	Owner's Capital
13	Compound journal entry	20	Posting
17	Credit	10	Posting reference (PR) column
15	Creditor	24	
9	Debit	4	Source documents
16	Debt ratio	7	T-account
21	Double-entry accounting	2	Trial balance
14	General journal	1	Unearned revenues

Problem VI

1. source documents or business papers

2. journal, ledger

3. journalizing, posting

4. Posting reference (PR) column

5. asset, liability

6. revenue, expense; capital, withdrawals

7. (a) debit; (b) credit; (c) credit; (d) debit; (e) credit; (f) debit

8. circling the amount or entering it in red

9. (1) Determine the balance of each account; (2) List in their ledger order the accounts having balances, with the debit balances in one column and the credit balances in another; (3) Add the debit balances; (4) Add the credit balances; (5) Compare the two totals for equality.

10. at least one error has been made

11. some types of errors do not create unequal debits and credits

12. transposition, nine

CHAPTER 3
ADJUSTING ACCOUNTS AND
PREPARING FINANCIAL STATEMENTS

Learning Objective C1:

Explain the importance of periodic reporting and the time period principle.

Summary

The value of information is often linked to its timeliness. To provide timely information, accounting systems prepare periodic reports at regular intervals. The time period principle assumes that an organization's activities can be divided into specific time periods for periodic reporting.

Learning Objective C2:

Explain accrual accounting and how it improves financial statements.

Summary

Accrual accounting recognizes revenue when earned and expenses when incurred—not necessarily when cash inflows and outflows occur. This information is viewed as valuable in assessing a company's financial position and performance.

Learning Objective C3:

Identify the types of adjustments and their purpose.

Summary

Adjustments can be grouped according to their timing of cash receipts and cash payments relative to when they're recognized as revenues or expenses as follows: prepaid expenses, unearned revenues, accrued expenses, and accrued revenues. Adjusting entries are necessary so that revenues, expenses, assets, and liabilities are correctly reported.

Learning Objective A1:

Explain how accounting adjustments link to financial statements.

Summary

Accounting adjustments bring an asset or liability account balance to its correct amount. They also update related expense or revenue accounts. Every adjusting entry affects one or more income statement accounts *and* one or more balance sheet accounts. An adjusting entry never affects cash.

Learning Objective A2:

Compute profit margin and describe its use in analyzing company performance.

Summary

Profit margin is defined as the reporting period's net income divided by its net sales. Profit margin reflects a company's earnings activities by showing how much income is in each dollar of sales.

Learning Objective P1:

Prepare and explain adjusting entries.

Summary

Prepaid expenses refer to items paid for in advance of receiving their benefits. Prepaid expenses are assets. Adjusting entries for prepaids involve increasing (debiting) expenses and decreasing (crediting) assets. Unearned (or prepaid) revenues refer to cash received in advance of providing products and services. Unearned revenues are a liability. Adjusting entries for unearned revenues involve increasing (crediting) revenues and decreasing (debiting) unearned revenues. Accrued expenses refer to costs incurred in a period that are both unpaid and unrecorded. Adjusting entries for recording accrued expenses involve increasing (debiting) expenses and increasing (crediting) liabilities. Accrued revenues refer to revenues earned in a period that are both unrecorded and not yet received in cash. Adjusting entries for recording accrued revenues involve increasing (debiting) assets and increasing (crediting) revenues.

Learning Objective P2:

Explain and prepare an adjusted trial balance.

Summary

An adjusted trial balance is a list of accounts and balances prepared after recording and posting adjusting entries. Financial statements are often prepared from the adjusted trial balance.

Learning Objective P3:

Prepare financial statements from an adjusted trial balance.

Summary

Revenue and expense balances are reported on the income statement. Asset, liability, and equity balances are reported on the balance sheet. We usually prepare statements in the following order: income statement, statement of owner's equity, balance sheet, and statement of cash flows.

Learning Objective P4[A] (Appendix 4A):

Explain alternatives in accounting for prepaids.

Summary

Charging all prepaid expenses to expense accounts when they are purchased is acceptable. When this is done, adjusting entries must transfer any unexpired amounts from expense accounts to asset accounts. Crediting all unearned revenues to revenue accounts when cash is received is also acceptable. In this case the adjusting entries must transfer any unearned amounts from revenue accounts to unearned revenue accounts.

Fundamental Accounting Principles, 18/e

Chapter Outline

I.   **Timing and Reporting**

    A. The Accounting Period
    To provide timely information, accounting systems prepare reports at regular intervals.

       1. Time-period principle assumes that an organization's activities can be divided into specific time periods such as a month, a three-month quarter, six-month interval or a year for periodic reporting. Interim and annual financial statements can then be prepared.

       2. Annual reporting period:

          a. Calendar year—January 1 to December 31.

          b. Fiscal year—Any twelve consecutive months used to base annual financial reports on.

          c. Natural business year—a fiscal year that ends when a company's sales activities are at their lowest point.

          d. Interim financial statements—statements prepared for any period less than a fiscal year.

    B. Accrual Basis versus Cash Basis

       1. Accrual basis—uses the adjusting process to recognize revenues when earned and match expenses when incurred with revenues. This means the economic effects of revenues and expenses are recorded when earned or incurred, not when cash is received or paid. Accrual basis is consistent with GAAP. Improves comparability of statements.

       2. Cash basis—revenues are recognized when cash is received and expenses are recognized when cash is paid. Cash basis is not consistent with GAAP.

    C. Recognizing Revenues and Expenses

       1. The revenue recognition principle requires revenue be recorded when earned, not before and not after.

       2. The matching principle aims to record expenses in the same period as the revenues earned as a result of these expenses.

II. **Adjusting Accounts**—An adjusting entry is recorded to bring an asset or liability account balance to its proper amount. This entry also updates the related expense or revenue account.

    A. Framework for Adjustments
    Adjustments are necessary for transactions that extend over more than one period.

B. Adjusting Prepaid (Deferred) Expenses

1. Prepaid expenses (including depreciation) are items *paid for* in advance of receiving their benefits. Prepaid expenses, also called deferred expenses, are assets. As the assets are used, their costs become expenses.

2. Common prepaid items are supplies, prepaid insurance, prepaid rent and depreciation.

3. Adjusting entries for prepaids involve increasing (debiting) expenses and decreasing (crediting) assets (with the exception of depreciation on plant and equipment).

C. Adjusting for Depreciation

1. Depreciation is the process of allocating the cost of plant assets over their expected useful lives.

2. Adjusting entries for depreciation expense involve increasing (debiting) expenses and increasing (crediting) a special account called Accumulated Depreciation. This account is classified as a contra-asset. It is linked to the asset as a subtraction and thus used to record the declining asset balance.

3. Book value is a term used to describe the asset less its contra-asset (accumulated-depreciation).

D. Adjusting Unearned (Deferred) Revenues

1. Unearned revenues (also called deferred revenues) are liabilities created by cash received in advance of providing products or services. The obligation is to provide the service or product. As they are provided, unearned revenues (liabilities) become *earned* revenues (revenues).

2. Adjusting entries for unearned revenues involve increasing (crediting) revenues and decreasing (debiting) unearned revenues.

E. Adjusting Accrued Expenses

1. Accrued expenses are costs or expenses incurred in a period but are both unpaid and unrecorded.

2. Common accrued expenses are salaries, interest, rent, and taxes.

3. Adjusting entries for recording accrued expenses involve increasing (debiting) expenses and increasing (crediting) liabilities. (The liability is a "payable.")

    F. Adjusting Accrued Revenues

        1. Accrued revenues are revenues earned in a period that are both unrecorded and not yet received in cash.

        2. Accrued revenues commonly result from partially completed jobs or interest earned.

        3. Adjusting entries for recording accrued revenues involve increasing (debit) assets and increasing (credit) revenues. (The asset is a "receivable.")

    G. Links to Financial Statements
        Each adjusting entry affects one or more income statement accounts *and* one or more balance sheet accounts. Failure to make a necessary adjustment will result in misstatements of amounts on each of these statements. (See textbook Exhibit 3-12, p.102 for a summary of adjustments and financial statement links.)

    H. Adjusted Trial Balance
        A list of accounts and balances prepared *after* adjusting entries are recorded and posted to the ledger.

III. **Preparing Financial Statements**—Prepare financial statements directly from information in the *adjusted* trial balance. The following preparation order shows the flow of information from one statement to another:

    A. Income Statement

    B. Statement of Owner's Equity
        Requires use of net income or loss from previous statement.

    C. Balance Sheet
        Requires use of ending equity from previous statement.

IV. **Decision Analysis—Profit Margin**

    A. Used to evaluate operating results by measuring the ratio of a company's net income to sales. Also called *return on sales*.

    B. Calculated as net income divided by net sales revenues.

    C. Interpreted as reflecting the portion of profit in each dollar of revenue.

V. **Appendix 3A—Alternative Accounting for Prepayments**

    A. Prepaid expenses may originally be recorded with debits to expense accounts instead of assets. If so, then adjusting entries must transfer the cost of the unused portions from expense accounts to prepaid expense (asset) accounts.

    B. Prepaid revenues or revenues collected in advance may originally be recorded with credits to revenue accounts instead of liabilities. If so, then adjusting entries must transfer the unearned portions from revenue accounts to unearned revenue (liability) accounts.

    C. Note that the financial statements are identical under either procedure, but the adjusting entries are different.

ACCRUAL BASIS ACCOUNTING

(Follows GAAP)

requires that the

Income Statement (for a period)

reports

GAAP Revenue Recognition

ALL REVENUES EARNED in period (Collected or Not)

Minus ALL EXPENSES INCURRED in period (Paid or Not)

Equals Net Income or Net Loss for the period

GAAP Matching

GAAP Periodicity

ACCOUNTS MUST BE ADJUSTED TO FOLLOW PRINCIPLES

DEFERRALS

The converse of statements in Visual #5A also applies.
Revenue not earned or expense not incurred results in <u>Deferrals</u>*

$$\boxed{\text{UNEARNED} = \text{LIABILITY}}\ *$$

A REVENUE <u>not</u> earned <u>cannot</u> be shown, even if collected.
An EXPENSE <u>not</u> incurred <u>cannot</u> be shown, even if paid.

$$\boxed{\text{PREPAID} = \text{ASSET}}\ *$$

*We defer or postpone the <u>reporting</u> of the collected revenues
(as revenues) and prepaid expenses (as expenses) until the
revenue is earned and the expense is incurred.

VISUAL #6

ADJUSTMENTS

TYPE	GENERALIZED* ENTRY	AMOUNT
1A. Prepaid (deferred) expenses—initially recorded as assets	Dr. _____ Expense Cr. the Asset* acct.	Amount used, or consumed, or expired
1B. Prepaid (deferred) expenses—that are depreciable (plant assets)	Dr. Depreciation Expense Cr. Accumulated Depreciation	Portion of cost allocated to this period as depreciation
1C. Prepaid (deferred) expenses—initially recorded as expenses (alternate treatment—appendix)	Dr. the Asset** acct. Cr. _____ Expense	Amount left, or not consumed, or unexpired
2A. Unearned revenues—(revenue received in advance) initially record as liability (unearned account)	Dr. Unearned _____ Cr. the Revenue** acct.	Amount earned to date
2B. Unearned revenues—(revenue received in advance) initially recorded as a revenue (alternate treatment—appendix)	Dr. the Revenue** acct. Cr. Unearned_____	Amount still not earned
3. Accrued expenses—(expenses incurred but not yet recorded)	Dr. _____ Expense Cr. _____ Payable	Amount accrued
4. Accrued revenues (revenues earned but not yet recorded)	Dr. _____ Receivable Cr. the Revenue** acct.	Amount accrued

*Note: (1) Each adjustment affects a Balance Sheet Account and an Income Statement Account and (2) CASH NEVER appears in an adjustment.
**Title or account name varies.

Problem I

The following statements are either true or false. Place a (T) in the parentheses before each true statement and an (F) before each false statement.

1. ( ) The effect of a debit to an unearned revenue account and a corresponding credit to a revenue account is to transfer the earned portion of the fee from the liability account to the revenue account.

2. ( ) If the accountant failed to make the end-of-period adjustment to remove from the Unearned Fees account the amount of fees earned, the omission would cause an overstatement of assets.

3. ( ) The financial effect of a revenue generally occurs when it is earned, not when cash is received.

4. ( ) Under the cash basis of accounting, revenues are recognized when they are earned and expenses are matched with revenues.

5. ( ) If a business follows the practice of debiting prepayments of expenses to expense accounts, the adjusting entries for prepaid expenses require debits to prepaid expense accounts. (Appendix 3A)

6. ( ) If a business records receipts of unearned revenues with debits to cash and credits to revenue accounts, no adjusting entries are required at the end of the period. (Appendix 3A)

7. ( ) Some companies initially record prepaid expenses with debits to expense accounts and then make end-of-period adjusting entries to transfer unexpired amounts to asset accounts. These companies may then use reversing entries to transfer the unexpired amounts back into expense accounts. (Appendix 3A)

Problem II

You are given several words, phrases, or numbers to choose from in completing each of the following statements or in answering the following questions. In each case select the one that best completes the statement or answers the question and place its letter in the answer space provided.

_____ 1. Time periods covered by statements are called:
   a. seasonal periods.
   b. fiscal years.
   c. operating cycles of a business.
   d. accounting periods.
   e. natural business years.

_____ 2. X Company has four employees who are each paid $40 per day for a five-day work week. The employees are paid every Friday. If the accounting period ends on Wednesday, X Company should make the following entry to accrue wages:

   a. Salaries Expense 800
         Salaries Payable   800
   b. Salaries Expense 800
         Cash   800
   c. Salaries Expense 480
         Salaries Payable..   480
   d. Salaries Expense...320
         Salaries Payable   320
   e. No entry should be made until the salaries are actually paid.

4×40×3 = 480

_____3   Lori Teach owns a sole proprietorship. During April, Lori's business received $250 cash in advance for future services. The following entry should be made when the money is received:

a. Cash 250

    Accounts Receivable   250

b. Accounts Receivable 250

    Unearned Revenue   250

c. Cash..250

    Unearned Revenue   250

d. Unearned Revenue 250

    Services Revenue   250

e. No entry should be made until services are actually rendered.

_____4.   On December 1, B & B Security Service collected three months' fees of $6,000 in advance of providing services and credited Unearned Security Service Fees. They provided the monthly service from that date forward. The December 31st adjustment will require that Unearned Service Fees be

a.   Credited for $ 2,000.

b.   Debited for $ 6,000.

c.   Credited for $ 6,000.

d.   Debited for $ 4,000.

e.   Debited for $ 2,000.

_____5.   The Epicure Restaurant prepares monthly financial statements. On January 31 the balance in the Supplies account was $1,600. During February $2,960 of supplies were purchased and debited to Supplies. What is the adjusting entry on February 28 to account for the supplies assuming a February 28 inventory showed that $1,300 of supplies were on hand?

a. Supplies Expense..300

    Supplies   300

b. Supplies 300

    Supplies Expense...   300

c. Supplies 3,260

    Cash   3,260

d. Supplies Expense...3,260

    Supplies   3,260

_____ 6. ABC Company's financial statements show the following:

Net income $195,000

Total revenues 850,000

Total expenses 655,000

ABC's profit margin is:

a. 22.9 %

b. 29.8 %

c. 435.9 %

d. 129.8 %

e. 77.1 %

_____ 7. (Appendix 3A) Hanover Company prepares monthly financial statements and follows the procedure of crediting revenue accounts when it records cash receipts of unearned revenues. During April, the business received $4,800 for services to be rendered during April and May. On April 30, $2,000 of the amounts received had been earned. What is the adjusting journal entry on April 30 for service fees?

a. Service Fees Earned 2,000

    Unearned Service Fees   2,000

b. Unearned Service Fees 2,800

    Service Fees Earned   2,800

c. Cash 2,000

    Service Fees Earned   2,000

d. Unearned Service Fees 2,000

    Service Fees Earned   2,000

e. Service Fees Earned 2,800

    Unearned Service Fees   2,800

(Appendix 3A) Xanadu Company prepares monthly financial statements. On August 31, the balance in the Office Supplies account was $300. During September, $500 of supplies were purchased and debited to Office Supplies Expense. What is the adjusting journal entry on September 30 to account for the supplies assuming a September inventory of supplies showed that $250 were on hand?

a. Office Supplies 350

      Office Supplies Expense..   350

b. Office Supplies Expense 250

      Office Supplies   250

c. Office Supplies Expense 50

      Office Supplies   50

d. Office Supplies Expense 350

      Office Supplies   350

e. Office Supplies 250

      Office Supplies Expense   250

Problem III

Many of the important ideas and concepts discussed in Chapter 3 are reflected in the following list of key terms. Test your understanding of these terms by matching the appropriate definitions with the terms. Record the number identifying the most appropriate definition in the blank space next to each term.

_____	Accounting period	_____	Fiscal year
_____	Accrual basis accounting	_____	Interim financial statements
_____	Accrued expenses	_____	Matching principle
_____	Accrued revenues	_____	Natural business year
_____	Adjusted trial balance	_____	Plant assets
_____	Adjusting entry	_____	Prepaid expenses
_____	Annual financial statements	_____	Profit margin
_____	Book value	_____	Straight-line depreciation method
_____	Cash basis accounting	_____	Time-period principle
_____	Contra account	_____	Unadjusted trial balance
_____	Depreciation	_____	Unearned revenues

1. Costs incurred in a period that are both unpaid and unrecorded; adjusting entries for recording these items involve increasing (debiting) expenses and increasing (crediting) liabilities.

2. Ratio of a company's net income to its revenues; measures the portion of profit in each dollar of revenue.

3. Allocates equal amounts of an asset's cost to depreciation expense during its useful life.

4. List of accounts and balances prepared after adjustments are recorded and posted to the ledger.

5. Revenues earned in a period that are both unrecorded and not yet received in cash; adjusting entries for recording these items involve increasing (debiting) assets and increasing (crediting) revenues.

6. List of accounts and balances prepared before adjustments have been recorded and posted.

7. Assumes activities of an organization can be divided into specific time periods such as months, quarters, or years.

8. Consecutive 12 months (or 52 weeks) chosen as an organization's annual accounting period.

9. Expense created by allocating the cost of plant and equipment to the periods in which they are used; represents the expense of using the assets.

10. Cash received in advance of providing products or services; a liability.

11. Journal entry at the end of an accounting period to bring an asset or liability account to its proper amount while also updating the related revenue or expense account.

12. Requires expenses to be reported in the same period as the revenues that were earned as a result of the expenses.

13. 12-month period that ends when a company's sales activities are at their lowest point.

14. Revenues are recognized when cash is received and expenses when cash is paid.

15. Accounting system that recognizes revenues when earned and expenses when incurred; the basis for GAAP.

16. Account linked with another account and having the opposite normal balance; reported as a subtraction from the other account's balance.

17. Length of time covered by periodic financial statements and other reports; also called *reporting period*.

18. Financial statements covering periods of less than one year; usually based on one- or three- or six-month periods.

19. Tangible long-lived assets used to produce or sell products and services; also called *plant assets* or *fixed assets*.

20. Financial statements covering a one-year period; often based on a calendar year, but any twelve consecutive month period is acceptable.

21. Items paid for in advance of receiving their benefits; classified as assets

22. Equals the assets original cost less its accumulated depreciation.

Problem IV

Complete the following by filling in the blanks.

1. Under the cash basis of accounting, revenues are reported as being earned in the accounting period in which _____; expenses are charged to the period in which _____; and net income for the period is the difference between _____ and _____.

2. Under the accrual basis of accounting, revenues are credited to the period in which _____, expenses are _____ with revenues, and no consideration is given as to when cash is received or disbursed.

Problem V

On October 1 of the current year, Harold Lloyd began business as a public stenographer. During the month he completed the following transactions:

October 1 Invested $3,000 in the business.

1 Paid three months' rent in advance on the office space, $1,245.

1 Purchased office equipment for cash, $925.50.

2 Purchased on credit office equipment, $700, and office supplies, $75.50.

31 Completed stenographic work during the month and collected cash, $1,725. (Combined into one entry to conserve space.)

31 Withdrew $725 for personal living expenses.

After the foregoing entries were recorded in the journal and posted, the accounts of Harold Lloyd appeared as follows:

GENERAL LEDGER

Cash   Account No. 101

DATE	EXPLANATION	P.R.	DEBIT	CREDIT	BALANCE
Oct. 1		G-1	3 0 0 0 00		3 0 0 0 00
1		G-1		1 2 4 5 00	1 7 5 5 00
1		G-1		9 2 5 50	8 2 9 50
31		G-2	1 7 2 5 00		2 5 5 4 50
31		G-2		7 2 5 00	1 8 2 9 50

Office Supplies   Account No. 124

DATE	EXPLANATION	P.R.	DEBIT	CREDIT	BALANCE
Oct. 2		G-1	7 5 50		7 5 50

Prepaid Rent   Account No. 131

DATE	EXPLANATION	P.R.	DEBIT	CREDIT	BALANCE
Oct. 1		G-1	1 2 4 5 00		1 2 4 5 00

Office Equipment   Account No. 163

DATE	EXPLANATION	P.R.	DEBIT	CREDIT	BALANCE
Oct. 1		G-1	9 2 5 50		9 2 5 50
2		G-1	7 0 0 00		1 6 2 5 50

Accumulated Depreciation, Office Equipment   Account No. 164

DATE	EXPLANATION	P.R.	DEBIT	CREDIT	BALANCE

Accounts Payable   Account No. 201

DATE	EXPLANATION	P.R.	DEBIT	CREDIT	BALANCE
Oct. 2		G-1	7 7 5 50		7 7 5 50

Harold Lloyd, Capital   Account No. 301

DATE	EXPLANATION	P.R.	DEBIT	CREDIT	BALANCE
Oct. 1		G-1		3 0 0 0 00	3 0 0 0 00

Harold Lloyd, Withdrawals   Account No. 302

DATE	EXPLANATION	P.R.	DEBIT	CREDIT	BALANCE
Oct. 31		G-2	7 2 5 00		7 2 5 00

Stenographic Services Revenue   Account No. 403

DATE	EXPLANATION	P.R.	DEBIT	CREDIT	BALANCE
Oct. 31		G-2		1 7 2 5 00	1 7 2 5 00

Depreciation Expense, Office Equipment   Account No. 612

DATE	EXPLANATION	P.R.	DEBIT	CREDIT	BALANCE

Rent Expense   Account No. 640

DATE	EXPLANATION	P.R.	DEBIT	CREDIT	BALANCE

Office Supplies Expense   Account No. 650

DATE	EXPLANATION	P.R.	DEBIT	CREDIT	BALANCE

On October 31, Harold Lloyd decided to adjust his accounts and prepare a balance sheet and an income statement. His adjustments were:

  a. One month's rent had expired.

  b. An inventory of office supplies showed $40 of unused office supplies.

  c. The office equipment had depreciated $35 during October.

Required:

1. Prepare and post general journal entries to record the adjustments.

2. After posting the adjusting entries, complete the adjusted trial balance.

3. From the adjusted trial balance complete the income statement, statement of changes in owner's equity, and balance sheet.

GENERAL JOURNAL

DATE	ACCOUNT TITLES AND EXPLANATION	P.R.	DEBIT	CREDIT

HAROLD LLOYD

Adjusted Trial Balance

October 31, 20—

	Cash								
	Office supplies								
	Prepaid rent								
	Office equipment								
	Accumulated depreciation, office equipment								
	Accounts payable								
	Harold Lloyd, capital								
	Harold Lloyd, withdrawals								
	Stenographic services revenue								
	Depreciation expense, office equipment								
	Rent expense								
	Office supplies expense								
	Totals								

HAROLD LLOYD

Income Statement

For Month Ended October 31, 20—

	Revenue:								
	Stenographic services revenue								
	Operating expenses:								
	Depreciation expense, office equipment								
	Rent expense								
	Office supplies expense								
	Total operating expenses								
	Net income								

HAROLD LLOYD

Statement of Changes in Owner's Equity

For Month Ended October 31, 20—

	Harold Lloyd, capital, October 1, 20—								
	October net income								
	Less withdrawals								
	Excess of income over withdrawals								
	Harold Lloyd, capital, October 31, 20—								

HAROLD LLOYD

Balance Sheet

October 31, 20—

	Assets							
	Cash							
	Office supplies							
	Prepaid rent							
	Office equipment							
	Less accumulated depreciation							
	Total assets							
	Liabilities							
	Accounts payable							
	Owner's Equity							
	Harold Lloyd, capital, October 31, 20—							
	Total liabilities and owner's equity							

Problem VI

a. Blade Company has one employee who earns $72.50 per day. The company operates with monthly accounting periods, and the employee is paid each Friday night for a workweek that begins on Monday. Assume the calendar for October appears as shown and enter the four $362.50 weekly wage payments directly in the T-accounts below. Then enter the adjustment for the wages earned but unpaid on October 31.

OCTOBER						
S	M	T	W	T	F	S
	1	2	3	4	5	6
7	8	9	10	11	12	13
14	15	16	17	18	19	20
21	22	23	24	25	26	27
28	29	30	31			

Cash	Wages Payable	Wages Expense

b. Blade Company's October income statement should show $_____ of wages expense, and its October 31 balance sheet should show a $_____ liability for wages payable. The wages earned by its employee but unpaid on October 31 are an example of an _____ expense.

c. In the space that follows give the general journal entry to record payment of a full week's wages to the Blade Company employee on November 2.

GENERAL JOURNAL   Page 1

DATE	ACCOUNT TITLES AND EXPLANATION	P.R.	DEBIT	CREDIT

Problem VII

Riverview Properties operates an apartment building. On December 31, at the end of an annual accounting period, its Rent Earned account had a $335,500 credit balance, and the Unearned Rent account had a $3,600 credit balance. The following information was available for the year-end adjustments: (a) the credit balance in the Unearned Rent account resulted from a tenant paying his rent for six months in advance beginning on November 1; (b) also, a tenant in temporary financial difficulties had not paid his rent for the month of December. The amount due was $475.

Required: Enter the necessary adjustments directly in the T-accounts below.

Rent Receivable	Unearned Rent	Rent Earned
	Nov. 1	Balance
	3,600	335,500

After the foregoing adjustments are entered in the accounts, the company's Rent Earned account has a $_____ balance which should appear on its income statement as revenue earned during the year. Its Unearned Rent account has a $_____ balance, and this should appear on the company's balance sheet as a _____. Likewise, the company's Rent Receivable account has a $_____ balance, and this should appear on its balance sheet as a _____.

Fundamental Accounting Principles, 18/e

Solutions for Chapter 3

Problem I

1. T
2. F
3. T
4. F
5. T
6. F
7. T

Problem II

1. D
2. C
3. C
4. E
5. D
6. A
7. E
8. C

Problem III

17	Accounting period	8	Fiscal year
15	Accrual basis accounting	18	Interim financial statements
1	Accrued expenses	12	Matching principle
5	Accrued revenues	13	Natural business year
4	Adjusted trial balance	19	Plant and equipment
11	Adjusting entry	21	Prepaid expenses
20	Annual financial statements	2	Profit margin
22	Book value	3	Straight-line depreciation method
14	Cash basis accounting	7	Time-period principle
16	Contra account	6	Unadjusted trial balance
9	Depreciation	10	Unearned revenues

Problem IV

1. they are received in cash; they are paid; revenue receipts; expense disbursements

2. earned; matched

Problem V

			Debit	Credit
Oct. 31	Rent Expense		415.00	
	Prepaid Rent			415.00
31	Office Supplies Expense		35.50	
	Office Supplies			35.50
31	Depreciation Expense, Office Equipment		35.00	
	Accumulated Depr., Office Equipment			35.00

Cash

Date	Debit	Credit	Balance
Oct 1	3,000.00		3,000.00
1		1,245.00	1,755.00
1		925.50	829.50
31	1,725.00		2,554.50
31		725.00	1,829.50

Office Supplies

Date	Debit	Credit	Balance
Oct. 2	75.50		75.50
31		35.50	40.00

Prepaid Rent

Date	Debit	Credit	Balance
Oct. 1	1,245.00		1,245.00
31		415.00	830.00

Office Equipment

Date	Debit	Credit	Balance
Oct. 1	925.50		925.50
2	700.00		1,625.50

Accumulated Depr., Office Equipment

Date	Debit	Credit	Balance
Oct. 31		35.00	35.00

Accounts Payable

Date	Debit	Credit	Balance
Oct. 2		775.50	775.50

Harold Lloyd, Capital

Date	Debit	Credit	Balance
Oct. 1		3,000.00	3,000.00

Harold Lloyd, Withdrawals

Date	Debit	Credit	Balance
Oct. 31	725.00		725.00

Stenographic Services Revenue

Date	Debit	Credit	Balance
Oct. 31		1,725.00	1,725.00

Depr. Expense, Office Equipment

Date	Debit	Credit	Balance
Oct. 31	35.00		35.00

Rent Expense

Date	Debit	Credit	Balance
Oct. 31	415.00		415.00

Office Supplies Expense

Date	Debit	Credit	Balance
Oct. 31	35.50		35.50

2.

HAROLD LLOYD
Adjusted Trial Balance
October 31, 20---

	Debit	Credit
Cash	$1,829.50	
Office supplies	40.00	
Prepaid rent	830.00	
Office equipment	1,625.50	
Accumulated depreciation, office equipment		$ 35.00
Accounts payable		775.50
Harold Lloyd, capital		3,000.00
Harold Lloyd, withdrawals	725.00	
Stenographic services revenue		1,725.00
Depreciation expense, office equipment	35.00	
Rent expense	415.00	
Office supplies expense	35.50	
Totals	$5,535.50	$5,535.50

3.

HAROLD LLOYD
Income Statement
For Month Ended October 31, 20---

Revenue:		
Stenographic services revenue		$1,725.00
Operating expenses:		
Depreciation expense, office equipment	$ 35.00	
Rent expense	415.00	
Office supplies expense	35.50	
Total operating expenses		485.50
Net income		$1,239.50

HAROLD LLOYD
Statement of Changes in Owner's Equity
For Month Ended October 31, 20---

Harold Lloyd, capital, October 1, 20---		$3,000.00
October net income	$1,239.50	
Less withdrawals	725.00	
Excess of income over withdrawals		514.50
Harold Lloyd, capital, October 31, 20---		$3,514.50

HAROLD LLOYD
Balance Sheet
October 31, 20---
Assets

Cash		$1,829.50
Office supplies		40.00
Prepaid rent		830.00
Office equipment	$1,625.50	
Less accumulated depreciation	35.00	1,590.50
Total assets		$4,290.00
Liabilities		
Accounts payable		$ 775.50
Owner's Equity		
Harold Lloyd, Capital, October 31, 20--		3,514.50
Total liabilities and owner's equity		$4,290.00

Problem VI

a.

Cash				Wages Expense		
	Oct. 5	362.50		Oct. 5	362.50	
	12	362.50		12	362.50	
	19	362.50		19	362.50	
	26	362.50		26	362.50	
				31	217.50	

Wages Payable		
	Oct. 31	217.50

b. $1,667.50; $217.50; accrued

c. Nov 2 Wages Expense... 145.00
        Wages Payable... 217.50
                Cash...   362.50

Problem VII

Rent Receivable				Unearned Rent			
Dec. 31	475			Dec. 31	1,200	Nov. 1	3,600

Rent Earned		
	Bal.	335,500
	Dec. 31	1,200
	31	475

Rent Earned, $337,175
Unearned Rent, $2,400, liability
Rent Receivable, $475, asset

CHAPTER 4
COMPLETING THE ACCOUNTING CYCLE

Learning Objective C1:

Explain why temporary accounts are closed each period.

Summary

Temporary accounts are closed at the end of each accounting period for two main reasons. First, the closing process updates the capital account to include the effects of all transactions and events recorded for the period. Second, it prepares revenue, expense, and withdrawal accounts for the next reporting period by giving them zero balances.

Learning Objective C2:

Identify steps in the accounting cycle.

Summary

The accounting cycle consists of 10 steps: (1) analyze transactions, (2) journalize, (3) post, (4) prepare an unadjusted trial balance, (5) adjust accounts, (6) prepare an adjusted trial balance, (7) prepare statements, (8) close, (9) prepare a post-closing trial balance, (10) prepare (optional) reversing entries.

Learning Objective C3:

Explain and prepare a classified balance sheet.

Summary

Classified balance sheets report assets and liabilities in two categories: current and noncurrent. Noncurrent assets often include long-term investments, plant assets, and intangible assets. They include at least two groups of liabilities: current and long-term. Owner's equity for proprietorships (and partnerships) report the capital account balance. A corporation separates equity into common stock and retained earnings.

Learning Objective A1:

Compute the current ratio and describe what it reveals about a company's financial condition.

Summary

A company's current ratio is defined as current assets divided by current liabilities. We use it to evaluate a company's ability to pay its current liabilities out of current assets.

Learning Objective P1:

Prepare a work sheet and explain its usefulness.

Summary

A work sheet can be a useful tool in preparing and analyzing financial statements. It is helpful at the end of a period in preparing adjusting entries, an adjusted trial balance, and financial statements. A work sheet often contains five pairs of columns: Unadjusted Trial Balance, Adjustments, Adjusted Trial Balance, Income Statement, and Balance Sheet & Statement of Owner's Equity.

Learning Objective P2:

Describe and prepare closing entries.

Summary

Closing entries involve four steps: (1) close credit balances in revenue (and gain) accounts to Income Summary, (2) close debit balances in expense (and loss) accounts to Income Summary, (3) close Income Summary to the capital account, and (4) close withdrawals account to owner's capital.

Learning Objective P3:

Explain and prepare a post-closing trial balance.

Summary

A post-closing trial balance is a list of permanent accounts and their balances after all closing entries are journalized and posted. Its purpose is to verify that (1) total debits equal total credits for permanent accounts and (2) all temporary accounts have zero balances.

Learning Objective P4[A] (Appendix 4A):

Prepare reversing entries and explain their purpose.

Summary

Reversing entries are an optional step. They are applied to accrued expenses and revenues. The purpose of reversing entries is to simplify subsequent journal entries. Financial statements are unaffected by the choice to use or not use reversing entries.

I. Work Sheet as a Tool

A. The work sheet is an internal document that serves as a useful tool for organizing accounting information. It is *not* a required report.

B. Benefits include: aids the preparation of financial statements, reduces possibility of errors, captures links accounts and adjustments to their impacts in financial statements, assists in planning and organizing an audit of financial statements, helps in preparing interim (monthly and quarterly) financial statements, and shows the effect of proposed or "what if" transactions.

C. Steps to prepare a work sheet:

1. Enter the unadjusted trial balance in the first two columns.

2. Enter the adjustments in the third and fourth columns. Total columns to verify debit adjustments equal credit adjustments.

3. Prepare the Adjusted Trial Balance. This is done by combining the unadjusted trial balance and adjustment columns. Total Adjusted Trial Balance columns to verify debits equal credits.

4. Sort the adjusted trial balance amounts to the appropriate financial statement columns.

5. Total statement columns, compute net income or loss and balance the columns by adding net income or loss.

D. Work Sheet Applications and Analysis—it does not substitute for financial statements. The financial statement columns yield pro forma financial statements because they show the statements *as if* the proposed transactions occurred.

II. Closing Process—The closing process is an important step at end of the accounting period *after* financial statements have been completed.

A Steps in closing process:

1. Identify accounts for closing.

2. Record and post closing entries.

3. Prepare a post-closing trial balance.

B. Purpose of closing process:

1. To reset revenues, expenses, and withdrawals account balances to zero at the end of every period to prepare these accounts for proper measurement in the next period.

2. To make owner's capital account reflect prior periods' revenues, expenses and withdrawals.

C. Temporary and Permanent Accounts

1. Temporary (or nominal) accounts accumulate data related to one accounting period. (All income statement accounts, withdrawals accounts, and the Income Summary.)

2. Permanent (or real) accounts report on activities related to one or more future accounting periods. They are all balance sheet accounts that are not closed.

D. Recording Closing Entries—the purpose is to transfer the end-of-period balances in revenues, expense, and withdrawals accounts to the permanent capital account.

1. Use a new temporary account called Income Summary. The four closing entries are:

   a. Close credit balances in revenue (and gain) accounts by debiting the accounts and crediting Income Summary. This transfers revenue balances to the credit side Income Summary.

   b. Close debit balances in expense (and loss) accounts by crediting the accounts and debiting Income Summary. This transfers the expense balances to the debit side of Income Summary.

   c. Close the Income Summary account to the owner's capital account.

   Note: The Income Summary account, prior to closing, will have a credit balance equal to net income or a debit balance equal to net loss. Therefore this entry will credit capital for the amount of net income (or debit capital for a net loss).

   d. Close withdrawals account by crediting the account and debiting the owner's capital account.

2. After all closing entries are posted, all temporary accounts have a zero balance and capital is up to date.

E. Post-Closing Trial Balance—a list of permanent accounts and their balances taken from the ledger.

1. Prepared after closing entries are journalized and posted.

2. Verifies that total debits equal total credits for permanent accounts and all temporary accounts have zero ending balances.

F. The Accounting Cycle (see Visual 7)
    The ten steps repeated each accounting cycle are as follows:

    1. Analyze transactions

    2. Journalize

    3. Post

    4. Prepare unadjusted trial balance

    5. Adjust

    6. Prepare an adjusted trial balance

    7. Prepare statements

    8. Close

    9. Prepare a post-closing trial balance.

    10. Reverse (optional)

III. **Classified Balance Sheet**—organizes assets and liabilities into important subgroups and provides more information for decision makers.

A. Classification Structure

    1. One of the more important classifications is the separation between current and noncurrent assets and liabilities.

    2. Current items are expected to come due (both collected and owed) within the longer of one year or the company's *operating cycle*.

    3. Operating cycle is the time span from when *cash is used* to acquire goods and services until *cash is received* from the sale of those goods and services.

B. Classification Categories

    1. Current assets—cash or other resources that are expected to be sold, collected, or used within one year or the operating cycle, whichever is longer. Examples: cash, short-term investments, accounts receivable, short-term notes receivable, merchandise inventory, and prepaid expenses.

    2. Long-term investments—assets held for more than one year, that are not used in business operations. Examples: stocks, bonds, long-term notes receivable, notes, and land held for future expansion.

    3. Plant assets—tangible, long-lived assets that are used to produce or sell goods and services. Examples: equipment, buildings, land.

      4. Intangible assets—long-term resources that benefit business operation. They lack physical form. Their value comes from the privileges or rights that are granted to or held by the owner. Examples: goodwill, patents, trademarks, franchises, copyrights.

      5. Current liabilities—obligations due to be paid or settled within the longer of one year or the operating cycle. Examples: accounts payable, notes payable, wages payable, taxes payable, interest payable, unearned revenues, current portions of long-term liabilities.

      6. Long-term liabilities—obligations that are not due to be paid within one year or the operating cycle of the business. Examples: notes payable, mortgage payable, bonds payable.

      7. Equity—owner's claim on assets. For a proprietorship it is reported in this section as the owner's capital account. In a corporation , equity is divided into two main subsections: capital stock and retained earnings.

IV.   **Decision Analysis—Current Ratio**

    A. Assesses a company's ability to pay its debts in the near future.

    B. Calculated as total current assets divided by total current liabilities.

V.   **Appendix 4A—Reversing Entries**

    A. Accounting with reversing entries

      1. An optional step.

      2. Linked to asset and liability account balances that arose from the accrual of revenues and expenses.

      3. Purpose is to simplify recordkeeping.

      4. They are prepared after closing entries and dated the first day of the new period.

      5. Procedure is to transfer accrued asset and liability account balances to related revenue and expense accounts creating an abnormal balance in these accounts.

      6. The full subsequent cash receipts (and payments) are recorded as increases in revenue (and expense) accounts creating a net balance equal to the amount earned or incurred in that period.

    B. Accounting without reversing entries

      1. To construct proper entries when the cash receipt/payment occurs in the new accounting period, the related accrual or deferral adjustment must be recalled and considered.

      2. Accounting with or without reversing entries must yield the same result.

THE ACCOUNTING CYCLE

STEPS	PURPOSE	TIMING
1. Analyze transactions	To determine accounts to be debited and credited	During the period
2. Journalize	To record the daily transactions	During the period
3. Post	To transfer the amounts from journal entries to the individual accounts affected by the recorded transaction	During the period
4. Prepare unadjusted trial balance	To summarize unadjusted ledger accounts and amount.	End of period
5. Journalizing and posting of adjusting entries	To bring the ledger accounts to adjusted balances	End of year
6. Prepare unadjusted trial balance	To summarize unadjusted ledger accounts and amounts	End of year
7. Preparing the statements	To report financial information	End of period*
8. Journalizing and posting of closing entries	To bring all temporary accounts to zero and the capital account up-to-date	End of year
9. Post-closing trial balance	To prove the accuracy of the adjusting and closing procedures	End of year
10. Reversing entries (optional)	To provide for recording in new fiscal period without consideration of accruals from previous periods adjustments.	Beginning of new year

*If statements are to be prepared for interim period (less than a year), a worksheet is generally used to project adjusted numbers for statements.

Steps 4, 6, and 9 can be done on a worksheet.

Steps 3, 4, 5, and 6 are automatic with a computerized system

MUSIC WORLD
BALANCE SHEET
DECEMBER 31, 20XX

Assets

Current Assets			
Cash		$30,360	
Short-Term Investments		2,000	
Notes Receivable		8,000	
Accounts Receivable		35,300	
Merchandise Inventory		60,400	
Prepaid Insurance		6,600	
Supplies		1,696	
Total Current Assets			$144,356
Investments			
Land Held for Future Use			13,950
Property, Plant, and Equipment			
Land		$ 4,500	
Building	$20,650		
Less Accumulated Depreciation	8,640	12,010	
Office Equipment	$ 8,600		
Less Accumulated Depreciation	5,000	3,600	
Total Property, Plant, and Equipment			20,110
Intangible Assets			
Trademark			500
Total Assets			$178,916

Liabilities

Current Liabilities			
Notes Payable	$15,000		
Accounts Payable	25,683		
Salaries Payable	2,000		
Mortgage Payable	10,200		
Total Current Liabilities		$52,883	
Long-Term Liabilities			
Mortgage Payable		27,600	
Total Liabilities			$ 80,483

Owner's Equity

Joy Melody, Capital			98,433
Total Liabilities and Owner's Equity			$178,916

Problem I

The following statements are either true or false. Place a (T) in the parentheses before each true statement and an (F) before each false statement.

1. ( ) If the Income Statement columns of a work sheet are equal after transferring from the Adjusted Trial Balance columns, then it can be concluded that there is no net income (or loss).

2. ( ) The only reason why the Statement of Owner's Equity or Balance Sheet columns of a work sheet might be out of balance would be if an error had been made in sorting revenue and expense data from the Adjusted Trial Balance columns of the work sheet.

3. ( ) After all closing entries are posted at the end of an accounting period, the Income Summary account balance is zero.

4. ( ) Throughout the current period, one could refer to the balance of the Income Summary account to determine the amount of net income or loss that was earned in the prior accounting period.

5. ( ) On a work sheet, net income would be understated if a liability was extended into the Income Statement—Credit column.

Problem II

You are given several words, phrases, or numbers to choose from in completing each of the following statements or in answering the following question. In each case select the one that best completes the statement or answers the question and place its letter in the answer space provided.

_____ 1. Equipment, Wages Expense, and The Owner, Capital would be sorted to which respective columns in completing a work sheet?

    a. Statement of Owner's Equity or Balance Sheet—Debit; Income Statement— Debit; and Statement of Owner's Equity or Balance Sheet—Debit.

    b. Statement of Owner's Equity or Balance Sheet—Debit; Income Statement— Debit; and Statement of Owner's Equity or Balance Sheet—Credit.

    c. Statement of Owner's Equity or Balance Sheet—Debit; Income Statement— Credit; and Statement of Owner's Equity or Balance Sheet—Debit.

    d. Statement of Owner's Equity or Balance Sheet—Debit; Income Statement— Credit; and Statement of Owner's Equity or Balance Sheet—Credit.

    e. Statement of Owner's Equity or Balance Sheet—Credit; Income Statement— Credit; and Statement of Owner's Equity or Balance Sheet—Credit.

2. Based on the following T-accounts and their end-of-period balances, what will be the balance of the Joe Cool, Capital account after the closing entries are posted?

Joe Cool, Capital				Joe Cool, Withdrawals				Income Summary		
	Dec. 31	7,000		Dec. 31	9,600					

Revenue				Rent Expense				Salaries Expense		
	Dec. 31	29,700		Dec. 31	3,600			Dec. 31	7,200	

Insurance Expense				Depr. Expense, Equipment				Accum. Depr. Equipment		
Dec. 31	920			Dec. 31	500				Dec.31	500

   a. $12,880 Debit.

   b. $12,880 Credit.

   c. $24,480 Credit.

   d. $14,880 Credit.

   e. $10,480 Debit.

3. The following items appeared on a December 31 work sheet. Based on the following information, what are the totals in the Statement of Owner's Equity or Balance Sheet columns?

	Unadjusted Trial Balance		Adjustments	
	Debit	Credit	Debit	Credit
Cash...	975			
Supplies..	180			70
Prepaid insurance	3,600			150
Equipment	10,320			
Accounts payable		1,140		
Unearned fees..		4,500	375	
The Owner, capital...		9,180		
The Owner, withdrawals	1,650			
Fees earned..		5,850		375
				300
Salaries expense	2,100		315	
Rent expense	1,500			
Utilities expense..	345			
	20,670	20,670		
Insurance expense			150	
Supplies expense...			70	
Depreciation expense, equipment			190	
Accumulated depreciation, equipment.................				190
Salaries payable..				315
Accounts receivable			300	
			1,400	1,400

   a. $16,805.

   b. $16,505.

   c. $14,950.

   d. $14,820.

   e. Some other amount.

_____ 4. In what order are the following steps in the accounting cycle performed?

  1) Preparing an unadjusted trial balance
  2) Recording and posting closing entries
  3) Journalizing transactions
  4) Preparing a post-closing trial balance
  5) Preparing the financial statements
  6) Completing the work sheet
  7) Journalizing and posting adjusting entries
  8) Posting the entries to record transactions

  a. (1),(3),(8),(7),(6),(2),(4),(5)
  b. (3),(8),(1),(6),(5),(7),(2),(4)
  c. (1),(3),(8),(6),(7),(2),(5),(4)
  d. (3),(1),(8),(7).(6),(5),(4),(2)
  e. (3),(8),(1),(7),(6),(2),(4),(5)

_____ 5. Real accounts are:

  a. Accounts that are closed at the end of the accounting period; therefore, the revenue, expense, Income Summary, and withdrawals accounts.

  b. Accounts used to record the owner's investment in the business plus any more or less permanent changes in the owner's equity.

  c. Accounts the balance of which is subtracted from the balance of an associated account to show a more current amount then recorded in the associated account.

  d. Also called temporary accounts.

  e. Also called permanent accounts.

_____ 6. The following information is available from the financial statements of Harvard Company:

Current assets	$ 195,000
Total assets	850,000
Current liabilities	113,500
Total liabilities	441,500
Stockholder's Equity	408,500

Harvard's current ratio is:

  a. 1.9
  b. 2.1
  c. 1.7
  d. 1.5
  e. 5.8

Problem III

Many of the important ideas and concepts discussed in Chapter 4 are reflected in the following list of key terms. Test your understanding of these terms by matching the appropriate definitions with the terms. Record the number identifying the most appropriate definition in the blank space next to each term.

_____ Accounting cycle		_____ Long-term liabilities
_____ Classified balance sheet		_____ Operating cycle
_____ Closing entries		_____ Permanent accounts
_____ Closing process		_____ Post-closing trial balance
_____ Current assets		_____ Pro forma statements
_____ Current liabilities		_____ Reversing entries
_____ Current ratio		_____ Temporary accounts
_____ Income Summary		_____ Unclassified balance sheet
_____ Intangible assets		_____ Working papers
_____ Long-term investments		_____ Work sheet

1. Assets such as notes receivable or investments in stocks and bonds that are held for more than the longer of one year or the operating cycle.

2. List of permanent accounts and their balances from the ledger after the closing entries are journalized and posted.

3. Recurring steps performed each accounting period, starting with analyzing transactions and continuing through the post-closing trial balance (or reversing entries).

4. Balance sheet that presents the assets and liabilities in relevant subgroups.

5. Accounts that are used to record revenues, expenses, and owner's withdrawals; they are closed at the end of the period.

6. Analyses and other informal reports prepared by accountants when organizing information for formal reports and financial statements.

7. Accounts that are used to report activities related to one or more periods; they include all balance sheet accounts whose balance it not closed.

8. Necessary steps to prepare the accounts for recording the transactions of the next period.

9. Temporary account used only in the closing process to which the balances of revenues and expenses are transferred; its balance is transferred to the owner's capital account.

10. Optional entries recorded at the beginning of a new period that prepare the accounts for new journal entries as if adjusting entries hadn't occurred.

11. Entries recorded at the end of each accounting period to transfer end-of-period balances in revenue, expense, and withdrawals accounts to the owner's capital.

12. Spreadsheet used to draft an unadjusted trial balance, adjusting entries, adjusted trial balance, and financial statements; an optional step in the accounting process.

13. Balance sheet that broadly groups the assets, liabilities and owner's equity.

14. Statements that show the effects of the proposed transactions as if the transactions had already occurred.

15. Long-term assets (resources) used to produce or sell products or services; these assets lack physical form and their benefits are uncertain.

16. Cash or other assets that are expected to be sold, collected, or used within the longer of one year or the company's operating cycle.

17. Obligations due to be paid or settled within the longer of one year or the operating cycle.

18. Ratio used to evaluate a company's ability to pay its short-term obligations; calculated by dividing current assets by current liabilities.

19. Obligations that are not due to be paid within the longer of one year or the operating cycle.

20. Normal time between paying cash for merchandise and receiving cash from customers.

Problem IV

Complete the following by filling in the blanks.

1. A work sheet is prepared after all transactions are recorded but before _____ _____.

2. Revenue accounts have credit balances; consequently, to close a revenue account and make it show a zero balance, the revenue account is _____ and the Income Summary account is _____ for the amount of the balance.

3. In extending the amounts in the Adjusted Trial Balance columns of a work sheet to the proper Income Statement or Statement of Owner's Equity and Balance Sheet columns, two decisions are:
   (a)_____ and
   (b)_____.

4. Expense accounts have debit balances; therefore, expense accounts are_____ and the Income Summary account is _____ in closing the expense accounts.

5. In preparing a work sheet for a concern, its unadjusted account balances are entered in the _____ of the work sheet form, after which the _____ are entered in the second pair of columns. Next, the unadjusted trial balance amounts and the amounts in the Adjustments columns are combined to secure an _____ in the third pair of columns.

6. Only balance sheet accounts should have balances appearing on the post-closing trial balance because the balances of all temporary accounts are reduced to _____ in the closing procedure.

7. Closing entries are necessary because if at the end of an accounting period the revenue and expense accounts are to show only one period's revenues and expenses, they must begin the period with _____ balances, and closing entries cause the revenue and expense accounts to begin a new period with _____ balances.

8. Closing entries accomplish two purposes: (1) they cause all _____ accounts to begin the new accounting period with zero balances, and (2) they transfer the net effect of the past period's _____, _____, and withdrawal transactions to the owner's capital account.

Problem V

The unfinished year-end work sheet of Homer's Home Shop appears on the next page.

©The McGraw-Hill Companies, Inc., 2007

Required:

1. Complete the work sheet using the following adjustments information:

    a. A $725 inventory of shop supplies indicates that $1,037 of shop supplies have been used during the year.

    b. The shop equipment has depreciated $475 during the year.

    c. On December 31, wages of $388 have been earned by the one employee but are unpaid because payment is not due.

2. After completing the work sheet, prepare the year-end adjusting and closing entries.

3. Post the adjusting and closing entries to the accounts that are provided in the abbreviated general ledger.

4. After posting the adjusting and closing entries, prepare a post-closing trial balance.

HOMER'S HOME SHOP
WORKSHEET FOR THE YEAR ENDED DECEMBER 31, 20--

ACCOUNT	UNADJUSTED TRIAL BALANCE DR.	UNADJUSTED TRIAL BALANCE CR.	ADJUSTMENTS DR.	ADJUSTMENTS CR.	ADJUSTED TRIAL BALANCE DR.	ADJUSTED TRIAL BALANCE CR.	INCOME STATEMENT DR.	INCOME STATEMENT CR.	STMT. OF O.E. AND BALANCE SHEET DR.	STMT. OF O.E. AND BALANCE SHEET CR.
Cash	2 875 00									
Accounts receivable	2 000 00									
Shop supplies	1 762 00									
Shop equipment	5 125 00									
Accumulated Depreciation shop equipment		725 00								
Accounts payable		575 00								
Homer Tonely, capital		5 500 00								
Homer Tonely, withdrawals	30 000 00									
Repair services revenue		55 785 00								
Wages expense	18 250 00									
Rent expense	2 500 00									
Miscellaneous expenses	73 00									
	62 585 00	62 585 00								
Shop supplies expense										
Depreciation expense, shop equipment										
Wages payable										

2.

DATE	ACCOUNT TITLES AND EXPLANATION	P.R.	DEBIT		CREDIT	

GENERAL LEDGER

3.

Cash

Date	Debit	Credit	Balance
Dec. 31			2,875.00

Accounts Receivable

Date	Debit	Credit	Balance
Dec. 31			2,000.00

Shop Supplies

Date	Debit	Credit	Balance
Dec. 31			1,762.00

Shop Equipment

Date	Debit	Credit	Balance
Dec. 31			5,125.00

Accum. Depr., Shop Equipment

Date	Debit	Credit	Balance
Dec. 31			725.00

Accounts Payable

Date	Debit	Credit	Balance
Dec. 31			575.00

Wages Payable

Date	Debit	Credit	Balance

Homer Tonely, Capital

Date	Debit	Credit	Balance
Dec. 31			5,500.00

Homer Tonely, Withdrawals

Date	Debit	Credit	Balance
Dec. 31			30,000.00

Repair Services Revenue

Date	Debit	Credit	Balance
Dec. 31			55,785.00

Depr. Expense, Shop Equipment

Date	Debit	Credit	Balance

Wages Expense

Date	Debit	Credit	Balance
Dec. 31			18,250.00

Rent Expense

Date	Debit	Credit	Balance
Dec. 31			2,500.00

Shop Supplies Expense

Date	Debit	Credit	Balance

Miscellaneous Expenses

Date	Debit	Credit	Balance
Dec. 31			73.00

Income Summary

Date	Debit	Credit	Balance

4.

HOMER'S HOME SHOP

Post-Closing Trial Balance

December 31, 20--

Cash							
Accounts receivable							
Shop supplies							
Shop equipment							
Accumulated depreciation, shop equipment							
Accounts payable							
Wages payable							
Homer Tonely, capital							
Totals							

Problem VI (This problem applies to Appendix 4A.)

The following statements are either true or false. Place a (T) in the parentheses before each true statement and a (F) before each false statement.

1. (   )   After the adjusting, closing, and reversing entries are posted to an account where there were end of-period adjustments of accrued items, the account will have an opposite from normal balance.

2. (   )   Reversing entries are used only for accruals of expense items such as Salaries Expense, Tax Expense, and Interest Expense.

3. (   )   Some companies initially record prepaid expenses with debits to expense accounts and then make end-of-period adjusting entries to transfer unexpired amounts to asset accounts. These companies may then use reversing entries to transfer the unexpired amounts back into expense accounts.

Problem VII (This problem applies to Appendix 4A.)

You are given several words, phrases, or numbers to choose from in completing each of the following statements or in answering the following questions. In each case select the one that best completes the statement or answers the question and place its letter in the answer space provided.

_____ 1. The December 31,2007, adjusting entries for Mary Swan's interior design company included accrual of $760 in secretarial salaries. This amount will be paid on January 10, as part of the normal $1,200 salary for two weeks. The bookkeeper for the company uses reversing entries where appropriate. When the secretary's salary was paid on January 10, 2008, the following entry was made:

| Jan. 10 | Salaries Expense.. | 1,200 | |
| | Cash... | | 1,200 |

What was the January 1, 2008, reversing entry?

a.	Salaries Payable	760	
	Salaries Expense	440	
	Cash..		1,200
b.	Salaries Payable	440	
	Salaries Expense..		440
c.	Salaries Payable	760	
	Salaries Expense..		760
d.	Cash..	1,200	
	Salaries Expense...		1,200

e. The bookkeeper would not make a reversing entry for this transaction.

_____ 2. On December 31, 2007, X Company accrued salaries expense with an adjusting entry. No reversing entry was made and the payment of the salaries during January 2008 was correctly recorded. If X Company had recorded an entry on January 1, 2008, to reverse the accrual, and the subsequent payment was correctly recorded, the effect on the 2008 financial statements of using the reversing entry would have been:

a. to increase net income and reduce liabilities.

b. to increase 2008 expense and reduce assets.

c. to decrease 2008 expense and increase liabilities.

d. to decrease 2008 expense and decrease liabilities.

e. No effect.

Problem VIII (This problem applies to Appendix 4A.)

Based on the following end-of-period information, prepare reversing entries assuming that adjusting and closing entries have been properly recorded.

1. Depreciation on office equipment, $3,000.

2. $350 of the $1,400 Prepaid Insurance balance has expired.

3. Employees have earned salaries of $1,000 that have not been paid. They will be paid $1,750 on the next pay date.

4. The company has earned $3,050 of service fees that have not been collected or recorded.

5. The Unearned Service Fees account balance includes $1,000 that has been earned.

6. An inventory of supplies shows $250 of unused supplies. The balance of supplies on the unadjusted trial balance for the period is $900.

7. The company pays $1,200 interest on a loan each quarter. The next quarterly payment is due in two months from the end of the current period.

GENERAL JOURNAL

Page 1

DATE	ACCOUNT TITLES AND EXPLANATION	P.R.	DEBIT	CREDIT

Solutions for Chapter 4

Problem I

1. T
2. F
3. T
4. F
5. F

Problem II

1. B
2. D
3. A
4. B
5. E
6. C

Problem III

3	Accounting cycle	19	Long-term liabilities
4	Classified balance sheet	20	Operating cycle
11	Closing entries	7	Permanent accounts
8	Closing process	2	Post-closing trial balance
16	Current assets	14	Pro forma statements
17	Current liabilities	10	Reversing entries
18	Current ratio	5	Temporary accounts
9	Income Summary	13	Unclassified balance sheet
15	Intangible assets	6	Working papers
1	Long-term investments	12	Work sheet

Problem IV

1. the adjustments are entered in the accounts

2. debited, credited

3. (a) Is the item a debit or a credit?

   (b) On which statement does it appear?

4. credited, debited

5. Unadjusted Trial Balance columns; adjustments; adjusted trial balance

6. zero

7. zero, zero

8. temporary, revenue, expense

Problem V

1.

HOMER'S HOME SHOP
Work Sheet for Year Ended December 31, 20--

	Unadjusted Trial Balance		Adjustments		Adjusted Trial Balance		Income Statement		Statement of Ch. in O.E. and Balance Sheet	
	Dr.	Cr.	Dr.	Cr.	Dr.	Cr.	Dr.	Cr.	Dr.	Cr.
Cash	2,875				2,875				2,875	
Accounts receivable	2,000				2,000				2,000	
Shop supplies	1,762			(a)1,037	725				725	
Shop equipment	5,125				5,125				5,125	
Accum. depr., shop equipment		725		(b) 475		1,200				1,200
Accounts Payable		575				575				575
Homer Tonely. capital		5,500				5,500				5,500
Homer Tonely, withdrawals	30,000				30,000				30,000	
Repair services revenue		55,785				55,785		55,785		
Wages expense	18,250		(c) 388		18,638		18,638			
Rent expense	2,500				2,500		2,500			
Miscellaneous expenses	73				73		73			
	62,585	62,585								
Shop supplies expense			(a)1037		1,037		1,037			
Depreciation expense, shop equipment			(b) 475		475		475			
Wages payable				(c) 388		388				388
			1,900	1,900	63,448	63,448	22,723	55,785	40,725	7,663
Net income							33,062			33,062
							55,785	55,785	40,725	40,725

Dec. 31	Shop Supplies Expense	1,037		
	Shop Supplies		1,037	
31	Depr. Expense, Shop Equipment	475		
	Accumulated Depr., Shop Equipment		475	
31	Wages Expense	388		
	Wages Payable		388	
31	Repair Services Revenue	55,785		
	Income Summary		55,785	
31	Income Summary	22,723		
	Rent Expense		2,500	
	Wages Expense		18,638	
	Miscellaneous Expenses		73	
	Shop Supplies Expense		1,037	
	Depr. Expense, Shop Equipment		475	
31	Income Summary	33,062		
	Homer Tonely, Capital		33,062	
31	Homer Tonely, Capital	30,000		
	Homer Tonely, Withdrawals		30,000	

GENERAL LEDGER

3.

Cash

Date	Debit	Credit	Balance
Dec. 31			2,875.00

Accounts Receivable

Date	Debit	Credit	Balance
Dec. 31			2,000.00

Shop Supplies

Date	Debit	Credit	Balance
Dec. 31			1,762.00
31		1,037.00	725.00

Shop Equipment

Date	Debit	Credit	Balance
Dec. 31			5,125.00

Accum. Depr., Shop Equipment

Date	Debit	Credit	Balance
Dec. 31			725.00
31		475.00	1,200.00

Accounts Payable

Date	Debit	Credit	Balance
Dec. 31			575.00

Wages Payable

Date	Debit	Credit	Balance
Dec. 31		388.00	388.00

Homer Tonely, Capital

Date	Debit	Credit	Balance
Dec. 31			5,500.00
31		33,062.00	38,562.00
31	30,000.00		8,562.00

Homer Tonely, Withdrawals

Date	Debit	Credit	Balance
Dec. 31			30,000.00
31		30,000.00	-0-

Repair Services Revenue

Date	Debit	Credit	Balance
Dec. 31			55,785.00
31	55,785.00		-0-

Depr. Expense, Shop Equipment

Date	Debit	Credit	Balance
Dec. 31	475.00		475.00
31		475.00	-0-

Wages Expense

Date	Debit	Credit	Balance
Dec. 31			18,250.00
31	388.00		18,638.00
31		18,638.00	-0-

Rent Expense

Date	Debit	Credit	Balance
Dec. 31			2,500.00
31		2,500.00	-0-

Shop Supplies Expense

Date	Debit	Credit	Balance
Dec. 31	1,037.00		1,037.00
31		1,037.00	-0-

Miscellaneous Expenses

Date	Debit	Credit	Balance
Dec. 31			73.00
31		73.00	-0-

Income Summary

Date	Debit	Credit	Balance
Dec. 31		55,785.00	55,785.00
31	22,723.00		33,062.00
31	33,062.00		-0-

4.

HOMER'S HOME SHOP

Post-Closing Trial Balance

December 31, 20--

Cash	$2,875	
Accounts receivable	2,000	
Shop supplies	725	
Shop equipment	5,125	
Accumulated depreciation, shop equipment		$1,200
Accounts payable		575
Wages payable		388
Homer Tonely, capital		8,562
	$10,725	$10,725

Problem VI

1. T

2. F

3. T

Problem VII

1. C

2. E

Problem VIII

1)	No reversing entry required.		
2)	No reversing entry required.		
3)	Salaries Payable	1,000.00	
	Salaries Expense		1,000.00
4)	Service Fees Earned	3,050.00	
	Accounts Receivable		3,050.00
5)	No reversing entry required.		
6)	No reversing entry required.		
7)	Interest Payable	400.00	
	Interest Expense		400.00

CHAPTER 5
ACCOUNTING FOR MERCHANDISING OPERATIONS

Learning Objective C1:

Describe merchandising activities and identify income components for a merchandising company.

Summary

Merchandisers buy products and resell them. Examples of merchandisers include Wal-Mart, Home Depot, The Limited, and Barnes & Noble. A merchandiser's costs on the income statement include an amount for cost of goods sold. Gross profit, or gross margin, equals sales minus cost of goods sold.

Learning Objective C2:

Identify and explain the inventory asset of a merchandising company.

Summary

The current asset section of a merchandising company's balance sheet includes *merchandise inventory* which refers to the products a merchandiser sells and are available for sale at the balance sheet date.

Learning Objective C3:

Describe both perpetual and periodic inventory systems.

Summary

A perpetual inventory system continuously tracks the cost of goods available for sale and the cost of goods sold. A periodic system accumulates the cost of goods purchased during the period and does not compute the amount of inventory or the cost of goods sold until the end of a period.

Learning Objective C4:

Analyze and interpret cost flows and operating activities of a merchandising company.

Summary

Cost of merchandise purchases flow into Merchandise Inventory and from there to Cost of Goods Sold on the income statement. Any remaining inventory is reported as a current asset on the balance sheet.

Learning Objective A1:

Compute the acid-test ratio and explain its use to assess liquidity.

Summary

The acid-test ratio is computed as quick assets (cash, short-term investments, and current receivables) divided by current liabilities. It indicates of a company's ability to pay its current liabilities with its existing quick assets. A ratio equal to or greater than 1.0 is often adequate.

Learning Objective A2:

Compute the gross margin ratio and explain its use to assess profitability.

Summary

The gross margin (or gross profit) ratio is computed as gross margin (net sales minus cost of goods sold) divided by net sales. It indicates a company's profitability before considering other expenses.

Learning Objective P1:

Analyze and record transactions for merchandise purchases using a perpetual system.

Summary

For a perpetual inventory system, purchases of inventory (net of trade discounts) are added to the Merchandise Inventory account. Purchase discounts and purchase returns and allowances are subtracted from Merchandise Inventory, and transportation-in costs are added to Merchandise Inventory.

Learning Objective P2:

Analyze and record transactions for sales of merchandise using a perpetual system.

Summary

A merchandiser records sales at list price less any trade discounts. The cost of items sold is transferred from Merchandise Inventory to Cost of Goods Sold. Refunds or credits given to customers for unsatisfactory merchandise are recorded in Sales Returns and Allowances, a contra account to Sales. If merchandise is returned and restored to inventory, the cost of this merchandise is removed from Cost of Goods Sold and transferred back to Merchandise Inventory. When cash discounts from the sales price are offered and customers pay within the discount period, the seller records Sales Discounts, a contra account to Sales.

Learning Objective P3:

Prepare adjustments and close accounts for a merchandising company.

Summary

With a perpetual inventory system, it is often necessary to make an adjustment for inventory shrinkage. This is computed by comparing a physical count of inventory with the Merchandise Inventory balance. Shrinkage is normally charged to Cost of Goods Sold. Temporary accounts closed to Income Summary for a merchandiser include Sales, Sales Discounts, Sales Returns and Allowances, and Cost of Goods Sold.

Fundamental Accounting Principles, 18/e

Learning Objective P4:

Define and prepare multiple-step and single-step income statements.

Summary

Multiple-step income statements include greater detail for sales and expenses than do single-step income statements. They also show details of net sales and report expenses in categories reflecting different activities.

Learning Objective P5 (Appendix 5A):

Record and compare merchandising transactions using both periodic and perpetual inventory systems.

Summary

Transactions involving the sale and purchase of merchandise are recorded and analyzed under both periodic and perpetual inventory systems. Adjusting and closing entries for both inventory systems are illustrated and explained.

I.   Merchandising Activities

A. Merchandise consists of products, also called goods, that a company acquires to resell to customers. Merchandisers can be either wholesalers (those that buy from manufacturers or other wholesalers and sell to retailers or other wholesalers) or retailers (those that buy from wholesalers or manufacturers and sell to consumers).

B. Reporting Income for a Merchandiser
Revenue from selling merchandise (*net sales*) minus the cost of goods (merchandise) sold to customers is called *gross profit*. Gross profit minus expenses (generally called *operating expenses*) determines the net income or loss for the period.

C. Reporting Inventory for a Merchandiser
A merchandiser's balance sheet is the same as service businesses with the exception of one additional *current* asset called:

1. *Merchandise Inventory,* or *Inventory*, refers to products a company owns and intends to sell.

2. The cost of this asset includes the cost incurred to buy the goods, ship them to the store, and make them ready for sale.

D. Operating Cycle for a Merchandiser
Begins by purchasing merchandise and ends by collecting cash from selling the merchandise.

E. Inventory Systems
Two alternative inventory systems that can be used to collect information about the cost of goods sold and the inventory (cost of goods available) are:

1. *Perpetual inventory system* which continually updates accounting records for merchandising transactions— specifically, those records of inventory available for sale and inventory sold. Technological advances and competitive pressures have dramatically increased the use of this method.

2. *Periodic inventory system* which updates the accounting records for merchandise transactions only at the *end of a period.*

Note: This outline describes the accounting using a Perpetual Inventory System. Periodic Inventory is only discussed in the appendix section of this outline. Also note, the terms inventory and merchandise inventory are synonymous. Inventory is used for brevity.

II.   **Accounting for Merchandise Purchases**
The *invoice* serves as a *source document* for this event.

   A.   Trade Discounts
   Deductions from list price (catalog price) to arrive at invoice price (actual selling price). Trade discounts are not entered into accounts.

      1.   Transactions are recorded using invoice price.

      2.   Entry to record purchase: debit Inventory, credit Cash or Accounts Payable.

   B.   Purchase Discounts
   Credit terms describe cash discounts offered to purchasers by seller for payment within a specified period of time called the *discount period.* Buyers view cash discounts as purchase discounts and sellers view them as sales discounts.

      1.   Example: *credit terms*, 2/10 n/30, offer a 2 % discount if invoice is paid within 10 days of invoice date, if not full payment is due within 30 days of invoice date.

      2.   Entry (for buyer) for payment within discount period: debit Accounts Payable (full invoice amount), credit Cash (amount paid = invoice – discount), credit Inventory (amount of discount).

   C.   Managing Discounts
   Missing out on cash discounts can be very costly. A system should be set-up to ensure that all invoices are paid on the last day of discount period.

   D.   Purchase Returns and Allowances

      1.   *Purchase returns* refers to merchandise a buyer acquires but then returns to the seller.

      2.   A *purchase allowance* is a reduction in the cost of defective merchandise that a buyer acquires.

      3.   A *debit memorandum* is a document that a buyer issues to inform the seller of a debit made to the seller's account in the buyer's records.

      4.   Entry on buyer's books: debit Accounts Payable or Cash (if refund given) and credit Inventory.

   E.   Discounts and Returns
   Discounts can only be taken on the remaining balance on the invoice after the return.

   F.   Transportation Costs and Ownership Transfer
   The point at which ownership is transferred (called FOB or *free on board*) determines who is responsible for paying any freight costs and/or bearing any loss. Two alternative points of title transfer are:

      1. FOB shipping point—title transfers at shipping point and buyer bears any loss and pays shipping costs.

          a. Increases cost of merchandise (cost principle)

          b. Debit Inventory, credit Cash or Accounts Payable (if to be paid for with merchandise later)

      2. FOB destination—title transfers at destination and seller bears any loss and pays shipping costs.

          a. Operating expense for seller

          b. Debit Delivery Expense (or Transportation-Out or Freight-Out), credit Cash.

  G. Recording Purchases Information

      The net cost of purchased merchandise according to the *cost principle* is recorded in the inventory account. (Inventory is debited, or increased, for invoice and transportation costs, and credited, or reduced, for returns, allowances, and discounts. *Supplemental records* are often used to collect information about each of the cost elements for management to evaluate and control.

III. **Accounting for Merchandise Sales—involves sales, sales discount, sales returns and allowances and cost of goods sold**

  A. Each sale of merchandise transaction involves two parts; the revenue and the cost.

      1. Recognize revenue—debit Accounts Receivable (or cash), credit Sales (both for the invoice amount).

      2. Recognize cost—debit Cost of Goods Sold, credit Inventory (both for the cost of the inventory sold).

  B. Sales Discounts

      Cash discounts awarded to customers for payment within the discount period. Recorded upon collection for sale.

      1. Collection after discount period—Debit Cash, Credit Accounts Receivable (full invoice amount).

      2. Collection within discount period—debit Cash (invoice amount less discount), debit Sales Discount (discount amount), credit Accounts Receivable (invoice amount).

      3. Sales Discounts is a contra-revenue account—subtraction from Sales.

  C. Sales Returns and Allowances

      1. *Sales returns*—merchandise that a customer returned to the seller after a sale.

      2. *Sales allowances*—reductions in the selling price of merchandise sold to customers (usually for damaged merchandise that a customer is willing to keep at a reduced price).

3. Entry: debit Sales Returns and Allowances and credit Accounts Receivable; additional entry to restore cost of returned goods to inventory if merchandise is returned and it is salable: debit Inventory, credit Cost of Goods Sold.

4. Sales Returns and Allowances is a contra-revenue account that is subtracted from Sales.

5. Net Sales = Sales – (Sales Discount + Sales Returns and Allowances).

6. Credit Memorandum—document issued by the seller to confirm a buyer's return or allowance and the credit to Accounts Receivable on the seller's books.

IV. **Completing the Accounting Cycle**

A. Adjusting Entries for Merchandisers
Generally same as discussed in chapter 4 for a service business with an additional adjustment needed to update inventory to reflect any loss referred to as *shrinkage*.

1. Shrinkage is determined by comparing a physical count of the inventory with recorded quantities.

2. Adjusting entry: debit Cost of Goods Sold, credit Inventory.

B. Preparing Financial Statements

Statements similar to service business with the following differences:

1. Income Statement includes the *cost of goods sold* and *gross profit*. Also, net sales is affected by discounts, returns and allowances and delivery expense as an additional possible expense.

2. Balance Sheet includes *merchandise inventory* as part of current assets.

C. Closing Entries
Similar to a service business except there are additional temporary accounts to close (sales, sales discounts, sales returns and allowances, and cost of goods sold). Debit balance accounts are closed with the expense accounts to Income Summary.

V. **Financial Statement Formats**—GAAP does not require any specific format. Common formats:

A. Multiple-Step Income Statement—shows details of net sales and other costs and expenses. Has three main parts:

1. *Gross profit*—net sales less cost of goods sold.

2. *Income from operations*—gross profit less operating expenses (classified into selling and general & administrative).

3. *Net income*—Income from operations adjusted for nonoperating items.

B. Single-Step Income Statement
Lists cost of goods sold as another expense and shows only one subtotal for total expenses, one subtraction to arrive at net income.

C. Classified Balance Sheet—reports merchandise inventory as a current asset, usually after accounts receivable (use liquidity order).

VI. **Decision Analysis—Acid Test Ratio and Gross Margin Ratio**

A. Acid-Test Ratio

1. Used to assess the company's liquidity or ability to pay its current debts. Differs from current ratio in that it is based on quick assets (which excludes less liquid current assets such as inventory and prepaid expenses) rather than all current assets.

2. Calculated by dividing *quick assets* by current liabilities.

3. Quick assets are cash, short-term investments, and receivables.

B. Gross Margin Ratio

1. Used to determine the percent of every sales dollar that is gross profit.

2. Calculated by dividing gross margin by net sales.

VII. **Periodic Inventory System (Appendix 5A)—textbook show comparison of periodic and perpetual in this appendix. The following chapter notes relate only to periodic inventory because the preceding notes outline the perpetual system.**

A. A periodic inventory system records merchandise acquisitions, discounts and returns in temporary accounts (Purchases, Purchase Returns, Purchases Discounts) rather than the merchandise inventory account.

B. Records only the revenue aspect of sales related events. Updates inventory and determines cost of goods sold only at the end of the accounting period. During the period, inventory account remains unchanged.

C. The inventory account can be updated as part of the adjusting or closing process.

D. Requires closing additional temporary accounts.

VISUAL #9

THE OUTDOOR STORE
Income Statement
For the Year Ended December 31, 20xx

Sales revenues			
Sales		$700,000	
Less: Sales returns and allowances...............	$ 5,000		
Sales discounts	3,000	8,000	
Net sales..			$692,000
Cost of goods sold			
Inventory, January 1		40,300	
Purchases	462,000		
Less: Purchase discounts $12,000			
Purchase returns and allowances.......................... 6,400	18,400		
Net purchases.......................................	443,600		
Add: Freight-in.................................	3,600		
Cost of goods purchased.............................		447,200	
Cost of goods available for sale		487,500	
Inventory, December 31		70,000	
Cost of goods sold			417,500
Gross profit on sales......................................			274,500
Operating expenses			
Selling expenses			
Sales salaries expense	76,000		
Sales commission expense..............	14,500		
Depreciation expense - Display equip.	13,300		
Utilities expense..........................	6,600		
Insurance expense........................	4,320		
Total selling expenses		114,720	
Administrative expenses			
Office salaries expense..................	32,000		
Depreciation expense – building	10,400		
Property tax expense....................	4,800		
Utilities expense..........................	4,400		
Insurance expense........................	2,880		
Total administrative expenses		54,480	
Total operating expenses			169,200
Income from operations................................			105,300
Other revenues and gains			
Interest revenue		4,000	
Other expenses and losses			
Interest expense.......................................		11,000	7,000
Net income			$ 98,300

©The McGraw-Hill Companies, Inc., 2007

COMPONENTS OF NET INCOME (FROM OPERATIONS)

	Steps:
(a)　Net Sales	X
(b) –Cost of Goods Sold*	–　X
(c)　Gross Profit on Sales	X
(d) –Operating Expenses	–　X
(e)　Net Income (Loss) from Operations	X

COMPONENTS OF COST OF GOODS SOLD

	Steps:
(a)　Inventory, Beginning of Period	X
(b) +Cost of Goods Purchased	+　X
(c)　Cost of Goods Available for Sale	X
(d) – Inventory, End of Period	–　X
(e)　Cost of Goods Sold	X

COMPONENTS COST OF GOODS PURCHASED

		Steps:
(a)　Purchases		X
(b) – (Purchase Returns & Allowances	X	
+ Purchases Discounts)	+　X	–　X
(c)　Net Purchases		X
(d) + Transportation In		+　X
(e)　Cost of Goods Purchased		X

* Perpetual inventory systems have a cost of goods sold account that continuously accumulates costs as items are sold. In a periodic inventory system, this amount is calculated at the end of period.

ACCOUNTS USED IN BASIC MERCHANDISING TRANSACTIONS
WITH A *PERPETUAL* INVENTORY SYSTEM

ASSETS	LIABILITIES	REVENUES & CONTRA-REV.

ASSETS   **LIABILITIES**   **REVENUES & CONTRA-REV.**

Cash   Accounts Payable   Sales

Dr. Bal. | | Cr. Bal. | Cr. Bal.

Accounts Receivable   Sales Returns & Allowance

Dr. Bal. | Dr. Bal. |

Merchandise Inventory   Sales Discount

Dr. Bal. | Dr. Bal. |

EXPENSE

Delivery Expense

Dr. Bal. |

ACCOUNTS USED IN BASIC MERCHANDISING TRANSACTIONS WITH A *PERIODIC* INVENTORY SYSTEM

ASSETS	LIABILITIES	REVENUES & CONTRA-REV.	COST & CONTRA-COST
Cash	Accounts Payable	Sales	Purchases
Dr. Bal.	Cr. Bal.	Cr. Bal.	Dr. Bal.
Accounts Receivable		Sales Returns & Allowance	Purchase Returns & Allowances
Dr. Bal.		Dr. Bal.	Cr. Bal.
Merchandise Inventory		Sales Discount	Purchases Discount
Dr. Bal.		Dr. Bal.	Cr. Bal.
			Transportation-In
			Dr. Bal.

EXPENSE

Delivery Expense

Dr.Bal.

Note: Problems I through VI assume the use of a perpetual inventory system. Problem VII (appendix 5A) assumes a periodic inventory system.

Problem I

The following statements are either true or false. Place a (T) in the parentheses before each true statement and an (F) before each false statement.

1. ( ) Sales returns and allowances or discounts are not included in the calculation of net sales.
2. ( ) On a classified multiple-step income statement, ending inventory is subtracted from the cost of goods available for sale to determine cost of goods sold.
3. ( ) Net sales minus cost of goods sold is gross profit on sales.
4. ( ) The balance sheet for a merchandising business is generally the same as for a service business with the exception of the addition of one account.
5. ( ) Quick assets include cash, short-term investments, receivables, and merchandise inventory.
6. ( ) A perpetual inventory system requires updating the inventory at the end of every fiscal period.
7. ( ) Cash discounts on merchandise purchased are debited to the inventory account.
8. ( ) Transportation costs on merchandise purchased are debited to the inventory account.
9. ( ) A debit or credit memorandum may originate with either party to a transaction, but the memorandum gets its name from the action of the selling party exclusively.
10. ( ) Recording the purchase of merchandise on account requires a debit to the inventory account and a credit to accounts payable.

Problem II

You are given several words, phrases, or numbers to choose from in completing each of the following statements or in answering the following questions. In each case select the one that best completes the statement or answers the question and place its letter in the answer space provided.

_____ 1. A method of accounting for inventories in which cost of goods sold is recorded each time a sale is made and an up-to-date record of goods available is maintained is called a:

    a. product inventory system.
    b. perpetual inventory system.
    c. periodic inventory system.
    d. parallel inventory system.
    e. principal inventory system.

_____ 2. Based on the following information, calculate the missing amounts.

Sales	$28,800	Cost of goods sold	?
Beginning inventory	?	Gross profit	$10,800
Purchases	18,000	Expenses	?
Ending inventory	12,600	Net income	3,600

    a. Beginning inventory, $16,200; Cost of goods sold, $12,600; Expenses, $1,800.
    b. Beginning inventory, $23,400; Cost of goods sold, $10,800; Expenses, $7,200.
    c. Beginning inventory, $9,000; Cost of goods sold, $14,400; Expenses, $3,600.
    d. Beginning inventory, $12,600; Cost of goods sold, $18,000; Expenses, $7,200.
    e. Beginning inventory, $19,800; Cost of goods sold, $25,200; Expenses, $14,400.

_____ 3. What is the effect on the income statement at the end of an accounting period in which the ending inventory of the prior period was understated and carried forward incorrectly?

a. Cost of goods sold is overstated and net income is understated.
b. Cost of goods sold is understated and net income is understated.
c. Cost of goods sold is understated and net Income is overstated.
d. Cost of goods sold is overstated and net income is overstated.
e. The errors of the prior period and the current period offset each other, so there is no effect on the income statement.

_____ 4. The following information is taken from a single proprietorship's income statement. Calculate ending inventory for the business.

Sales	$165,250	Purchase returns	$ 390
Sales returns	980	Purchase discounts	1,630
Sales discounts	1,960	Transportation-in	700
Beginning inventory	16,880	Gross profit	58,210
Purchases	108,380	Net income	17,360

a. $19,840.
b. 22,080.
c. $21,160.
d. 44,250.
e. Some other amount.

_____ 5. On July 18, Double Aught Sales Company sold merchandise on credit, terms 2/10, n/30, for $1,080. On July 21, Double Aught issued a $180 credit memorandum to the customer of July 18 who returned a portion of the merchandise purchased. In addition to the journal entry that debits inventory and credits cost of goods sold, what other journal entry is necessary to record the July 21 transaction?

a.	Accounts Receivable..	180.00	
	Sales..		180.00
b.	Sales Returns and Allowances	180.00	
	Accounts Receivable		180.00
c.	Accounts Receivable..	900.00	
	Sales Returns and Allowances	180.00	
	Sales..		1,080.00
d.	Sales	180.00	
	Accounts Receivable		180.00
e.	Sales Returns and Allowances	180.00	
	Sales..		180.00

_____ 6. The following information is available from the balance sheet of Foster Company:

Cash...	$22,300
Short-term investments	10,500
Accounts receivable	47,360
Merchandise inventory..	52,100
Accounts payable	66,800
J. Foster, capital..	57,300

Foster's acid-test ratio is:

a. 0.5
b. 1.2
c. 2.0
d. 1.4
e. 2.3

Problem III

Many of the important ideas and concepts discussed in Chapter 5 are reflected in the following list of key terms. Test your understanding of these terms by matching the appropriate definitions with the terms. Record the number identifying the most appropriate definition in the blank space next to each term.

_____	Acid-test ratio	_____ List price
_____	Cash discount	_____ Merchandise
_____	Cost of goods sold	_____ Merchandise inventory
_____	Credit memorandum	_____ Merchandiser
_____	Credit period	_____ Multiple-step income statement
_____	Credit terms	_____ Periodic inventory system
_____	Debit memorandum	_____ Perpetual inventory system
_____	Discount period	_____ Purchases discount
_____	EOM	_____ Retailer
_____	FOB	_____ Sales discount
_____	General and administrative expenses	_____ Selling expenses
_____	Gross margin	_____ Shrinkage
_____	Gross margin ratio	_____ Single-step income statement
_____	Gross profit	_____ Supplementary records
_____	Inventory	_____ Trade discount
		_____ Wholesaler

1. Net sales minus cost of goods sold; also called *gross profit*.

2. Accounting method that maintains continuous records of the cost of inventory available and the cost of goods sold.

3. Reduction below a list or catalog price that can vary for wholesalers, retailers, and customers.

4. Term used by a seller to describe a cash discount granted to customers for paying within the discount period.

5. Notification that the sender has debited the recipient's account in the sender's records.

6. Merchandise a company owns and expects to sell in its normal operations.

7. Abbreviation for *end of month;* used to describe credit terms for some transactions.

8. Catalog price of an item before any trade discount is deducted.

9. Products that a company owns to sell to their customers; also called merchandise.

10. Description of the amounts and timing of payments that a buyer agrees to make in the future.

11. Time period that can pass before a customer's payment is due.

12. Ratio used to assess a company's ability to settle its current debts with its most liquid assets; defined as quick assets (cash, short-term investments, and current receivables) over current liabilities.

13. Term used by a purchaser to describe a cash discount granted to the purchaser for paying within the discount period.

14. Notification that the sender has credited the recipient's account in the sender's records.

15. Method that records the cost of inventory purchased but does not continuously track the quantity available or sold to customers; records are updated at the end of each period to reflect the physical count and costs of goods available.

16. Time period in which a cash discount is available and the buyer can make a reduced payment.

17. Income statement format that includes cost of goods sold as an operating expense and shows only one subtotal for total expenses.

18. Reduction in the price of merchandise that is granted by a seller to a buyer when payment is made within the discount period.

19. Expenses of promoting sales such as displaying and advertising merchandise, making sales, and delivering goods to customers.

20. Products that a company owns to sell to their customers.

21. Expenses that support the operating activities of a business.

22. Abbreviation for *free on board;* the point at which ownership of goods passes to the buyer; FOB *shipping point* (or *factory*) means the buyer pays shipping costs and accepts ownership of the goods at the seller's place of business; FOB *destination* means the seller pays shipping costs and accepts ownership of the goods until at the buyer's place of business;

23. Income statement format that shows subtotals between sales and net income and details of net sales.

24. Inventory losses that occur as a result of theft or deterioration.

25. Cost of inventory sold to customers during a period.

26. Gross margin (sales minus cost of goods sold) divided by sales; also called *gross profit ratio*.

27. Entity that earns net income by buying and selling merchandise.

28. A intermediary that buys products from manufacturers or other wholesalers and sells them to retailers or other wholesalers.

29. Information outside the usual accounting records and accounts.

30. Intermediary that buys products from manufacturers or wholesalers and sells them to customers.

31. Net sales minus cost of goods sold; also called gross margin.

Problem IV

The following amounts appeared on Valentine Variety Store's adjusted trial balance as of December 31, 2007, the end of its fiscal year:

	Debit	Credit
Cash	$ 4,000	
Merchandise inventory	15,000	
Other assets	8,000	
Liabilities		$ 4,000
Violet Valentine, capital		22,300
Violet Valentine, withdrawals	10,000	
Sales		80,000
Sales returns and allowances	600	
Cost of goods sold	47,700	
General and administrative expenses	8,000	
Selling expenses	13,000	
Totals	$106,300	$106,300

On December 31, 2006, the company's merchandise inventory amounted to $13,000. *Supplementary records* of merchandising activities during the 2007 year disclosed the following:

Invoice cost of merchandise purchases	$48,500
Purchase discounts received	900
Purchase returns and allowances received	400
Cost of transportation-in	2,500

Required: Using the data above, complete the Income Statement for Valentine Variety Store for December 31, 2007. Use the form provided below.

©The McGraw-Hill Companies, Inc., 2007

VALENTINE VARIETY STORE

Income Statement

For the Year Ended December 31, 2007

Revenue:										
Sales										
Less: Sales returns and allowances										
Net sales										
Cost of goods sold:										
Merchandise inventory, December 31, 2006										
Purchases										
Less: Purchases returns										
and allowances $_____										
Purchase discounts _____										
Net purchases										
Add: Transportation-in										
Cost of goods purchased										
Goods available for sale										
Merchandise inventory, December 31, 2007										
Cost of goods sold										
Gross profit from sales										
Operating expenses:										
General and administrative expenses										
Selling expenses										
Total operating expenses										
Net income										

Problem V

Use the adjusted trial balance presented above to prepare the closing entries for Valentine Variety Store. Do not give explanations, but skip a line after each entry.

GENERAL JOURNAL   Page 1

DATE	ACCOUNT TITLES AND EXPLANATION	P.R.	DEBIT			CREDIT		

Problem VI

1. If a company determines cost of goods sold by counting the inventory at the end of the period and subtracting the inventory from the cost of goods available for sale, the system of accounting for inventories is called a(an)_____.

2. Trade discounts _____ (are, are not) credited to the Inventory account.

3. A reduction in a payable that is granted if it is paid within the discount period is a _____ discount.

4. A store received a credit memorandum from a wholesaler for unsatisfactory merchandise that the store sent back for credit. The store should record the memorandum with a _____ (debit, credit) to its Inventory account and a _____ (debit, credit) to its Accounts Payable account.

5. The two common systems of accounting for merchandise inventories are the _____ inventory system and the _____ inventory system. Before the availability of computers, the _____ inventory system was most likely used in stores that sold a large volume of relatively low-priced items.

Problem VII (Appendix 5A)

The trial balance that follows was taken from the ledger of Sporthaus Lindner at the end of its annual accounting period. Fritz Lindner, the owner of Sporthaus Lindner, did not make additional investments in the business during 2007.

SPORTHAUS LINDNER
Unadjusted Trial Balance
December 31, 2007

Cash	$ 1,840	
Accounts receivable	2,530	
Merchandise inventory	3,680	
Store supplies	2,070	
Accounts payable		$ 4,370
Salaries payable	---	---
Fritz Lindner, capital		5,980
Fritz Lindner, withdrawals	1,380	
Sales		14,260
Sales returns and allowances	1,150	
Purchases	5,750	
Purchase discounts		920
Transportation-in	1,150	
Salaries expense	4,370	
Rent expense	1,610	
Store supplies expense	---	---
Totals	$25,530	$25,530

Use the adjusting entry approach to account for merchandise inventories and prepare adjusting journal entries and closing journal entries for Sporthaus Lindner using the following information:

    a.   Ending store supplies inventory, $1,150.

    b.   Accrued salaries payable, $690.

    c.   Ending merchandise inventory, $4,830.

Record the adjusting journal entries and closing journal entries in the general journal set forth below.

                                                      Fundamental Accounting Principles, 18/e

DATE	ACCOUNT TITLES AND EXPLANATION	P.R.	DEBIT			CREDIT		

Solutions for Chapter 5

Problem I

1. F	6. F
2. T	7. F
3. T	8. T
4. T	9. F
5. F	10. T

Problem II

1. B
2. D
3. C
4. A
5. B
6. B

Problem III

12	Acid-test ratio	8	List price
18	Cash discount	20	Merchandise
25	Cost of goods sold	6 or 9	Merchandise inventory
14	Credit memorandum	27	Merchandiser
11	Credit period	23	Multiple-step income statement
10	Credit terms	15	Periodic inventory system
5	Debit memorandum	2	Perpetual inventory system
16	Discount period	13	Purchases discount
7	EOM	30	Retailer
22	FOB	4	Sales discount
21	General and administrative expenses	19	Selling expenses
1	Gross margin	24	Shrinkage
26	Gross margin ratio	17	Single-step income statement
31	Gross Profit	29	Supplementary records
9 or 6	Inventory	3	Trade discount
		28	Wholesaler

Problem IV

VALENTINE VARIETY STORE
Income Statement
For the Year Ended December 31, 2007

Revenue:			
Sales		$80,000	
Less: Sales returns and allowances		600	
Net sales			$79,400
Cost of goods sold:			
Merchandise inventory, December 31, 2006		$13,000	
Purchases	$48,500		
Less: Purchases returns and allowances	$400		
Purchase discounts	900	1,300	
Net purchases		47,200	
Add: Transportation-in		2,500	
Cost of goods purchased		49,700	
Goods available for sale		62,700	
Merchandise inventory, December 31, 2007		15,000	
Cost of goods sold			47,700
Gross profit from sales			31,700
Operating expenses:			
General and administrative expenses		8,000	
Selling expenses		13,000	
Total operating expenses			21,000
Net income			$10,700

Problem V

Dec. 31	Sales	80,000	
	Income Summary		80,000
31	Income Summary	69,300	
	Sales Returns and Allowances		600
	Cost of Goods Sold		47,700
	General and Administrative Expenses		8,000
	Selling Expenses		13,000
31	Income Summary	10,700	
	Violet Valentine, Capital		10,700
31	Violet Valentine, Capital	10,000	
	Violet Valentine, Withdrawals		10,000

©The McGraw-Hill Companies, Inc., 2007

Problem VI

1. periodic inventory system

2. are not

3. cash

4. credit, debit

5. periodic, perpetual, periodic

Problem VII (Appendix 5A)

Adjusting Entries

Dec. 31	Store Supplies Expense	920	
	Store Supplies		920
31	Salaries Expense	690	
	Salaries Payable		690
31	Income Summary	3,680	
	Merchandise Inventory		3,680
31	Merchandise Inventory	4,830	
	Income Summary		4,830

Closing Entries

Dec. 31	Sales	14,260	
	Purchase Discounts	920	
	Income Summary		15,180
31	Income Summary	15,640	
	Sales Returns and Allowances		1,150
	Purchases		5,750
	Transportation-in		1,150
	Salaries Expense		5,060
	Rent Expense		1,610
	Store Supplies Expense		920
31	Income Summary	690	
	Fritz Lindner, Capital		690
31	Fritz Lindner, Capital	1,380	
	Fritz Lindner, Withdrawals		1,380

Learning Objective C1:

Identify the items making up merchandise inventory.

Summary

Merchandise inventory refers to goods owned by a company and held for resale. Three special cases merit our attention. Goods in transit are reported in inventory of the company that holds ownership rights. Goods on consignment are reported in the consignor's inventory. Goods damaged or obsolete are reported in inventory at their net realizable value.

Learning Objective C2:

Identify the costs of merchandise inventory.

Summary

Costs of merchandise inventory include expenditures necessary to bring an item to a salable condition and location. This includes its invoice price minus any discount plus any added or incidental costs necessary to put it in a place and condition for sale.

Learning Objective A1:

Analyze the effects of inventory methods for both financial and tax reporting.

Summary

When purchase costs are rising or falling, the inventory costing methods are likely to assign different cost to inventory. Specific identification exactly matches costs and revenues. Weighted average smoothes out cost changes. FIFO assigns an amount to inventory closely approximating current replacement cost. LIFO assigns the most recent costs incurred to cost of goods sold, and likely better matches current costs with revenues.

Learning Objective A2:

Analyze the effects of inventory errors on current and future financial statements.

Summary

An error in the amount of ending inventory affects assets (inventory), net income (cost of goods sold), and equity for that period. Since ending inventory is next period's beginning inventory, an error in ending inventory affects next period's cost of goods sold and net income. Inventory errors in one period are offset in the next period.

Learning Objective A3:

Assess inventory management using both inventory turnover and days' sales in inventory.

Summary

We prefer a high inventory turnover, provided that goods are not out of stock and customers are not turned away. We use days' sales in inventory to assess the likelihood of goods being out of stock. We prefer a small number of days' sales in inventory if we can serve customer needs and provide a buffer for uncertainties.

Learning Objective P1:

Compute inventory in a perpetual system using the methods of specific identification, FIFO, LIFO, and weighted average.

Summary

Costs are assigned to the cost of goods sold account *each time* a sale occurs in a perpetual system. Specific identification assigns a cost to each item sold by referring to its actual cost (for example, its net invoice cost). Weighted average assigns a cost to items sold by dividing the current balance in the inventory account by the total items available for sale to determine the cost per unit. We then multiply the number of units sold by this cost per unit to get the cost of each sale. FIFO assigns cost to items sold assuming that the earliest units purchased are the first units sold. LIFO assigns cost to items sold assuming that the most recent units purchased are the first units sold

Learning Objective P2:

Compute the lower of cost or market amount of inventory.

Summary

Inventory is reported at market cost when market is *lower* than recorded cost, called the *lower of cost or market (LCM) inventory*. Market is typically measured as replacement cost. Lower of cost or market can be applied separately to each item, to major categories of items, or to the entire inventory.

Learning Objective P3[A] (Appendix 6A):

Compute inventory in a periodic system using the methods of specific identification, FIFO, LIFO, and weighted average.

Summary

Periodic inventory systems allocate the cost of goods available for sale between cost of goods sold and ending inventory *at the end of a period*. Specific identification and FIFO give identical results whether the periodic or perpetual system is used. LIFO assigns costs to cost of goods sold assuming the last units purchased for the period are the first units sold. The weighted average cost per unit is computed by dividing the total cost of beginning inventory and net purchases for the period by the total number of units available. Then, it multiplies cost per unit by the number of units sold to give cost of goods sold.

Learning Objective P4[B] (Appendix 6B):

Apply both the retail inventory and gross profit methods to estimate inventory.

Summary

The retail inventory method involves three steps: (1) goods available at retail minus net sales at retail equals ending inventory at retail, (2) goods available at cost divided by goods available at retail equals the cost-to-retail ratio, and (3) ending inventory at retail multiplied by the cost-to-retail ratio equals estimated ending inventory at cost. The gross profit method involves two steps: (1) net sales at retail multiplied by 1 minus the gross profit ratio gives estimated cost of goods sold, and (2) goods available at cost minus estimated cost of goods sold equals estimated ending inventory at cost.

I.   Inventory Basics

    A. Determining Inventory Items
        Includes all goods that a company owns and holds for sale.

        1. Goods in transit—included if ownership has passed.

        2. Goods on consignment—owned by consignor.

        3. Goods damaged or obsolete—not included if they cannot be sold. If salable, included at a conservative estimate of their *net realizable value* (sales price minus cost of making the sale).

    B. Determining Inventory Costs
        Includes cost of expenditures necessary, directly or indirectly, in bringing an item to a salable condition and location.

        1. Cost example: invoice price minus any discount, plus any incidental costs such as import duties, transportation-in, storage, insurance, etc.

        2. *Matching principle* states that inventory costs should be recorded against revenue in the period when inventory is sold.

        3. Exception: Under the *materiality principle* or the *cost-to-benefit constraint* (effort outweighs benefit), incidental costs of acquiring inventory maybe deemed immaterial and allocated to cost of goods sold in the period when they are incurred.

    C. Internal Controls and Taking a Physical Count

        1. The Inventory account under a perpetual system is updated for each purchase and sale.

        2. Physical count is generally taken at the end of its fiscal year or when inventory amounts are low (at least once per year).

        3. Physical inventory is used to adjust the Inventory account balance to the actual inventory on hand and thus account for theft, loss, damage, and errors.

        4. Internal controls (such as pre-numbered inventory tickets, assigned primary and secondary counters, and manager confirmations) are applied when a physical count is taken.

II.   Inventory Costing Under a Perpetual System—Accounting for inventory affects both the balance sheet and the income statement. There are 4 commonly used inventory costing methods. Each assumes a particular pattern of how cost flow through inventory. **Physical flow and cost flow need not be the same.**

Chapter Outline

(Note: The following assumes a perpetual inventory system. The periodic system is addressed in the appendix 6A outline.)

A. Inventory Cost Flow Assumptions

Four methods of assigning costs to inventory and cost of goods sold are:

1. Specific identification—when each item in inventory can be identified with a specific purchase and invoice, we can use this method to assign actual cost of units sold to cost of goods sold and leave actual cost of units on hand in the inventory account.

2. First-in, first-out (FIFO)—when sales occur, the costs of the earliest units acquired are charged to cost of goods sold, leaving costs of most recent purchases in inventory.

3. Last-in, first-out (LIFO)—when sales occur, costs of the most recent purchases are charged to cost of goods sold, leaving costs of earliest purchases in inventory. (Note: LIFO comes closest to matching current costs against revenues.)

4. Weighted average (also called average cost)—requires we compute the weighted average cost per unit of inventory at the time of each sale (cost of goods available divided by units available). We charge this weighted average cost per unit times units sold to cost of goods sold.

Note: Advanced computing technology has made perpetual inventory systems more affordable and more widely used.

B. Financial Statement Effects of Costing Methods

When purchase prices are different, the 4 costing methods nearly always assign different cost amounts. When costs *regularly rise*, note the following results:

1. FIFO assigns the lowest amount to cost of goods sold yielding the highest gross profit and the highest net income.

2. LIFO assigns the highest amount to cost of goods sold yielding the lowest gross profit and the lowest net income.

3. Weighted average method yields results between FIFO and LIFO.

4. Specific identification always yields results that depend on which units are sold.

Note: When costs *regularly decline* the reverse of above occurs for FIFO and LIFO.

All 4 methods are acceptable. Companies must disclose the method used in its financial statements or notes. Each method offers certain advantages:

1. FIFO assigns an amount to inventory on the balance sheet that approximates current replacement costs.

  2. LIFO better matches current costs with revenues on the income statement.

  3. Weighted average tends to smooth out erratic changes in costs.

  4. Specific identification exactly matches costs with revenues they generate.

 C. Tax Effects of Costing Methods
  Since inventory costs affect net income, they have potential tax effects. Companies can use different methods for financial reporting and tax reporting. *Exception*: When LIFO is used for tax purposes, IRS requires it be used for financial statements.

 D. Consistency in Using Costing Methods

  The *consistency principle* requires that a company use the same accounting methods period after period (for comparability) *unless* a change will improve financial reporting. *Full-disclosure principle* requires any change, its justification and effect of net income be reported.

III. **Valuing Inventory at LCM and the Effects of Inventory Errors**

 A. Lower of Cost or Market (*LCM*)
  Accounting principles require that inventory be reported on the balance sheet at market value when market is *lower* than cost.

  1. *Market* in the term *LCM* is defined as replacement cost.

  2. LCM is applied in *one* of three ways:

   a. to each individual item separately

   b. to major categories of products

   c. to the entire inventory.

  3. When recorded cost is higher than replacement cost (market), inventory is adjusted downward and an increase to cost of goods sold is recorded.

  4. LCM is often justified with reference to *conservatism principle*.

 B. Financial Statement Effects of Inventory Errors

  1. Inventory errors cause misstatements in cost of goods sold, gross profit, net income, current assets, and equity.

  2. Erroneous ending inventory of one period becomes erroneous beginning inventory of the next and results in misstatements in that next period's statements.

  3. An inventory error, although serious, is said to be *self-correcting* because it always yields an *offsetting* error in the next period.

©The McGraw-Hill Companies, Inc., 2007

140   *Fundamental Accounting Principles, 18/e*

    4. Understated ending inventories result in understated assets and equity (on balance sheet), and an understated net income (on income statement) that period. Note: overstated ending inventories have the reverse effects.

    5. Beginning inventory errors do not affect the balance sheet but do affect the current period's net income.

IV. **Decision Analysis—Inventory Turnover and Days' Sales in Inventory**

  A. Inventory Turnover

    1. Calculated by dividing cost of goods sold by average merchandise inventory.

    2. Reveals how many *times* a company turns over (sells) it, inventory during a period.

    3. Users apply it to analyze short-term liquidity and to assess management's ability to control inventory availability.

    4. A low ratio (in comparison to competitors) suggests inefficient use of assets and a high ratio suggests inventory may be too low.

  B. Days' Sales in Inventory

    1. Reveals how much inventory is available in terms of the number of days' sales (how many days one can sell from inventory if no new items are purchased).

    2. Calculated by dividing ending inventory by cost of goods sold, and then multiplying the result by 365.

  C. Analysis of inventory management
    A major emphasis for most merchandisers to both plan and control inventory purchases and sales.

V. **Inventory Costing Under a Periodic System (Appendix 6A)**

  A. The basic aim of the periodic and perpetual system is the same. The aim is to assign costs to inventory and cost of goods sold.

  B. The same four methods of assigning costs are used in each system but the results may differ by inventory system due to timing of cost assignment (Note: perpetual—cost assigned at point of sale vs. periodic—costs assigned at year end when physical count is taken).

    1. Specific identification—periodic results will be same as perpetual since specific cost will always be the same regardless of system used.

    2. First-in, first-out (FIFO)—periodic results will be same results as perpetual since first costs will always be the same regardless of system used.

    3. Last-in, first-out (LIFO)—periodic results differ from

perpetual because timing of cost assignment changes what is identified as the last cost. Perpetual LIFO identifies last cost at point of sale, whereas periodic LIFO identifies last cost at year end.

4. Weighted average—periodic results differ from perpetual because timing of cost assignment changes what costs are averaged. Periodic weighted average is computed once at year end and is based on total cost of goods available for sale and total units available for sale.

C. Financial Statement Effects

A periodic system has the same general affects on financial statements as perpetual system.

VI. **Inventory Estimation Methods (Appendix 6B)**

A. Retail Inventory Method
Estimates the cost of ending inventory for interim statements in a periodic inventory system when a physical count is taken only annually. Also used to estimate if casualty loss makes physical count impossible.

Steps:

1. Subtract sales (general ledger amount) from goods available measured at retail price (retail data in supplementary records) to get ending inventory at retail.

2. Find cost ratio by dividing total of goods available at cost by total of goods available at retail.

3. Apply cost ratio to ending inventory at retail to convert to ending inventory at cost.

B. Gross Profit Method
Estimates the cost of ending inventory for insurance claims when inventory is destroyed, lost or stolen.

Preliminary steps:

1. Determine the normal gross profit percentage from recent years.

2. Find the cost of goods percentage (100% less gross profit percentage).

Steps to estimate inventory using gross profit method:

a) Multiply actual sales by the cost of goods sold percentage to get estimated cost of goods sold.

b) Subtract estimated cost of goods sold from the actual amount of cost of goods available for sale to get estimated ending inventory at cost.

Schedule of Cost of Goods Available

		Units		Cost		Total
Jan. 1	Beginning Inventory	60	@	$10	=	$ 600
Jan. 7	Purchase	90	@	11	=	990
Jan. 15	Purchase	100	@	13	=	1,300
Jan 25	Purchase	50	@	16	=	800
Goods available for sale		300				$3,690

Sold a total of 230 units for $20 per unit. Timing of sales is as follows:

Jan. 1- Sold 30 units (actual CPU $10)
Jan. 9- Sold 70 units (actual CPU: 20 @ $10 and 50 @ $11)
Jan 17-Sold 100 units (actual CPU: 50 @ $13, 30 @ $11 and 20 @ $10)
Jan 28-Sold 30 units (actual CPU: 20 @ 16, 10 @ $13)
*CPU= Cost per unit

Cost Flow Assumptions or

Methods of Assigning Cost to Units as Sold (CGS)

(Using a Perpetual Inventory System)

(1) **Specific Identification** – Each time a sale occurs, the <u>actual</u> invoice cost of the units sold is identified and charged to cost of goods sold. This leaves the actual cost of units left in inventory.

(2) **Weighted Average** – Each time a sale occurs, the weighted average cost per unit is determined (based on total cost of goods available *at point of sale* divided by total number of units of goods available *at point of sale*). This cost is charged to cost of goods sold, leaving a weighted average cost in inventory.

(3) **First-in, First-out (FIFO)** – Each time a sale occurs, the costs of the earliest units acquired are charged to cost of goods sold, leaving costs of most recent purchases in inventory.

(4) **Last-in, First-out (LIFO)** – Each time a sale occurs, costs of the most recent purchases are charged to cost of goods sold, leaving costs of earliest purchases in inventory.

Schedule of Cost of Goods Available

	Units		Cost		Total
Jan. 1 Beginning Inventory	60	@	$10	=	$ 600
Mar. 27 Purchase	90	@	11	=	990
Aug. 15 Purchase	100	@	13	=	1,300
Nov. 6 Purchase	50	@	16	=	800
Goods available for sale	300				$3,690
Units in physical count at year end	70				

Cost Flow Assumptions or

Methods of Assigning Cost to Units in Ending Inventory

(Using a Periodic Inventory System)

(1) **Specific Identification** - requires that each item in an inventory be assigned its <u>actual</u> invoice cost.

(2) **Weighted Average** - a weighted average cost per unit is determined based on total cost and units of goods available for sale. This cost is assigned to units in the ending inventory.

(3) **First-in, First-out (FIFO)** - assumes the first units acquired (beginning inventory) are the first to be sold and that additional sales flow is in the order purchased. Therefore, the costs of the last items received are assigned to the ending inventory.

(4) **Last-in, First-out (LIFO)** - assumes the last units acquired (most recent purchase) are the first units sold. Therefore, the cost of the first items acquired (starting with beginning inventory) is assigned to the ending inventory.

Note: In all methods, *Cost of Good Sold* equals *Cost of Good Available* minus *Ending Inventory* (as computed by chosen method).

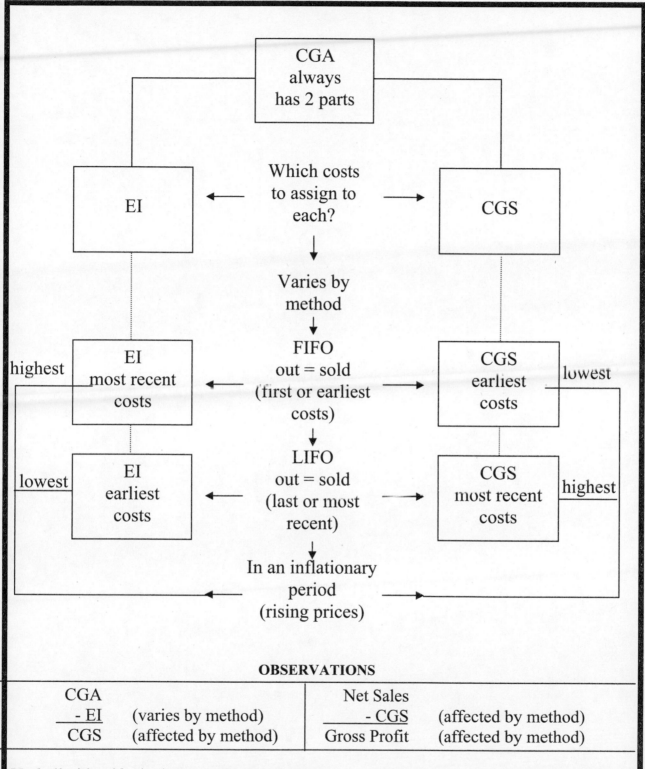

OBSERVATIONS

CGA		Net Sales	
- EI	(varies by method)	- CGS	(affected by method)
CGS	(affected by method)	Gross Profit	(affected by method)

Verbally identify the impact of LIFO & FIFO on net income in a period of rising prices <u>and</u> a period of declining prices.

Which method(s) will result in the same EI and CGS under both a Perpetual and Periodic Inventory System?

Problem I

The following statements are either true or false. Place a (T) in the parentheses before each true statement and an (F) before each false statement.

1. ( ) The merchandise inventory of a business includes goods sold FOB destination if they are not yet delivered.

2. ( ) When a perpetual inventory system is used, the dollar amount of ending inventory is determined by counting the units of product on hand, multiplying the count for each product by its cost, and adding the costs for all products.

3. ( ) If prices of goods purchased remain unchanged, then all four methods of assigning costs to goods in the ending inventory would yield the same cost figures.

4. ( ) When first-in, first-out inventory pricing is used in a perpetual inventory system, as sales occur the costs of the first items purchased are assigned to cost of goods sold.

5. ( ) If prices are rising, then using the LIFO method of pricing inventory will result in the highest net income.

6. ( ) The conservatism principle supports the lower of cost or market rule.

7. ( ) A misstatement of ending inventory will carry forward and cause misstatements in the succeeding period's cost of goods sold, gross profit, and net income.

8. ( ) The perpetual inventory system uses a Purchases account to record items purchased.

9. ( ) Using FIFO, the perpetual and periodic inventory systems do not result in the same amounts of sales, cost of goods sold, and end-of-period merchandise inventory.

10. ( ) Lower of cost or market may be applied separately to each product, to major categories of products, or to the merchandise inventory as a whole.

Problem II

You are given several words, phrases, or numbers to choose from in completing each of the following statements or in answering the following questions. In each case select the one that best completes the statement or answers the question and place its letter in the answer space provided.

_____ 1. Cisco Company's ending inventory consists of the following:

Product	Units on Hand	Unit Cost	Replacement Cost per Unit
X	100	$10	$ 8
Y	90	15	14
Z	75	8	10

Replacement cost is determined to be the best measure of market. Lower of cost or market for the inventory applied separately to each product is:

a. $2,950

b. $2,810

c. $2,660

d. $3,1 00

e. Cannot be determined from the information given.

The following information is to be used for questions 2 to 5:

Serese Co. made purchases of a particular product in the current year (2007) as follows:

Jan.	1	Beginning inventory ...	120 units	@	$5.00	=	$ 600
Mar.	7	Purchased..................	250 units	@	$5.60	=	1,400
July	28	Purchased..................	500 units	@	$5.80	=	2,900
Oct.	3	Purchased..................	450 units	@	$6.00	=	2,700
Dec.	19	Purchased..................	100 units	@	$6.20	=	620
		Total	1,420 units				$8,220

Serese Co. made sales on the following dates at $15 a unit:

Jan.	10	70 units
Mar.	15	125 units
Oct.	5	600 units
Total		795 units

The business uses a perpetual inventory system, and the ending inventory consists of 625 units, 500 from the July 28 purchase and 125 from the Oct. 3 purchase.

_____ 2. Using the specific identification cost assignment method, the amounts to be assigned to cost of goods sold and ending inventory respectively are:

   a. $4,465, $3,755
   b. $4,537.50, $3,682.50
   c. $4,570, $3,650
   d. $4,620, $3,600
   e. None of the above.

_____ 3. Using the LIFO cost assignment method, the amounts to be assigned to cost of goods sold and ending inventory respectively are:

   a. $4,465, $3,755
   b. $4,537.50, $3,682.50
   c. $4,570, $3,650
   d. $4,620, $3,600
   e. None of the above.

_____ 4. Using the FIFO cost assignment method, the amounts to be assigned to cost of goods sold and ending inventory respectively are:

   a. $4,465, $3,755
   b. $4,537.50, $3,682.50
   c. $4,570, $3,650
   d. $4,620, $3,600
   e. None of the above.

5. Using the weighted average cost assignment method, the amounts to be assigned to cost of goods sold and ending inventory respectively are:

    a. $4,465, $3,755
    b. $4,537.50, $3,682.50
    c. $4,570, $3,650
    d. $4,620, $3,600
    e. None of the above.

6. Atlantis Company made an error at the end of year 1 that caused its year 1 ending inventory to be understated by $5,000. What effect does this error have on the company's financial statements?

    a. Net income is understated; assets are understated.
    b. Net income is understated; assets are overstated.
    c. Net income is overstated; assets are understated.
    d. Net income is overstated; assets are overstated.
    e. Net income is overstated; assets are correctly stated.

7. Trador Company's ending inventory at December 31, 2008 and 2007, was $210,000 and $146,000, respectively. Cost of goods sold for 2008 was $832,000 and $780,000 for 2007. Calculate Trador's inventory turnover for 2008.

    a. 4.7 times.
    b. 4.5 times.
    c. 4.0 times.
    d. 3.8 times.
    e. Cannot be determined from the information given.

8. Refer to the information presented in question 7. Calculate Trador's days' sales in inventory for 2008.

    a. 78.1 days.
    b. 80.6 days.
    c. 66.1 days.
    d. 92.1 days.
    e. 68.3 days.

Note: Questions 9-12 relate to Appendix 6A.

9. Magnum Company began a year and purchased merchandise as follows:

Jan.	1	Beginning inventory	40 units	@ $17.00
Feb.	4	Purchased	80 units	@ $16.00
May	12	Purchased	80 units	@ $16.50
Aug.	9	Purchased	60 units	@ $17.50
Nov.	23	Purchased	100 units	@ $18.00

The company uses a periodic inventory system and the ending inventory consists of 60 units, 20 from each of the last three purchases. Determine ending inventory assuming costs are assigned on the basis of FIFO.

    a. $1,040
    b. $1,000
    c. $1,069
    d. $1,080
    e. $1,022

_____ 10. Linder Company began a year and purchased merchandise as follows:

Jan.	1	Beginning inventory	40 units	@ $17.00
Feb.	4	Purchased	80 units	@ $16.00
May	12	Purchased	80 units	@ $16.50
Aug.	9	Purchased	60 units	@ $17.50
Nov.	23	Purchased	100 units	@ $18.00

The company uses a periodic inventory system and the ending inventory consists of 60 units, 20 from each of the last three purchases. Determine ending inventory assuming costs are assigned on the basis of LIFO.

a. $1,040

b. $1,000

c. $1,022

d. $980

e. $1,080.

_____ 11. Box Company began a year and purchased merchandise as follows:

Jan.	1	Beginning inventory	40 units	@ $17.00
Feb.	4	Purchased	80 units	@ $16.00
May	12	Purchased	80 units	@ $16.50
Aug.	9	Purchased	60 units	@ $17.50
Nov.	23	Purchased	100 units	@ $18.00

The company uses a periodic inventory system and the ending inventory consists of 60 units, 20 from each of the last three purchases. Determine ending inventory assuming costs are assigned on the basis of specific invoice prices.

a. $1,000

b. $1,022

c. $1,040

d. $1,080

e. $990

_____ 12. Crow Company began a year and purchased merchandise as follows:

Jan.	1	Beginning inventory	40 units	@ $17.00
Feb.	4	Purchased	80 units	@ $16.00
May	12	Purchased	80 units	@ $16.50
Aug.	9	Purchased	60 units	@ $17.50
Nov.	23	Purchased	100 units	@ $18.00

The company uses a periodic inventory system and the ending inventory consists of 60 units, 20 from each of the last three purchases. Determine ending inventory assuming costs are assigned on a weighted average basis.

a. $1,022.00

b. $1,040.00

c. $1,080.00

d. $1,000.00

e. $1,042.50

Note: Question 13 relates to Appendix 6B.

_____ 13. Sanders Company wants to prepare interim financial statements for the first quarter of 2007. The company uses a periodic inventory system and has an average gross profit rate of 30%. Based on the following information, use the gross profit method to prepare an estimate of the March 31 inventory.

January 1, beginning inventory........................	$ 97,000
Purchases..	214,000
Purchases returns...	2,000
Transportation-in...	4,000
Sales	404,000
Sales returns	5,000

   a. $ 33,700.
   b. $193,300.
   c. $119,700.
   d. $179,900.
   e. $ 26,700.

Problem III

Many of the important ideas and concepts discussed in Chapter 6 are reflected in the following list of key terms. Test your understanding of these terms by matching the appropriate definitions with the terms. Record the number identifying the most appropriate definition in the blank space next to each term.

_____ Average cost	_____ Interim statements
_____ Conservatism principle	_____ Inventory turnover
_____ Consignee	_____ Last-in, first-out (LIFO)
_____ Consignor	_____ Lower of cost or market (LCM)
_____ Consistency principle	_____ Net realizable value
_____ Days' sales in inventory	_____ Retail inventory method
_____ First-in, first-out (FIFO)	_____ Specific identification
_____ Gross profit inventory method	_____ Weighted average inventory pricing

1. Method required to report inventory at market when it is lower than cost; market value is the current replacement.

2. Method of assigning cost to inventory that assumes items are sold in the order acquired; the earliest items purchased are the first items sold.

3. Method to assign cost to inventory that assumes that the unit costs of the items are weighted by the number of units of each item in inventory. The total is then divided by the total number of units available for sale to find the average unit cost of inventory and of the units sold.

4. Number of times a company's average inventory is sold during a period; computed by dividing cost of goods sold by the average inventory balance; also called _merchandise turnover_.

5. Principle that a company use the same accounting methods period after period so that the financial statements are comparable across periods.

6. Estimate of days needed to convert inventory at the end of the period into receivables or cash; equals the ending inventory divided by cost of goods sold and multiplying by 365; also called _days' stock on hand._

7. Expected selling price of an item minus the cost of making the sale.

8. Owner of goods who ships them to another party who will then sell them for the owner.

9. Procedure to estimate inventory when the past gross profit rate is used to estimate cost of goods sold, which is then subtracted from the cost of goods available for sale to yield estimated inventory.

10. Method to assign cost to inventory when the purchase cost of each item in inventory is identified and used to compute the cost of inventory.

11. Another name for weighted average inventory method.

12. Method to assign cost to inventory that assumes costs for the most recent items purchased are sold first and charged to cost of goods sold.

13. The principle that seeks to select the less optimistic estimate when two estimates are about equally likely.

14. Financial statements prepared for periods of less than one year.

15. Method to estimate ending inventory based on the ratio of the amount of goods for sale at cost to the amount of goods for sale at retail prices.

16. One who receives and holds goods owned by another for purposes of selling the goods for the owner.

Problem IV

Complete the following by filling in the blanks.

1. Consistency in the use of an inventory costing method is particularly important if there is to be _____.

2. If a running record is maintained for each inventory item of the number of units received as units are received, the number of units sold as units are sold, and the number of units remaining after each receipt or sale, the inventory system is called _____.

3. When a company changes its accounting procedures, the _____ principle requires that the nature of the change, justification for the change, and the effect of the change on _____ be disclosed in the notes accompanying the financial statements.

4. An error in stating an end-of-period inventory will cause a misstatement of periodic net income for _____ (one, two) accounting periods because _____ _____ _____.

5. When identical items are purchased during an accounting period at different costs, a problem arises as to which costs apply to the cost of goods sold and which apply goods remaining in inventory. There are at least four commonly used ways of assigning costs to goods sold and to inventory. They are:

   a. _____;

   b. _____;

   c. _____;

   d. _____;

6. A major objective of accounting for inventories is the proper determination of periodic net income through the process of matching _____ and _____. The matching process consists of determining how much of the cost of the goods that were for sale during an accounting period should be deducted from the period's _____ and how much should be carried forward as _____, to be matched against a future period's revenues.

7. Although changing back and forth from one inventory costing method to another might allow management to report the incomes it would prefer, the accounting principle of _____ requires a company to use the same pricing method period after period unless it can justify the change.

8. Cost of an inventory item includes

   _____

   _____

   _____

9. Use of the lower-of-cost-or-market rule places an inventory on the balance sheet at a _____ figure. The argument in favor of this rule provides that any loss should be _____ in the year the loss occurs.

10. When recording a sale of merchandise using a _____ (perpetual, periodic) inventory system, two journal entries must be made. One entry records the revenue received for the sale and the second entry debits the _____ account.

Note: Question 11 relates to Appendix 6B.

11. In the gross profit method of estimating an ending inventory, an average _____ _____ rate is used to determine estimated cost of goods sold, and the ending inventory is then estimated by subtracting estimated _____ from the cost of goods available for sale.

Problem V

A company uses a perpetual inventory system and during a year had the following beginning inventory, purchases, and sales of Product Z:

Jan.	1	Inventory	200 units	@	$0.50 =	$100
Mar.	15	Purchased	400 units	@	0.50 =	200
Apr.	1	Sold	300 units	@		
June	3	Purchased	300 units	@	0.60 =	180
July	1	Sold	200 units	@		
Oct.	8	Purchased	600 units	@	0.70 =	420
Nov.	1	Sold	500 units	@		
Dec.	15	Purchased	500 units	@	0.80 =	400

In the spaces below show the cost that should be assigned to the ending inventory and to the goods sold under the following assumptions:

	Portions Assigned to—	
	Ending Inventory	Cost of Goods Sold
1. A first-in, first-out basis was used to price the ending inventory..	$	$
2. A last-in, first-out basis was used to price the ending inventory..	$	$

Problem VI—Relates to Appendix 6B

The following end-of-period information about a store's beginning inventory, purchases, and sales is available.

	At Cost	At Retail
Beginning inventory	$ 9,600	$13,000
Net purchases	54,400	69,100
Transportation-in	1,680	
Net sales		69,000

The above information is to be used to estimate the store's ending inventory by the retail method.

1. The store had goods available for sale during the year calculated as follows:

	At Cost	At Retail
Beginning inventory	$_____	$_____
Net purchases	_____	_____
Transportation-in	_____	
Goods available for sale	$_____	$_____

2. The store's cost ratio was:_____
   $_____ / $_____ x 100 = _____

3. Of the goods the store had available for sale at retail prices during the year, the following is gone because of sales at retail_____
   Which left the store an estimated ending inventory at retail_____ $_____

4. And when the store's cost ratio is applied to this estimated ending inventory at retail, the estimated ending inventory at cost is_____ $_____

The store took a physical inventory and counted only $12,850 of merchandise on hand (at retail). Calculate the inventory shortage at cost.

Solutions for Chapter 6

Problem I

1. T	6. T
2. F	7. T
3. T	8. F
4. T	9. F
5. F	10. T

Problem II

1. C	7. A
2. C	8. D
3. D	9. D
4. A	10. B
5. B	11. C
6. A	12. A
7. A	13. A

Problem III

11	Average-cost method	14	Interim statements
13	Conservatism principle	4	Inventory turnover
16	Consignee	12	Last-in, first-out (LIFO)
8	Consignor	1	Lower of cost or market (LCM)
5	Consistency principle	7	Net realizable value
6	Days' sales in inventory	15	Retail inventory method
2	First-in, first-out (FIFO)	10	Specific identification
9	Gross profit inventory method	3	Weighted average inventory pricing

Problem IV

1. comparability in the financial statements prepared period after period

2. a perpetual inventory system

3. full-disclosure, net income

4. two, the ending inventory of one period becomes the beginning inventory of the next

5.   (a) specific invoice prices; (b) weighted average cost; (c) first-in, first-out; (d) last-in, first-out

6. costs, revenues, revenues, merchandise inventory

7. consistency

8. the invoice price, less the discount, plus any additional incidental costs necessary to put the item in place and in condition for sale

9. conservative, recognized

10. perpetual, cost of goods sold

11. gross profit, cost of goods sold

Problem V

	Portions Assigned to	
	Ending Inventory	Cost of Goods Sold
1.	$750	$550
2.	680	620

Problem VI

	At Cost	At Retail
Goods for sale		
Beginning inventory	$ 9,600	$13,000
Net purchases	54,400	69,100
Transportation-in..	1,680	
Goods available for sale.................................	$65,680	82,100
Cost ratio: $65,680/$82,100 x 100 = 80 %.....		
Net sales at retail		69,000
Ending inventory at retail..............................		$13,100
Ending inventory at cost ($13,100 x 80 %)	$10,480	

Inventory shortage at cost:
$13,100 - $12,850 = $250
$250 x 80% = $200

CHAPTER 7
ACCOUNTING INFORMATION SYSTEMS

Learning Objective C1:

Identify fundamental principles of accounting information systems.

Summary

Accounting information systems are governed by five fundamental principles: control, relevance, compatibility, flexibility, and cost-benefit.

Learning Objective C2:

Identify components of accounting information systems.

Summary

The five basic components of an accounting information system are source documents, input devices, information processors, information storage, and output devices.

Learning Objective C3:

Explain the goals and uses of special journals.

Summary

Special journals are used for recording transactions of similar type, each meant to cover one kind of transaction. Four of the most common special journals are the sales journal, cash receipts journal, purchases journal, and cash disbursements journal. Special journals are efficient and cost-effective tools in journalizing and posting processes.

Learning Objective C4:

Describe the use of controlling accounts and subsidiary ledgers.

Summary

A general ledger keeps controlling accounts such as Accounts Receivable or Accounts Payable, but details on individual accounts making up the controlling account are kept in subsidiary ledgers (such as an accounts receivable ledger). The balance in a controlling account must equal the sum of its subsidiary account balances after posting is complete.

Learning Objective C5:

Explain how technology-based information systems impact accounting.

Summary

Technology-based information systems aim to increase the accuracy, speed, efficiency, and convenience of accounting procedures.

Learning Objective A1:

Compute segment return on assets and use it to evaluate segment performance.

Summary

A business segment is a part of a company that is separately identified by its products or services or by the geographic market it serves. Analysis of a company's segments is aided by the segment return on assets (segment operation income divided by segment average assets).

Learning Objective P1:

Journalize and post transactions using special journals.

Summary

Each special journal is devoted to similar kinds of transactions. Transactions are journalized on one line of a special journal, with columns devoted to specific accounts, dates, names, posting references, explanations and other necessary information. Posting is threefold: (1) individual amounts in the Other Accounts column are posted to their general ledger accounts on a regular (daily) basis, (2) individual amounts in a column whose total is *not* posted to a controlling account at the end of a period (month) are posted regularly (daily) to their accounts in the general ledger, and (3) total amounts for all columns except the Other Accounts column are posted at the end of a period (month) to their column's account title in the general ledger.

Learning Objective P2:

Prepare and prove the accuracy of subsidiary ledgers.

Summary

Account balances in the general ledger and its subsidiary ledgers are tested for accuracy after posting is complete. This procedure is twofold: (1) prepare a trial balance of the general ledger to confirm debits equal credits, and (2) prepare a schedule to confirm that the controlling account's balance equals the subsidiary ledger's balance.

Learning Objective P3[A] (Appendix 7A):

Journalize and post transactions using special journals in a periodic inventory system.

Summary

Transactions are journalized and posted using special journals in a periodic inventory system. The methods are similar to those in a perpetual system; the primary difference is that both cost of goods sold and inventory are not adjusted at the time of each sale. This usually results in the deletion (or renaming) of one or more columns devoted to these accounts in each special journal.

Chapter Outline

I. **Fundamental System Principles**—Accounting information systems (AIS) collect and process data from transactions and events, organize them in useful reports and communicate results to decision makers. *The five fundamental principles* of accounting information systems are:

A. Control Principle
Prescribes that AIS have *internal controls*—methods and procedures allowing managers to control and monitor activities.

B. Relevance Principle
Prescribes that AIS report useful, understandable, timely and pertinent information for effective decision making.

C. Compatibility Principle
Prescribes that AIS conform with a company's activities, personnel and structure. It also must adapt to the company's unique characteristics.

D. Flexibility Principle
Prescribes that AIS be able to adapt to changes in the company, business environment, and needs of decisions makers.

E. Cost-Benefit Principle
Requires that the benefits from an activity in AIS outweigh the costs of that activity. Decisions regarding the other system principles are affected by this principle.

II. **Components of Accounting Systems**—AIS consist of people, records, methods and equipment. *Five basic components* of AIS are:

A. Source Documents
Documents (paper and electronic) that provide the basic information processed by an accounting system.

B. Input Devices
Capture information from source documents and enable its transfer to the information system's processing component.

C. Information Processors
Systems that interpret, transform, and summarize information for use in analysis and reporting.

D. Information Storage
System component that keeps data in a form accessible to information processors.

E. Output Devices
Means to take information out of an accounting system and make available to users.

III. Special Journals in Accounting

A. Basics of Special Journals

A special journal is used to record and post transactions of similar type. Use reduces recording and posting labor by grouping similar transactions and periodically posting totals accumulated. Use allows an efficient division of labor—an effective control procedure.

B. Subsidiary Ledgers

List of individual accounts with a common characteristic. Contains detailed information on specific general ledger accounts which are referred to as the *control account*.

1. Two of the most important subsidiary ledgers are:

a. Accounts receivable ledger—stores transaction data of individual customers; controlled by Accounts Receivable in General Ledger.

b. Accounts payable ledger—stores transaction data of individual suppliers; controlled by Accounts Payable in General Ledger.

2. Subsidiary ledgers are common for other general ledger accounts such as equipment or investments.

C. Sales Journal

Used to record sales of inventory *on credit*.

1. Generally contains two columns. The first column is use to record each sale and the *total* is posted to Accounts Receivable (debit) and to Sales (credit) in the General Ledger. It has a second column to record the tracking of the perpetual inventory cost. This column *total* is posted to Cost of Goods Sold (debit) and Inventory (credit).

2. Debits to the accounts of particular customers are *individually* posted to the customers account in a subsidiary accounts receivable ledger.

3. A *schedule* (list) *of accounts receivable* is used to prove the accuracy of the subsidiary ledger. The total of this schedule must equal the balance of the Accounts Receivable controlling account in the general ledger.

D. Cash Receipts Journal

Multicolumn journal used to record all receipts of cash.

1. Every transaction increases Cash and is recorded in special Cash *debit* column. Only the *total* of this column is posted.

2. Special *credit* columns are usually established for Accounts Receivable and Sales. A special *debit* column may be used for Sales Discounts. A special column is established to record the tracking of the perpetual inventory cost. Amounts in this column are *debits* to Cost of Goods Sold and *credits* to Inventory. Only the *totals* of special columns are posted to the General Ledger.

3. A column titled "Other Accounts - Credit" is used to record all types of receipts that are not frequent enough to justify having special columns. Each credit in the Other Accounts column must be posted *individually*.

4. Credits to the accounts of particular customers are *individually* posted to the customer's account in a subsidiary Accounts Receivable Ledger.

E. Purchases Journal
    Multicolumn journal used to record all purchases on credit.

1. In addition to a special column for Inventory *debit* and Accounts Payable *credit,* separate columns may be established for frequent credit purchases, such as Store Supplies *debit* and Office Supplies *debit*.

2. Only the *totals* of special columns are posted to the General Ledger. Amounts in "Other Accounts" columns are posted *individually*.

3. *Credits* to the accounts of particular creditors are *individually* posted to the subsidiary Accounts Payable Ledger.

4. A *schedule* (list) *of accounts payable* is used to prove the accuracy of the subsidiary ledger. The total of this schedule must equal the balance of the Accounts Payable controlling account in the general ledger

F. Cash Disbursements (Payments) Journal
    Used to record all payments of cash.

1. A Check Register is a cash disbursements journal that includes a column for entering the number of each check.

2. A special Cash *credit* column is established. Only the *total* of this column is posted.

3. Special columns are usually established for Accounts Payable *debit* and Inventory *credit* (for purchase discounts received). Only the *totals* of special columns are posted to the General Ledger.

4. A column titled "Other Accounts -*Debit*" is used to record all types of payments that are not frequent enough to justify a special columns. Each debit in the Other Accounts column must be posted *individually*.

5. *Debits* to the accounts of particular creditors are *individually* posted to the supplier's account in a subsidiary Accounts Payable Ledger.

G. General Journal Transactions
Used to record transactions that do not fit in any of the special journals. Examples:

1. Adjusting entries.

2. Closing entries.

3. Correcting entries.

4. Other transactions may include sales returns, purchases returns, and purchases of plant assets by issuing a note and receipt of notes from customers.

IV. **Technology-Based Accounting Systems**—AIS are supported with technology ranging from simple calculators to advanced computerized systems

A. Computer Technology in Accounting—provides accuracy, speed, efficiency, and convenience in performing accounting tasks.

1. Multipurpose off-the-shelf software programs are designed to be user friendly and menu driven (Examples: Peachtree and QuickBooks).

2. Some software can operate efficiently as an *integrated* system—actions in one part of the system automatically affect related parts (For example: recording automatically results in posting).

3. Technology has reduced recordkeeping time and thereby allows more time for analysis and managerial decision making.

B. Data Processing in Accounting—systems differ with regard to how input is entered and processed.

1. On-line processing—enters and processes data as soon as source documents are available. Updates databases immediately. Examples: airline reservations, credit card records, and rapid mail-order processing.

2. Batch processing accumulates source documents for a period of time and then processes them all at once such as daily, weekly, or monthly.

C. Computer Networks in Accounting
Links among computers giving different users and different computers access to a common database and programs.

1. Local area network (LAN)—links computers with hard-wire hookups.

2. Large computer networks extending over long distances often rely on modem or wireless communication.

    D. Enterprise-Resource Planning (ERP) Software
Programs that manage a company's vital operations.

V.   **Decision Analysis—Segment Return on Assets**

    A. A *segment* is a part of a company that is separately identified by its products or services or by the geographic market it serves.

    B. Segment return on assets ratio—one measure of success for a business segment.

    C. Segment return on assets ratio equals the segment operating income divided by segment average assets.

VI.   **Special Journals Under A Periodic System. (Appendix 7A)**

    A. Transactions are journalized and posted using special journals in a periodic system using methods similar to those in a perpetual system.

    B. Primary difference is that cost of goods sold and inventory do not need adjusting at the time of each sale. This results in the deletion of the columns used to record this in the sales and cash receipt journal. Also, in the purchases journal the Inventory debit column is replaced with a Purchases debit column and in the cash disbursements journal the Inventory credit column is replaced with a Purchases Discount credit column.

Problem I

The following statements are either true or false. Place a (T) in the parentheses before each true statement and an (F) before each false statement.

1. (   ) A Purchases Journal is used to record all purchases.

2. (   ) At month-end, the total sales recorded in the Sales Journal is debited to Accounts Receivable and credited to Sales.

3. (   ) Sales is a General Ledger account.

4. (   ) Transactions recorded in a journal do not necessarily result in equal debits and credits to General Ledger accounts.

5. (   ) If a general journal entry is used to record a charge sale, the credit of the entry must be posted twice.

6. (   ) A printer is one example of an input device for a computer system.

7. (   ) Business segment information is required of all U.S. companies.

Problem II

You are given several words, phrases or numbers to choose from in completing each of the following statements or in answering the following questions. In each case select the one that best completes the statement or answers the question and place its letter in the answer space provided.

_____ 1. A company that uses a Sales Journal, a Purchases Journal, a Cash Receipts Journal, a Cash Disbursements Journal, and a General Journal borrowed $1,500 from the bank in exchange for a note payable to the bank. In which journal would the transaction be recorded?

    a. Sales Journal

    b. Purchases Journal

    c. Cash Receipts Journal

    d. Cash Disbursements Journal

    e. General Journal

_____ 2. A company that uses a Sales Journal, a Purchases Journal, a Cash Receipts Journal, a Cash Disbursements Journal, and a General Journal paid a creditor for office supplies purchased on account. In which journal would the transaction be recorded?

    a. Sales Journal

    b. Purchases Journal

    c. Cash Receipts Journal

    d. Cash Disbursements Journal

    e. General Journal

_____ 3. A book of original entry that is designed and used for recording only a specified type of transaction is a:

    a. Check Register

    b. Subsidiary Ledger

    c. General Ledger

    d. Special Journal

    e. Schedule of Accounts Payable

_____ 4. A company that accumulates source documents for a period of time and then processes all of them at the same time:

    a. is most likely an airline company.

    b. must be using a manual accounting system.

    c. uses batch processing.

    d. uses on-line processing.

    e. always has an up-to-date data base.

Problem III

Many of the important ideas and concepts discussed in Chapter 7 are reflected in the following list of key terms. Test your understanding of these terms by matching the appropriate definitions with the terms. Record the number identifying the most appropriate definition in the blank space next to each term.

_____ Accounting information system	_____ Flexibility principle
_____ Accounts Payable Ledger	_____ General Journal
_____ Accounts Receivable Ledger	_____ Information processor
_____ Batch processing	_____ Information storage
_____ Cash Disbursements Journal	_____ Input device
_____ Cash Receipts Journal	_____ Internal controls
_____ Check Register	_____ Online processing
_____ Columnar journal	_____ Output devices
_____ Compatibility principle	_____ Purchases Journal
_____ Components of accounting systems	_____ Relevance principle
_____ Computer network	_____ Sales Journal
_____ Controlling account	_____ Schedule of accounts payable
_____ Control principle	_____ Schedule of accounts receivable
_____ Cost-benefit principle	_____ Segment return on assets
Enterprise resource planning (ERP)	
_____ software	_____ Special journal
	_____ Subsidiary ledger

1. Means of capturing information from source documents that enables its transfer to the information processing component of an accounting system.

2. Another name for a cash disbursements journal when the journal has a column for check numbers.

3. The component of an accounting system that keeps data in a form accessible to information processors.

4. List of balances of all the accounts in the accounts receivable ledger that are summed to show the total amount of accounts receivable outstanding.

5. General ledger account, the balance of which (after posting) equals the sum of the balances of the accounts in a related subsidiary ledger.

6. People, records, methods, and equipment that collect and process data from transactions and events, organize them into useful forms, and communicate results to decision makers.

7. Special journal used to record all payments of cash; also called cash payments journal.

8. Any journal used for recording and posting transactions of a similar type.

9. Information system principle that requires an accounting system to be able to adapt to changes in the company, business, and needs of decision makers.

10. A subsidiary ledger listing individual creditor accounts.

11. List of the balances of all accounts in the accounts payable ledger that are summed to show the total amount of accounts payable outstanding.

12. Component of an accounting system that interprets, transforms, and summarizes information for use in analyses and reporting.

13. A subsidiary ledger listing individual credit customer accounts.

14. Information system principle that requires an accounting information system conform with a company's activities, personnel, and structure.

15. List of individual accounts with a common characteristic; linked to a controlling account in the general ledger.

16. Means by which information is taken out of the accounting system and made available for use.

17. Journal with more than one column.

18. Special journal used to record all receipts of cash.

19. Source documents, input devices, information processors, information storage, and output devices..

20. Segment operating income divided by segment average (identifiable) assets..

21. Journal used to record sales of merchandise on credit.

22. Information system principle requiring that an accounting system report be useful, understandable, timely and pertinent for decision making.

23. A journal that is used to record all purchases on credit.

24. Information system principle that requires the benefits from an activity in an accounting information system to outweigh the costs of that activity.

25. Information system principle that requires an accounting information system to aid managers in controlling and monitoring business activities.

26. All policies and procedures used to protect assets, ensure reliable accounting, promote efficient operations, and urge adherence to company policies..

27. All-purpose journal for recording the debits and credits of transactions and events..

28. Linkage giving different users and different computers access to common databases and programs.

29. Programs that manage a company's vital operation, which range from order taking to manufacturing to accounting.

30. Approach to inputting data on each source document as soon as the document is available.

31. Approach that accumulates source documents for a period of time and then processes them all at once such as once a day, week, or month.

Problem IV

Complete the following by filling in the blanks.

1. The five basic components of an accounting system are: source documents, _____, the information processor, _____, and output devices.

2. When a company records sales returns with general journal entries, the credit of an entry recording such a return is posted to two different accounts. This does not cause the trial balance to be out of balance because_____

    _____.

3. Cash sales _____ (are, are not) normally recorded in the Sales Journal.

4. When special journals are used, credit purchases of store supplies or office supplies should be recorded in the_____.

5. The posting principle upon which a subsidiary ledger and its controlling account operate requires that the controlling account be debited for an amount or amounts equal to the sum of _____ _____ to the subsidiary ledger and that the controlling account be credited for an amount or amounts equal to the sum of _____ to the subsidiary ledger.

6. Cash purchases of store supplies or office supplies should be recorded in a(n)_____ _____.

7. When a subsidiary Accounts Receivable Ledger is maintained, the equality of the debits and credits posted to the General Ledger is proved by preparing _____. At the same time the balances of the customer accounts in the Accounts Receivable Ledger are proved by preparing_____.

8. Computer technology provides _____,_____,_____, and _____ in performing accounting tasks.

9. A segment refers to a part of a company that is separately identified by its _____ or _____, or by the _____ it serves.

10. Segment return on assets ratio is computed by dividing _____ by _____.

Problem V

Below are nine transactions completed by McGuff Company on September 30 of the current year. Following the transactions are the company's journals with prior September transactions recorded therein.

Requirement One: Record the nine transactions in the company's journals.

Sept. 30   Received an $808.50 check from Ted Clark in full payment of the September 20, $825 sale, less the $16.50 discount.

30   Received a $550 check from a tenant in payment of his September rent.

30   Sold merchandise costing $840 to Inez Smythe for $1,675 on credit, Invoice No. 655.

30   Received merchandise and an invoice dated September 28, terms 2/10, n/60 from Johnson Company, $4,000.

30   Purchased store equipment on account from Olson Company, invoice dated September 30, terms n/10, EOM, $950.

30   Issued Check No. 525 to Kerry Meadows in payment of her $650 salary.

30   Issued Check No. 526 for $1,715 to Olson Company in full payment of its September 20 invoice, less–a $35 discount.

30   Received a credit memorandum from Olson Company for unsatisfactory merchandise received on September 24 and returned for credit, $625.

30   Cash sales for the last half of the month totaled $9,450.50. This merchandise cost $ 4,275.

GENERAL JOURNAL

DATE	ACCOUNT TITLES AND EXPLANATION	P.R.	DEBIT	CREDIT

SALES JOURNAL

DATE	ACCOUNT DEBITED	INVOICE NUMBER	P.R.	Accts Receivable Dr Sales Cr.	Cost of Goods Sold Dr. Inventory Cr.
20--- SEPT. 3	N.R. Boswell	651	√	1 8 7 5 00	9 5 0 00
15	Inez Smythe	652	√	1 5 0 0 00	8 0 0 00
20	Ted Clark	653	√	8 2 5 00	4 2 0 00
24	N.R. Boswell	654	√	2 2 5 0 00	1 2 5 00

PURCHASES JOURNAL

DATE	ACCOUNT	DATE OF INVOICE	TERMS	P.R.	ACCOUNTS PAYABLE CREDIT	INVENTORY DEBIT	OTHER ACCOUNTS DEBIT
20--- Sept. 8	Johnson Company	9/6	2/10, n/60	√	3 7 5 0 00	3 7 5 0 00	
22	Olson Company	9/20	2/10, n/60	√	1 7 5 0 00	1 7 5 0 00	
24	Olson Company	9/22	2/10. n/60	√	5 6 2 5 00	5 6 2 5 00	

CASH RECEIPTS JOURNAL

DATE	ACCOUNT CREDITED	P.R.	CASH DEBIT	SALES DISCOUNT DEBIT	ACCOUNTS RECEIVABLE CREDIT	SALES CREDIT	OTHER ACCOUNTS CREDIT	Cost of Goods Sold Dr. Inventory Cr.
20--								
Sept. 1	Rent Earned	406	5 5 0 00				5 5 0 00	
13	N.R. Boswell	√	1 8 3 7 50	3 7 50	1 8 7 5 00			
15	Sales	√	9 0 0 00			9 0 0 00		4 6 0 00

CASH DISBURSEMENTS JOURNAL

DATE	CH. NO.	PAYEE	ACCOUNT DEBITED	P.R.	CASH CREDIT	INVENTORY CREDIT	OTHER ACCOUNTS DEBIT	ACCOUNTS PAYABLE DEBIT
20--								
Sept. 15	523	Kerry Meadows	Salaries Expense	622	6 5 0 00		6 5 0 00	
16	524	Johnson Company		√	3 6 7 5 00	7 5 00		3 7 5 0 00

Requirement Two: The individual postings from the journals of McGuff Company through September 29 have been made. Complete the individual postings from the journals.

Requirement Three: Foot and crossfoot the journals and make the month-end postings.

Requirement Four: Complete the trial balance and test the subsidiary ledgers by preparing schedules of accounts receivable and accounts payable.

ACCOUNTS RECEIVABLE LEDGER

N.R. Boswell

2200 Falstaff Street

DATE	EXPLANATION	P.R.	DEBIT			CREDIT			BALANCE		
20--- Sept. 3		S-8	1	8 7 5	00				1	8 7 5	00
13		R-9				1	8 7 5	00			
24		S-8	2	2 5 0	00				2	2 5 0	00

Ted Clark

10765 Catonsville Avenue

DATE	EXPLANATION	P.R.	DEBIT			CREDIT			BALANCE		
20--- Sept. 20		S-8		8 2 5	00					8 2 5	00

Inez Smythe

785 Violette Circle

DATE	EXPLANATION	P.R.	DEBIT			CREDIT			BALANCE		
20--- Sept. 15		S-8	1	5 0 0	00				1	5 0 0	00

ACCOUNTS PAYABLE LEDGER

Johnson Company

118 E. Seventh Street

DATE	EXPLANATION	P.R.	DEBIT			CREDIT			BALANCE		
20--- Sept. 8		P-8				3	7 5 0	00	3	7 5 0	00
16		D-7	3	7 5 0	00					- 0 -	

Olson Company

788 Hazelwood Avenue

DATE	EXPLANATION	P.R.	DEBIT	CREDIT	BALANCE
20--- Sept. 22		P-8		1 7 5 0 00	1 7 5 0 00
24		p-8		5 6 2 5 00	7 3 7 5 00

GENERAL LEDGER

Cash   Account No. 101

DATE	EXPLANATION	P.R.	DEBIT	CREDIT	BALANCE

Accounts Receivable   Account No. 106

DATE	EXPLANATION	P.R.	DEBIT	CREDIT	BALANCE

Inventory   Account No.107

DATE	EXPLANATION	P.R.	DEBIT	CREDIT	BALANCE

Store Equipment   Account No. 165

DATE	EXPLANATION	P.R.	DEBIT	CREDIT	BALANCE

Accounts Payable   Account No.201

DATE	EXPLANATION	P.R.	DEBIT	CREDIT	BALANCE

Rent Earned   Account No.406

DATE	EXPLANATION	P.R.	DEBIT	CREDIT	BALANCE
20--- Sept. 1		R-9		5 5 0 00	5 5 0 00

Sales   Account No.413

DATE	EXPLANATION	P.R.	DEBIT	CREDIT	BALANCE

Sales Discounts   Account No.415

DATE	EXPLANATION	P.R.	DEBIT	CREDIT	BALANCE

Cost of Goods Sold   Account No.613

DATE	EXPLANATION	P.R.	DEBIT	CREDIT	BALANCE

Salaries Expense   Account No.622

DATE	EXPLANATION	P.R.	DEBIT	CREDIT	BALANCE
20--- Sept. 15		D-7	6 5 0 00		6 5 0 00

MCGUFF COMPANY

Trial Balance

September 30, 20--

Cash										
Accounts receivable										
Inventory										
Store equipment										
Accounts payable										
Rent earned										
Sales										
Sales discounts										
Cost of goods sold										
Salaries expense										

MCGUFF COMPANY

Schedule of Accounts Receivable

September 30, 20--

MCGUFF COMPANY

Schedule of Accounts Payable

September 30, 20--

Fundamental Accounting Principles, 18/e

Solutions for Chapter 7

Problem I

1. F
2. T
3. T
4. F
5. F
6. F
7. F

Problem II

1. C
2. D
3. D
4. C

Problem III

6	Accounting information system		9	Flexibility principle
10	Accounts Payable Ledger		27	General Journal
13	Accounts Receivable Ledger		12	Information processor
31	Batch processing		3	Information storage
7	Cash Disbursements Journal		1	Input device
18	Cash Receipts Journal		26	Internal controls
2	Check Register		30	Online processing
17	Columnar journal		16	Output devices
14	Compatibility principle		23	Purchases Journal
19	Components of accounting systems		22	Relevance principle
28	Computer network		21	Sales Journal
5	Controlling account		11	Schedule of accounts payable
25	Control principle		4	Schedule of accounts receivable
24	Cost-benefit principle		20	Segment return on assets
29	Enterprise resource planning (ERP) software		8	Special journal
			15	Subsidiary ledger

Problem IV

1. input devices, information storage
2. only the balance of one of the accounts, Accounts Receivable account, appears on the trial balance.
3. are not
4. Purchases Journal
5. the debits posted, the credits posted
6. Cash Disbursements Journal
7. a trial balance, a schedule of accounts receivable
8. accuracy, speed, efficiency, convenience
9. products, services, geographic area
10. segment operating income, segment average assets

Problem V

DATE	GENERAL JOURNAL		DEBIT	CREDIT
Sept 30	Accounts Payable-Olson Company	201/√	625.00	
	Inventory..	107		625.0

SALES JOURNAL

DATE	ACCOUNT DEBITED	INVOICE NUMBER	P.R.	Accts Receivable Dr Sales Cr.					Cost of Goods Sold Dr. Inventory Cr.				
20---SEPT. 3	N.R. Boswell	651	√	1	8	7	5	00		9	5	0	00
15	Inez Smythe	652	√	1	5	0	0	00		8	0	0	00
20	Ted Clark	653	√		8	2	5	00		4	2	0	00
24	N.R. Boswell	654	√	2	2	5	0	00		1	2	5	00
30	Inez Smythe	655	√	1	6	7	5	00		8	4	0	00
30	Totals.			8	1	2	5	00	3	1	3	5	00
				(106/413)					(501/107)				

PURCHASES JOURNAL

DATE	ACCOUNT	DATE OF INVOICE	TERMS	P.R.	ACCOUNTS PAYABLE CREDIT				INVENTORY DEBIT				OTHER ACCOUNTS DEBIT			
20---Sept. 8	Johnson Company	9/6	2/10, n/60	√	3	7 5 0		00	3	7 5 0		00				
22	Olson Company	9/20	2/10, n/60	√	1	7 5 0		00	1	7 5 0		00				
24	Olson Company	9/22	2/10. n/60	√	5	6 2 5		00	5	6 2 5		00				
30	Johnson Company	9/28	2/10, n/60	√	4	0 0 0		00	4	0 0 0		00				
30	Str Equip/Olsn Co.	9/30	n/10 EOM	165√		9 5 0		00					9 5 0		00	
30	Totals				16	0 7 5		00	15	1 2 5		00	9 5 0		00	
					(201)				(107)				(√)			

CASH RECEIPTS JOURNAL

DATE	ACCOUNT CREDITED	P.R.	CASH DEBIT	SALES DISCOUNT DEBIT	ACCOUNTS RECEIVABLE CREDIT	SALES CREDIT	OTHER ACCOUNTS CREDIT	Cost of Goods Sold Debit Inventory Cr.
20--								
Sept. 1	Rent Earned	406	550 00				550 00	
13	N.R. Boswell	√	1 837 50	37 50	1 875 00			
15	Sales	√	9 000 00			9 000 00		4 600 00
30	Ted Clark	√	808 50	16 50	825 00			
30	Rent Earned	406	550 00				550 00	
30	Sales	√	9 450 50			9 450 50		4 275 00
30	Totals		22 196 50	54 00	2 700 00	18 450 50	1 100 00	8 875 00
			(101)	(415)	(106)	(413)	(√)	(501/107)

CASH DISBURSEMENTS JOURNAL

DATE	CH. NO.	PAYEE	ACCOUNT DEBITED	P.R.	CASH CREDIT	INVENTORY CREDIT	OTHER ACCOUNTS DEBIT	ACCOUNTS PAYABLE DEBIT
20--								
Sept. 15	523	Kerry Meadows	Salaries Expense	622	650 00		650 00	
16	524	Johnson Company		√	3 675 00	75 00		3 750 00
30	525	Kerry Meadows	Salaries Expense	622	650 00		650 00	
30	526	Olson Company		√	1 715 00	35 00		1 750 00
30			Totals		6 690 00	110 00	1 300 00	5 500 00
					(101)	(107)	(√)	(201)

GENERAL LEDGER

Cash   No. 101

Date	Debit	Credit	Balance
Sept. 30	22,196.50		22,196.50
30		6,690.00	15,506.50

Accounts Receivable   No. 106

Date	Debit	Credit	Balance
Sept. 30	8,125.00		8,125.00
30		2,700.00	5,425.00

Inventory   No. 107

Date	Debit	Credit	Balance
Sept. 30	15,125.00		15,125.00
30		625.00	14,500.00
30		110.00	14,390.00
30		3,135.00	11,255.00
30		8,875.00	2,380.00

Store Equipment   No. 165

Date	Debit	Credit	Balance
Sept. 30	950.00		950.00

Accounts Payable   No. 201

Date	Debit	Credit	Balance
Sept 30		16,075.00	16,075.00
30	5,500.00		10,575.00
30	625.00		9,950.00

Rent Earned   No. 406

Date	Debit	Credit	Balance
Sept. 1		550.00	550.00
30		550.00	1,100.00

Sales   No. 413

Date	Debit	Credit	Balance
Sept. 30		8,125.00	8,125.00
30		18,450.50	26,575.50

Sales Discounts   No. 415

Date	Debit	Credit	Balance
Sept. 30	54.00		54.00

Cost of Goods Sold   No. 501

Date	Debit	Credit	Balance
Sept. 30	3,135.00		3,135.00
30	8,875.00		12,010.00

Salaries Expense   No. 622

Date	Debit	Credit	Balance
Sept. 15	650.00		650.00
30	650.00		1,300.00

ACCOUNTS PAYABLE LEDGER

Johnson Company

Date	Debit	Credit	Balance
Sept. 8		3,750.00	3,750.00
16	3,750.00		-0-
30		4,000.00	4,000.00

Olson Company

Date	Debit	Credit	Balance
Sept. 22		1,750.00	1,750.00
24		5,625.00	7,375.00
30		950.00	8,325.00
30	1,750.00		6,575.00
30	625.00		5,950.00

ACCOUNTS RECEIVABLE LEDGER

N.R. Boswell

Date	Debit	Credit	Balance
Sept. 3	1,875.00		1,875.00
13		1,875.00	-0-
24	2,250.00		2,250.00

Inez Smythe

Date	Debit	Credit	Balance
Sept. 15	1,500.00		1,500.00
30	1,675.00	5,625.00	3,175.00

Ted Clark

Date	Debit	Credit	Balance
Sept. 20	825.00		825.00
30		825.00	-0-

MCGUFF COMPANY
Trial Balance
September 30, 20--

Cash	$15,506.50	
Accounts receivable	5,425.00	
Inventory	2,380.00	
Store equipment	950.00	
Accounts payable		$ 9,950.00
Rent earned		1,100.00
Sales		26,575.50
Sales discounts	54.00	
Cost of goods sold	12,010.00	
Salaries expense	1,300.00	
Totals	$37,625.50	$37,625.50

MCGUFF COMPANY
Schedule of Accounts Receivable
September 30, 20--

N.R. Boswell	$2,250.00
Inez Smythe	3,175.00
Total accounts receivable	$5,425.00

MCGUFF COMPANY
Schedule of Accounts Payable
September 30, 20--

Johnson Company	$4,000.00
Olson Company	5,950.00
Total accounts payable	$9,950.00

CHAPTER 8
CASH AND INTERNAL CONTROLS

Learning Objective C1:

Define internal control and identify its purpose and principles.

Summary

An internal control system consists of the policies and procedures managers use to protect assets, ensure reliable accounting, promote efficient operations, and urge adherence to company policies. It can prevent avoidable losses and help managers both plan operations and monitor company and human performance. Principles of good internal control include establishing responsibilities, maintaining adequate records, insuring assets and bonding employees, separating recordkeeping from custody of assets, dividing responsibilities for related transactions, applying technological controls, and performing regular independent reviews.

Learning Objective C2:

Define cash and cash equivalents and explain how to report them.

Summary

Cash includes currency, coins and amounts on (or acceptable for) deposit in bank checking and savings accounts. Cash equivalents are short-term, highly liquid investment assets readily convertible to a known cash amount and sufficiently close to their maturity date so that market value is not sensitive to interest rate changes. Cash and cash equivalents are liquid assets because they are readily converted into other assets or can be used to paying for goods, services or liabilities.

Learning Objective C3:

Identify control features of banking activities.

Summary

Banks offer several basic services that promote the control and safeguarding of cash. A bank account is a record set up by a bank permitting a customer to deposit money for safekeeping and to draw checks on it. A bank deposit is money contributed to the account with a deposit ticket as proof. A check is a document signed by the depositor instructing the bank to pay a specified amount of money to a designated recipient.

Learning Objective A1:

Compute days' sales uncollected ratio and use it to assess liquidity.

Summary

Many companies attract customers by selling to them on credit. This means that cash receipts from customers are delayed until accounts receivable are collected. Users want to know how quickly a company can convert its accounts receivable into cash. The days' sales uncollected ratio, one measure reflecting a company's liquidity, is computed by dividing the ending balance of receivables by annual net sales, and then multiplying by 365.

Learning Objective P1:

Apply internal control to cash receipts and disbursements.

Summary

Internal control of cash receipts ensures that all cash received is properly recorded and deposited. Attention focuses on two important types of cash receipts: over-the-counter and by mail. Good internal control for over-the-counter cash receipts includes use of a cash register, customer review, use of receipts, a permanent transaction record, and the separation of the custody of cash from its recordkeeping. Good internal control for cash receipts by mail includes assigning at least two people to open mail and a listing of each sender's name, amount, and explanation.

Learning Objective P2:

Explain and record petty cash fund transactions.

Summary

Petty cash disbursements are payments of small amounts for items such as postage, courier fees, minor repairs, and supplies. A company usually sets up one or more petty cash funds. A petty fund cashier is responsible for the safekeeping of the cash, making payments from this fund, and keeping receipts and records. A Petty Cash account is debited only when the fund is established or increased in amount. When the fund is replenished, petty cash disbursements are recorded with debits to expense (or asset) accounts and a credit to cash.

Learning Objective P3:

Prepare a bank reconciliation.

Summary

A bank reconciliation proves the accuracy of the depositor's and the bank's records. The bank statement balance is adjusted for items such as outstanding checks and unrecorded deposits made on or before the bank statement date but not reflected on the statement. The book balance is adjusted for items such as service charges, bank collections for the depositor, and interest earned on the account.

Learning Objective P4[A]:

Describe the voucher system to control cash disbursements.

Summary

A voucher system is a set of procedures and approvals designed to control cash disbursements and acceptance of obligations. The voucher system of control relies on several important documents including the voucher and its files. A key factor in this system is that only approved departments and individuals are authorized to incur certain obligations.

Learning Objective P5^B:

Apply the net method to control purchase discounts.

Summary

The net method aids management in monitoring and controlling purchase discounts. When invoices are recorded at gross amounts, the amount of discounts taken is deducted from the balance of the Inventory account. This means that the amount of any discounts lost is not reported in any account and is unlikely to come to the attention of management. When purchases are recorded at net amounts, a Discounts Lost account is brought to management's attention as an operating expense. Management can then seek to identify the reason for discounts lost, such as oversight, carelessness, or unfavorable terms.

Chapter Outline

I. **Internal Control**

    A. Purpose of Internal Control
        An *internal control system* consists of policies and procedures managers use to:

        1. Protect assets.

        2. Ensure reliable accounting.

        3. Promote efficient operations.

        4. Urge adherence to company policies.

    B. Principles of Internal Control:

        1. Establish responsibilities.

        2. Maintain adequate records.

        3. Insure assets and bond key employees.

        4. Separate recordkeeping from custody of assets.

        5. Divide responsibility for related transactions.

        6. Apply technological controls.

        7. Perform regular and independent reviews.

    C. Technology and Internal Control
        Technology provides quick access to databases and information. Examples of how technology impacts internal control:

        1. Reduces processing errors.

        2 Allows more extensive testing of records.

        3. Limits hard copy evidence of processing steps but can electronically store additional evidence.

        4. Requires that crucial separation of responsibilities be carefully distributed among fewer employees.

        5. Increased e-commerce increases risks of credit card theft, computer viruses and online impersonation.

    D. Limitations of Internal Control

        1. Human error and/or human fraud

        2. *Cost-benefit principle*—the costs of internal controls must not exceed their benefits.

II. **Control of Cash**—Basic guidelines for control of cash and cash equivalents include: handling of cash must be separate from recordkeeping of cash, cash receipts are promptly deposited in bank, and disbursements of cash are by check.

    A. Cash, Cash Equivalents, and Liquidity

        1. *Liquidity* refers to a company's ability to pay for its near term obligations.

2. *Cash* includes currency and coins, deposits in bank and checking accounts (called demand deposits), many savings accounts (called time deposits), and items that are acceptable for deposit in those accounts (customers checks, cashier checks, certified checks, and money orders).

3. *Cash equivalent* (examples; short-term U.S. Treasury bills and money market funds) are short-term, highly liquid investment assets meeting two criteria:

   a. Readily convertible to a known cash amount.

   b. Sufficiently close to their maturity date so that market value is not sensitive to interest rate changes.

   Note: Only investments purchased within three months of their maturity dates usually satisfy these criteria.

B. Control of Cash Receipts
   Procedures for protecting cash received over-the-counter and by mail:

   1. Apply internal control principles.

   2. Record cash shortages and overages in and income statement account called Cash Over and Short.

C. Control of Cash Disbursements
   To safeguard against theft:

   1. Require all expenditures be made by checks. (Exception— small payments made from petty cash fund.)

   2. Deny access to the accounting records to anyone, other than the owner, who has authority to sign checks.

   3. Use a *voucher system* of control that establishes procedures for:
      a. verifying, approving and recording obligations for eventual cash disbursement.
      b. issuing checks for payment of verified, approved, and recorded obligations.
      (Documents in a voucher system are listed and explained in appendix notes)

   4. Use a petty cash system of control as follows:

      a. Write and cash a check to establish petty cash fund. Record as a debit to Petty Cash and credit to Cash. (Use the Petty Cash account only when the fund is established or <u>size</u> of fund is increased or decreased.)

      b. Assigning a petty cashier (custodian) to account for the amounts expended and to keep receipts.

        c. Reimbursement—debit the expenses or other items paid for with petty cash and credit Cash for the amount reimbursed to the petty cash fund.

        d. Record any petty cash shortages/overages.

III.   **Banking Activities as Controls**

  A. Basic Bank Services
     Bank accounts permit depositing money for safeguarding and helps control withdrawals.

  B. Electronic Funds Transfer (EFT)
     Electronic communication transfer of cash from one party to another.

  C. Bank Statement
     Shows activities of a bank account and is used to prove the accuracy of the depositor's cash records by preparing a bank reconciliation.

     1. *Bank reconciliation* –a report that explains *(reconciles)* the difference between the balance of a checking account according to the depositor's records and the balance reported on the bank statement.

     2. Factors causing the bank statement balance to differ from the depositor's book balance are:

        a. Outstanding checks.

        b. Deposits in transit.

        c. Deductions for uncollectible items and services

        d. Additions for collections and interest.

        e. Errors.

     3. Steps in preparing the bank reconciliation:

        a. Identify the bank balance of the cash account (*balance per bank*).

        b. Identify and list any unrecorded deposits and any bank errors understating the bank balance. Add them to the bank balance.

        c. Identify and list any outstanding checks and any bank errors overstating the bank balance. Deduct them from the bank balance.

        d. Compute the *adjusted bank balance*, also called corrected or reconciled balance.

        e. Identify the company's balance of the cash account (*balance per book*).

        f. Identify and list any unrecorded credit memoranda from the bank, interest earned, and errors understating the book balance. Add them to the book balance.

      g. Identify and list any unrecorded debit memoranda from the bank, service charges, and errors overstating the book balance. Deduct them from the book balance.

      h. Compute the *adjusted book balance*, also called corrected or reconciled balance.

      i. Verify the two adjusted balances from steps d and h are equal. If yes, they are reconciled. If not, check for accuracy and missing data to achieve reconciliation.

   4. Adjusting entries from a bank reconciliation

      a. All reconciling additions to book balance are debits to cash. Credit depends on reason for addition (Examples: Credit Interest Income for interest on balance and Notes Receivable when bank collected note).

      b. All reconciling subtractions from book balance are credits to cash. Debit depends on reason for subtraction (Examples: Debit Miscellaneous Expense for bank service charge and Accounts Receivable/customer for NSF checks.).

IV.   **Decision Analysis—Days' Sales Uncollected**

   A. Also called *days' sales in receivables*.

   B. Used to evaluate the liquidity of a company; estimates how quickly a company will convert its accounts receivable into cash.

   C. Calculated by dividing current balance of accounts receivable by net sales and multiplying the result by 365.

V.   **Documents in a Voucher System—Appendix 8A**

Important documents of a voucher system of control include:

   A. Purchase Requisition—lists the merchandise needed and requests that it be purchased.

   B. Purchase Order—used by purchasing department to place an order with a vendor (seller or supplier).

   C. Invoice—an itemized statement of goods prepared by the vendor (copy sent to buyer) listing the customer's name, items sold, sales prices, and terms of sale.

   D. Receiving report—used by receiving department to verify that goods conform to purchase order.

   E. Invoice Approval—used by accounting department to verify all necessary documents related to a purchase are assembled and approve payment of the related invoice.

   F. Voucher—can be a folder used to hold all documents related to a given transaction and authorizes the recording.

VI   **Controls of Purchases Discounts—Appendix 8B**

    A. Recording inventory purchases using *net method* provides more control than *gross method*.

    B. Gross method in a perpetual inventory system—records the purchase (debit inventory, credit accounts payable) at the gross amount and later reduces the inventory account by the amount of the discount if invoice is paid within the discount period. If the invoice is not paid within the discount period the inventory account is not affected.

    C. Net method in a perpetual inventory system—records purchases (debit inventory, credit accounts payable) at net amount and later records *Discount Lost* and increases accounts payable if the invoice not paid within discount period.

    D. Periodic inventory system differs from perpetual (under either method) in that increases to inventory are recorded in Purchases account and decreases to inventory for the discount are recorded in Purchases Discount.

BANK RECONCILIATION

<u>Reasons for discrepancies between
bank statement balance and checkbook
balance:</u>

<u>Handle as follows:</u>

Unrecorded deposits	Add to Bank Balance
Outstanding checks	Deduct from Bank Balance
Bank service charges	Deduct from Book Balance
Debit memos	Deduct from Book Balance
Credit memos	Add to Book Balance
NSF checks	Deduct from Book Balance
Interest	Add to Book Balance
Errors	Must analyze individually (bank errors affect bank balance and book errors affect book balance)

Problem I

The following statements are either true or false. Place a (T) in the parentheses before each true statement and an (F) before each false statement.

1. ( ) One of the fundamental principles of internal control states that the person who has access to or is responsible for an asset should not maintain the accounting record for that asset.

2. ( ) Procedures for controlling cash disbursements are as important as those for cash receipts.

3. ( ) In order to approve an invoice for payment for the purchase of assets, the accounting department of a large company should require copies of the purchase requisition, purchase order, invoice, and receiving report.

4. ( ) After the petty cash fund is established, the Petty Cash account is not debited or credited again unless the size of the fund is changed.

5. ( ) The Cash Over and Short account is usually shown on the income statement as part of miscellaneous revenues if it has a credit balance at the end of the period.

6. ( ) If 20 canceled checks are listed on the current month's bank statement, then no less than 20 checks could have been issued during the current month.

Note: Question 7 relates to appendix 8B

7. ( ) Under the periodic inventory system, when the net method of recording invoices is used, cash discounts lost are reported as an expense in the income statement; when the gross method is used, cash discounts taken are deducted from purchases in the income statement.

Problem II

You are given several words, phrases, or numbers to choose from in completing each of the following statements or in answering the following questions. In each case select the one that best completes the statement or answers the question and place its letter in the answer space provided.

_____ 1. A voucher system:

    a. Permits only authorized individuals to incur obligations that will result in cash disbursements.

    b. Establishes procedures for incurring such obligations and for their verification, approval, and recording.

    c. Permits checks to be issued only in payment of properly verified, approved, and recorded obligations.

    d. Requires that every obligation be recorded at the time it is incurred and every purchase be treated as an independent transaction, complete in itself.

    e. Does all of the above.

_____ 2. Liquidity is:

    a. The portion of a corporation's equity that represents investments in the corporation by its stockholders.

    b. Cash or other assets that are reasonably expected to be realized in cash or be sold or consumed within one year or one operating cycle of the business.

    c. A characteristic of an asset indicating how easily the asset can be converted into cash or used to buy services or satisfy obligations.

    d. Obligations that are due to be paid or liquidated within one year or one operating cycle of the business.

    e. Economic benefits or resources without physical substance, the value of which stems from the privileges or rights that accrue to their owner.

_____ 3. A voucher is:

a. An internal business paper (or folder) used to accumulate other papers and information needed to control cash disbursements and to ensure that the transaction is properly recorded.

b. A business form used within a business to ask the purchasing department of the business to buy needed items.

c. A document, prepared by a vendor, on which are listed the items sold, the sales prices, the customer's name, and the terms of sale.

d. A form used within a business to notify the proper persons of the receipt of goods ordered and of the quantities and condition of the goods.

e. A document on which the accounting department notes that it has performed each step in the process of checking an invoice and approving it for recording and payment.

_____ 4. Each of the following items would cause Brand X Sales Company's book balance of cash to differ from its bank statement balance.

A. A service charge made by the bank.

B. A check listed as outstanding on the previous month's reconciliation and that is still outstanding.

C. A customer's check returned by the bank marked "NSF."

D. A deposit which was mailed to the bank on the last day of November and is unrecorded on the November bank statement.

E A check paid by the bank at its correct $422 amount but recorded in error in the General Journal at $442.

F. An unrecorded credit memorandum indicating the bank had collected a note receivable for Brand X Sales Company and deposited the proceeds in the company's account.

G. A check written during November and not yet paid and returned by the bank.

Which of the above items require entries on the books of Brand X Sales Company?

a. A., B., C., and E.

b. A., C., E., and F.

c. A., B., D., and F.

d. A., B., D., E., and G.

e. C., D., E., and F.

_____ 5 A company reported net sales for 2007 and 2008 of $560,000 and $490,000 respectively. The year-end balances of accounts receivable were $34,000 and $31,000. Days' sales uncollected for 2008 is:

a. 6 days

b. 20.2 days

c. 15.8 days

d. 23.1 days

e. 24.2 days

Problem III

Many of the important ideas and concepts discussed in Chapter 8 are reflected in the following list of key terms. Test your understanding of these terms by matching the appropriate definitions with the terms. Record the number identifying the most appropriate definition in the blank space next to each term.

_____	Bank reconciliation	_____	Liquid asset
_____	Bank statement	_____	Liquidity
_____	Canceled checks	_____	Net method
_____	Cash	_____	Outstanding checks
_____	Cash equivalents	_____	Petty cash
_____	Cash Over and Short	_____	Principles of internal control
_____	Check	_____	Purchase order
_____	Days' sales uncollected	_____	Purchase requisition
_____	Deposit in transit	_____	Receiving report
_____	Deposit ticket	_____	Signature card
_____	Discounts lost	_____	Vendee
_____	Electronic funds transfer (EFT)	_____	Vendor
_____	Gross method	_____	Voucher
_____	Internal control system	_____	Voucher register
_____	Invoice	_____	Voucher system
_____	Invoice approval		

1. Form used to report that ordered goods are received and to describe their quantity and condition.

2. Company's ability to pay for its short-term obligations.

3. Expense resulting from failing to take advantage of cash discounts on purchases.

4. Checks written and recorded by the depositor but not yet paid by the bank at the bank statement date.

5. Seller of goods or services.

6. Itemized record of goods prepared by the vendor that lists the customer's name, the items sold, the sales prices, and the terms of sale.

7. Internal business file that is used to accumulate documents and information to control the cash disbursements and to ensure that a transaction is properly recorded.

8. Method of recording purchases at the full invoice price without deducting any cash discounts.

9. Asset such as cash that is easily converted into other types of assets or used to pay for goods, services or liabilities.

10. Checks that the bank has paid and deducted from the customer's account during the period.

11. Document containing a checklist of steps necessary for approving an invoice for recording and payment; also called *check authorization*.

12. Document listing merchandise needed by a department and requesting it be purchased.

13. An income statement account used to record cash overages and cash shortages arising from missing petty cash receipts or from errors in making change.

14. All policies and procedures used to protect assets, ensure reliable accounting, promote efficient operations, and urge adherence to company policies.

15. Set of procedures and approvals designed to control cash disbursements and acceptance of obligations.

16. Document used by the purchasing department to place an order with a seller (vendor).

17. Report that explains the difference between the balance of a checking account in the depositor's records and the balance reported on the bank statement.

18. A measure of the liquidity of receivables computed by dividing the current balance of receivables by the annual (or net) sales and then multiplying by 365; also called *days' sales in receivables*.

19. Method of recording purchases at the full invoice price less any cash discounts.

20. Buyer or purchaser of goods or services.

21. Short-term, highly liquid investments that are readily converted into a known cash amount and sufficiently close to their maturity date so that market value is not sensitive to interest rate changes.

22. Includes the signatures of each person authorized to sign checks on the account.

23. Principles requiring management to establish responsibility, maintain records, insure assets, separate recordkeeping from custody of assets, divide responsibility for related transactions, apply technological controls, and perform reviews.

24. Use of electronic communication to transfer cash from one party to another.

25. Lists items such as currency, coins, and checks deposited and their corresponding dollar amounts.

26. Document signed by the depositor instructing the bank to pay a specified amount to a designated recipient.

27. Includes currency, coins, and amounts on deposit in bank checking or savings accounts.

28. Bank report on the depositor's beginning and ending cash balances, and a listing of its changes, for a period.

29. Deposits recorded by the company but not yet by its bank.

30. Small amount of cash in a fund to pay minor expenses.

31. A journal used to record approved vouchers.

Problem IV
Complete the following by filling in the blanks.

1. If a cashier errs while making change and gives a customer too much money back, the resulting cash shortage is recorded with a debit to an account called

   _____.

2. A (n) _____ form is used by the accounting department in checking and approving an invoice for recording and payment.

3. Cash discounts offered but not taken are _____.

4. If the size of the petty cash fund remains unchanged, the Petty Cash account _____ (is, is not) debited in the entry to replenish the petty cash fund.

5. Control of a small business is commonly gained through the direct supervision and active participation of the _____ in the affairs and activities of the

business. However, as a business grows, it becomes necessary for the manager to delegate responsibilities and rely on _____ rather than personal contact in controlling the affairs and activities of the business.

6. A properly designed internal control system encourages adherence to prescribed managerial policies; and it also (a) _____

_____ ;

   (b) _____

   _____ ; and (c) _____

   _____ .

7. A good system of internal control for cash requires a _____
   of duties so that the people responsible for handling cash and for its custody are not the same people who _____ . It also requires that all cash receipts be deposited in the bank _____ and that all payments, except petty cash payments, be made by _____ .

8. A bank reconciliation is prepared to account for the difference between the
   _____ and the _____ .

9. An accounting system used to control the incurrence and payment of obligations requiring the disbursement of cash is a _____ .

10. A _____ is commonly used by a selling department to notify the purchasing department of items which the selling department wishes the purchasing department to purchase.

11. The business form commonly used by the purchasing department of a large company to order merchandise is called a(n) _____ .

12. Good internal control follows certain broad principles. These principles are:

    (a) Responsibilities should be clearly established, and in every situation
    _____ should be made responsible for each task.

    (b) Adequate records should be maintained since they provide an important means of protecting _____ .

    (c) Assets should be _____ and employees _____ .

    (d) Record-keeping for assets and _____ of assets should be separated.

    (e) Responsibility for related transactions should be _____ so that the work of one department or individual may act as a check on the work of others.

    (f) Mechanical devices _____ where practicable.

    (g) Regular and independent _____ of internal control procedures should be conducted.

13. After preparing a bank reconciliation, journal entries _____ (should, should not) be made to record those items listed as outstanding checks.

14. Days' sales uncollected is used in evaluating the _____ of a company.

©The McGraw-Hill Companies, Inc., 2007

Problem V

On November 5 of the current year Cullen Company drew Check No. 23 for $50 to establish a petty cash fund.

1. Give the general journal entry to record the establishment of the fund.

DATE	ACCOUNT TITLES AND EXPLANATION	P.R.	DEBIT	CREDIT

After making a payment from petty cash on November 25, the petty cashier noted that there was only $2.50 cash remaining in the fund. The cashier prepared the following list of expenditures from the fund and requested that the fund be replenished.

Nov. 9	Express freight on merchandise purchased	$ 9.75
12	Miscellaneous expense to clean office	10.00
15	Office supplies	3.50
18	Delivery of merchandise to customer	8.00
23	Miscellaneous expense for collect telegram	3.25
25	Express freight on merchandise purchased	13.00

Check No. 97 in the amount of $47.50 was drawn to replenish the fund.

2. In the General Journal below give the entry to record the check replenishing the petty cash fund.

DATE	ACCOUNT TITLES AND EXPLANATION	P.R.	DEBIT	CREDIT

Problem VI

Information about the following eight items is available to prepare Verde Company's December 31 bank reconciliation.

Two checks (1) No. 453 and (2) No. 457 were outstanding on November 30. Check No. 457 was returned with the December bank statement but Check No. 453 was not. (3) Check No. 478, written on December 26, was not returned with the canceled checks; and (4) Check No. 480 for $96 was incorrectly entered in the Cash Disbursements Journal and posted as though it were for $69. (5) A deposit placed in the bank's night depository after banking hours on November 30 appeared on the December bank statement, but (6) one placed there after hours on December 31 did not. (7) Enclosed with the December bank statement was a debit memorandum for a bank service charge and (8) a check received from a customer and deposited on December 27 but returned by the bank marked "Not Sufficient Funds."

1. If an item in the above list should not appear on the December 31 bank reconciliation, ignore it. However, if an item should appear, enter its number in a set of parentheses to show where it should be added or subtracted in preparing the reconciliation.
2.

VERDE COMPANY
Bank Reconciliation
December 31, 20--

Book balance of cash	$X,XXX	Bank statement balance	$X,XXX
Add:		Add:	
( )		( )	
( )		( )	
( )		( )	
Deduct:		Deduct:	
( )		( )	
( )		( )	
( )		( )	
Reconciled balance	$X,XXX	Reconciled balance	$X,XXX

2. Certain of the above items require entries on Verde Company's books. Place the numbers of these items within the following parentheses:

( ), ( ), ( ), ( ), ( ), ( )

Problem VII

On May 8 a company that records purchases at net amounts received a shipment of merchandise having a $3,750 invoice price. Attached to the merchandise was the invoice, which was dated May 6, terms 2/10, n/60, FOB the vendor's warehouse. The vendor, Vee Company, had prepaid the shipping charges on the goods, $125, adding the amount to the invoice and bringing its total to $3,875. The invoice was recorded and filed in error for payment on May 26. Give in General Journal form the entries to record the (1) purchase, (2) discovery on May 26 of the discount lost, and (3) payment of the invoice on July 5. Do not give explanations but skip a line between entries.

DATE	ACCOUNT TITLES AND EXPLANATION	P.R.	DEBIT	CREDIT

Problem VIII—Relates to Appendix 8B

1. The ABC Company uses a perpetual inventory system and records all purchases at gross amounts. Give in general journal form the entries to record the following transactions (do not give explanations but skip a line between entries):

 June 1   Received shipment of merchandise having $2,000 invoice price, terms 2/10, n/30.
 June 2   Received shipment of merchandise having $500 invoice price, terms 1/10, n/60.
 June 7   Paid for merchandise received on June 1.
 July 30 Paid for merchandise received on June 2.

DATE	ACCOUNT TITLES AND EXPLANATION	P.R.	DEBIT	CREDIT

2. Show the appropriate general journal entries for the ABC Company if they had recorded purchases at net amounts (do not give explanations but skip a line between entries):

DATE	ACCOUNT TITLES AND EXPLANATION	P.R.	DEBIT	CREDIT

Problem IX

The bank statement dated September 30, 2007, for the Smith Company showed a balance of $2,876.35 which differs from the $1,879.50 book balance of cash on that date. In attempting to reconcile the difference, the accountant noted the following facts:

1. The bank recorded a service fee of $15 that was not recorded on the books of Smith Company.

2. A deposit of $500 was made on the last day of the month but was not recorded by the bank.

3. A check for $176 had been recorded on the Smith Company books as $167. The bank paid the correct amount.

4. A check was written during September but has not been processed by the bank. The amount was $422.85.

5. A check for $1,000 is still outstanding from August.

6. A check for $100 deposited by Smith Company was returned marked "Not Sufficient Funds."

7. A credit memorandum stated that the bank collected a note receivable of $200 for Smith Company and charged Smith a $2 collection fee. Smith Company had not previously recorded the collection.

Prepare, in good form, a bank reconciliation which shows the correct cash balance on September 30, 2007.

Solutions for Chapter 8

Problem I

1. T
2. T
3. T
4. T

5. T
6. F
7. T

Problem II

1. E
2. C
3. A
4. B
5. D

Problem III

17	Bank reconciliation	9	Liquid asset
28	Bank statement	2	Liquidity
10	Canceled checks	19	Net method
27	Cash	4	Outstanding checks
21	Cash equivalents	30	Petty cash
13	Cash Over and Short	23	Principles of internal control
26	Check	16	Purchase order
18	Days' sales uncollected	12	Purchase requisition
29	Deposit in transit	1	Receiving report
25	Deposit ticket	22	Signature card
3	Discounts lost	20	Vendee
24	Electronic funds transfer (EFT)	5	Vendor
8	Gross method	7	Voucher
14	Internal control system	31	Voucher register
6	Invoice	15	Voucher system
11	Invoice approval		

Problem IV

1. Cash Over and Short
2. invoice approval
3. discounts lost
4. is not
5. owner-manager, a system of internal control
6. (a) promotes operational efficiencies; (b) protects the business assets from waste, fraud, and theft; and (c) ensures accurate and reliable accounting data
7. separation, keep the cash records, intact each day, check
8. book balance of cash, bank statement balance
9. voucher system
10. purchase requisition
11. purchase order
12. (a) one person; (b) assets; (c) insured, bonded; (d) custody; (e) divided; (f) should be used; (9) reviews
13. should not
14. liquidity

Problem V

1. Nov. 5   Petty Cash 50.00

              Cash 50.00

              Established a petty cash fund.

2. Nov. 25   Transportation-In 22.75

              Miscellaneous Expenses 13.25

              Office Supplies 3.50

              Delivery Expense 8.00

              Cash 47.50

              Reimbursed the petty cash fund.

Problem VI

1. Book balance of cash .... $X,XXX   Bank statement balance .... $X,XXX

    Add: Add:

      ( )   (6)

    Deduct: Deduct:

      (4)   (1)

      (7)   (3)

      (8)   ( )

2.   (4), (7), (8)

                                                         Fundamental Accounting Principles, 18/e

Problem VII

May 8	Purchases...	3,675.00	
	Transportation-In..	125.00	
	Accounts Payable—Vee Company		3,800.00
	$3,750 - ($3,750 \times .02) = $3,675 + 125		
26	Discounts Lost..	75.00	
	Accounts Payable—Vee Company		75.00
July 5	Accounts Payable—Vee Company	3,875.00	
	Cash..		3,875.00

Problem VIII

1.	June 1	Merchandise Inventory	2,000.00	
		Accounts Payable...		2,000
	2	Merchandise Inventory	500.00	
		Accounts Payable...		500.00
	7	Accounts Payable...	2,000.00	
		Merchandise Inventory		40.00
		Cash		1,960.00
	July 30	Accounts Payable...	500.00	
		Cash		500.00
2.	June 1	Merchandise Inventory ($2,000 x 98%)...............................	1.960.00	
		Accounts Payable...		1,960.00
	2	Merchandise Inventory ($500 x 99%)	495.00	
		Accounts Payable...		495.00
	7	Accounts Payable...	1,960.00	
		Cash		1,960.00
	July 30	Discounts Lost	5.00	
		Accounts Payable...		5.00
	30	Accounts Payable...	500.00	
		Cash		500.00

Problem IX

SMITH COMPANY
Bank Reconciliation
September 30, 2007

Book balance of cash		$1,879.50	Bank statement balance	$2,876.35
Add:			Add:	
Proceeds of note less				
Collection fee		198.00	Deposit on 9/30/07	500.00
		2,077.50		3,376.35
Deduct:			Deduct:	
NSF check	$100.00		Outstanding checks:	
Service fee	15.00		August	$1,000.00
Recording error	9.00	124.00	September	422.85	1,422.85
Reconciled balance		$1,953.50	Reconciled balance	$1,953.50

Learning Objective C1:

Describe accounts receivable and how they occur and are recorded.

Summary

Accounts receivable are amounts due from customers for credit sales. A subsidiary ledger lists amounts owed by each customer. Credit sales arise from at least two sources: (1) sales on credit and (2) credit card sales. *Sales on credit* refers to a company's granting credit directly to customers. Credit card sales involve customers' use of third-party's credit cards.

Learning Objective C2:

Describe a note receivable and the computation of its maturity date and interest.

Summary

A note receivable is a written promise to pay a specified amount of money at a definite future date. The maturity date is the day the note (principal and interest) must be repaid. Interest rates are normally stated in annual terms. The amount of interest on a note is computed by expressing time as a fraction of one year and multiplying the note's principal by this fraction and the annual interest rate.

Learning Objective C3:

Explain how receivables can be converted to cash before maturity.

Summary

Receivables can be converted to cash before maturity in three ways. First, a company can sell accounts receivable to a factor, who charges a factoring fee. Second, a company can borrow money by signing a note payable that is secured by pledging the accounts receivable. Third, notes receivable can be discounted at (sold to) a financial institution.

Learning Objective A1:

Compute accounts receivable turnover and use it to help assess financial condition.

Summary

Accounts receivable turnover is a measure of both the quality and liquidity of accounts receivable. The accounts receivable turnover measure indicates how often, on average, receivables are received and collected during the period. Accounts receivable turnover is computed as net sales divided by average accounts receivable.

Learning Objective P1:

Apply the direct write-off and allowance methods to account for accounts receivable.

Summary

The direct write-off method charges Bad Debts Expense when accounts are written off as uncollectible. This method is acceptable only when the amount of bad debts expense is immaterial. Under the allowance method, bad debts expense is recorded with an adjustment at the end of each accounting period that debits the Bad Debts Expense account and credits the Allowance for Doubtful Accounts. The uncollectible accounts are later written off with a debit to the Allowance for Doubtful Accounts.

Learning Objective P2:

Estimate uncollectibles using methods based on sales and accounts receivable.

Summary

Uncollectibles are estimated by focusing on either (1) the income statement relation between bad debts expense and credit sales or (2) the balance sheet relation between accounts receivable and the allowance for doubtful accounts. The first approach emphasizes the matching principle using the income statement. The second approach emphasizes realizable value of accounts receivable using the balance sheet.

Learning Objective P3:

Record the receipt of a note receivable.

Summary

A note received is recorded at its principal amount by debiting the Notes Receivable account. The credit amount is to the asset, product, or service provided in return for the note.

Learning Objective P4:

Record the honoring and dishonoring of a note and adjustments for interest.

Summary

When a note is honored, the payee debits the money received and credits both Notes Receivable and Interest Revenue. Dishonored notes are credited to Notes Receivable and debited to Accounts Receivable (to the account of the maker in an attempt to collect) and Interest Revenue is recorded for the interest earned for the time the note is held.

I. **Accounts Receivable**—Amounts due from customers for credit sales. They occur when a customer uses credit cards issued by third parties and when a company gives credit directly to customers.

   A. Recognizing Accounts Receivable:

     1. Sales on credit—Increase (debit) Accounts Receivable for the full amount of the sale and increase (credit) Sales.

        a. The General Ledger continues to keep a single (total) accounts receivable.

        b. A supplementary record, called the Accounts Receivable (subsidiary) Ledger, maintains a separate account receivable for each customer.

        c. A *Schedule of Accounts Receivable* shows that the sum of the individual accounts in the subsidiary ledger equals the debit balance of the Accounts Receivable account in the general ledger.

     2. Credit card sales (Examples: Visa, MasterCard, American Express).

        a. advantages: (1) eliminates the company's need to evaluate each customer's credit standing (2) avoids seller's risk (3) seller receives cash sooner than when they grant credit directly (4) more credit options potentially increase sales.

        b. Credit card sales (when cash is received upon deposit of sales receipt) results in debit to Cash for the amount of sale less the credit card company charge, debit to Credit Card Expense for this fee and credit to Sales for full invoice amount.

        c. Credit card sales (when cash receipt is delayed until payment is made by credit card) results in debit to Accounts Receivable for the amount to be collected, and a debit to Credit Card expense for the amount of the fee and credit to Sales for full invoice. Later, when payment is received, debit Cash and credit Accounts Receivable.

   B. Installment Sales and Receivables
      Amounts owed by customers from credit sales where payment is required in periodic amounts over an extended time period.

     1. Customer is usually charged interest.

     2. Should be classified as current assets even if credit period exceeds year if the company regularly offers customers such terms.

   C. Valuing Accounts Receivable
      Accounts of customers who do not pay are uncollectible accounts, commonly called *bad debts*. Two methods are used to account for uncollectible accounts:

1. Direct Write-off Method
   Records the loss from an uncollectible account receivable when it is determined to be uncollectible.

   a. To write off uncollectible and recognize loss: debit Bad Debt Expense, credit Accounts Receivable.

   b. If a written off account is later collected, this results in a reversal of the write-off (see above) and a normal collection of account entry.

   c. This method violates the matching principle since it frequently results in expense being charged in a period after that of the credit sale.

   d. Materiality principle states that an amount can be ignored if its effect on the financial statements is unimportant to users' decisions. This principle permits use of direct write-off when bad debts expenses are very small in relation to other financial statement items such as sales and net income.

2. Allowance Method
   Matches the *estimated* loss from uncollectibles against the sales they helped produce.

   a. At the end of each accounting period, bad debts expense is *estimated* and recorded in an adjusting entry.

   b. To record estimate of bad debt expense, Debit Bad Debt Expense, credit a contra-asset account called Allowance for Doubtful Accounts.

   c. Advantages of method:

      i. Satisfies the matching principle because expense is charged in the period of the corresponding sale.

      ii. Reports accounts receivable on balance sheet at the estimated amount of cash to be collected.

   d. To write-off an uncollectible: debit Allowance for Doubtful Accounts, credit Accounts Receivable.

   e. Writing off an uncollectible does not change the estimated amount of cash to be collected (realizable value of accounts receivable).

   f. If a written off account is later recovered (collected) , this results of a reversal of the write off (see d above) and a normal collection of account entry.

D. Estimating Bad Debts Expense—two methods:

1. Percent of Sales Method (uses income statement relations to estimate)—bad debts expense is computed as a percentage of sales for the period.

       a.   Sales figure chosen as base is usually *credit* sales but it can be total or net sales if cash sales are small.

       b.   The estimate is used in the adjusting entry. Note that the resulting reported allowance account balance is rarely equal the reported expense because the allowance account was not likely to be zero prior to adjustment.

   2.   Accounts Receivable methods (uses balance sheet relations to estimate)—desired credit balance in Allowance for Doubtful Accounts is computed:

       a.   As a percentage of outstanding receivables (simplified approach) or

       b.   By aging accounts receivable.

       a.   The amount in the adjustment is calculated by determining the amount necessary to bring allowance account to a credit balance equivalent to the estimated uncollectibles.

II.   **Notes Receivable**— *Promissory note* that is a written promise to pay a specified amount of money *(principal)* either on demand or on a definite future date. Most notes are interest bearing. Promissory notes are notes payable to the *maker* (person promising to pay) and notes receivable to the *payee* (person to be paid).

   A. Computations for Notes

     1.   *Maturity date* is the date the note must be repaid.

     2.   Amount to be repaid is principal plus interest (*maturity value*).

     3.   The *period* of the note is the time from the note's date to its maturity date.

     4.   Formula for computing annual interest:

	Annual	Time of note		
Principal of **x**	rate of **x**	expressed	=	Interest
note	interest	in years		

   B. Recognizing Notes Receivable—debit Notes Receivable for principal or face amount of note. Credit will vary; depends on reason note is received. Note that interest is not recorded until earned.

   C. Valuing and Settling Notes

     1.   Recording an honored note—debit Cash for maturity value (face and interest), credit Note Receivable for face amount and credit Interest Revenue for the interest amount.

2. Recording a dishonored note—debit Accounts Receivable for maturity value, credit Note Receivable for face amount and credit Interest Revenue for the interest amount. If account receivable remains uncollected, it will be written-off.

3. Recording End-of-Period Interest Adjustment—record accrued interest by debiting Interest Receivable and crediting Interest Revenue.

4. Collection entry if some interest was accrued requires a debit to Cash for full amount received, credits to Interest Receivable (amount previously accrued), Interest Revenue (amount earned since accrual date) and Notes Receivable (face amount of note).

III. **Disposing of Receivables**—Companies can convert receivables to cash before they are due. Reasons for this include the need for cash or a desire to not be involved in collection activities.

A. Selling Receivables

1. Buyer, called a *factor*, charges the seller a *factoring fee* and then collects the receivables as they come due.

2. Entry: debit Cash (amount received), and Factoring Fee Expense (amount charged) and credit Accounts Receivable (amount sold).

B. Pledging Receivables

1. Company borrows money by pledging its receivables as security.

2. Borrower retains ownership of the receivables.

3. If borrower defaults, the lender has right to be paid from receipts on accounts receivable when collected.

4. The pledge should be disclosed in financial statement footnotes.

5. The loan is recorded as a debit to Cash and a credit to Notes Payable.

IV. **Decision Analysis—Accounts Receivable Turnover**

A. Measures both the quality (likeliness of collecting) and liquidity (speed of collection) of accounts receivable,

B. Indicates how often, on average, receivables are received and collected during the period.

C. Calculated by dividing net sales by average accounts receivable.

VISUAL #17
METHODS OF ACCOUNTING FOR BAD DEBTS

	DIRECT WRITE-OFF METHOD Accounts for bad debts from an uncollectible account receivable at the time the account is determined to be uncollectible.	ALLOWANCE METHOD At the end of each accounting period, bad debts expense is estimated and recorded.
Year-end	No adjusting entry	Adjusting entry required: **Bad Debt Expense** XXX **Allowance for Uncollectible Accounts** XXX (The amount is an estimate based on a percentage of sales or a percentage of outstanding accounts receivable. If the estimate is based on sales, the full estimate is used in the adjusting entry. If the estimate is based on accounts receivable the allowance account balance is brought to the amount of the estimate.)

When an account is determined to be uncollectible	Write-off entry required:
	Bad Debts Expense XXX
	    Accounts Receivable/Customer XXX
	(The amount is the balance of the uncollectible account.)
		Write-off entry required:
		Allowance for Uncollectible Accounts XXX
		    Accounts Receivable/Customer XXX
		(The amount is the balance of the uncollectible account.)

When an account previously written off is recovered	1. Reinstate account *by reversing write-off:*
	Accounts Receivable/Customer XXX
	    Bad Debts Expense XXX
	(The amount is the account balance that was written off.)
	2. Record collection on account normally:
	Cash XXX
	    Accounts Receivable/Customer XXX
	(The amount is the amount collected.)
		1. Reinstate account *by reversing write-off:*
		Accounts Receivable/Customer XXX
		    Allowance for Uncollectible Accounts XXX
		(The amount is the account balance that was written off.)
		2. Record collection on account normally:
		Cash XXX
		    Accounts Receivable/Customer XXX
		(The amount is the amount collected.)

Advantages:	• **Does not require adjusting entry.** • **Does not require year-end estimating of uncollectibles.**	• **Matches expense against related revenues.** • **Reports the net realizable accounts receivable on the balance sheet (a more accurate reporting of assets).**
Disadvantages:	• **Violates matching, therefore only allowed if qualified under materiality principle. (May be used by a business that anticipates an immaterial amount of uncollectibles.)**	• **Requires adjusting entry.** • **Requires year-end estimating of uncollectibles.**

PROMISSORY NOTE

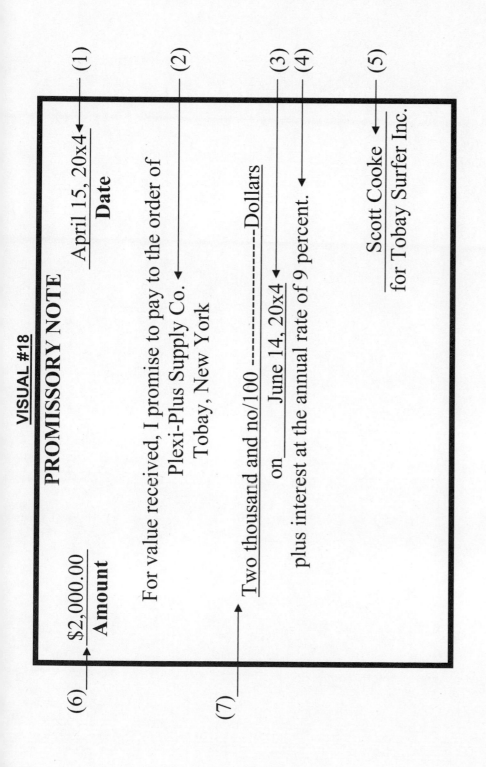

$2,000.00
Amount (6)

April 15, 20x4 (1)
Date

For value received, I promise to pay to the order of (2)
Plexi-Plus Supply Co.
Tobay, New York

Two thousand and no/100 ----------Dollars (3) (7)

on   June 14, 20x4

plus interest at the annual rate of 9 percent. (4)

Scott Cooke (5)
for Tobay Surfer Inc.

Problem I

The following statements are either true or false. Place a (T) in the parentheses before each true statement and an (F) before each false statement.

1. ( ) If cash from credit card sales is received immediately when the credit card receipts are deposited at the bank, the credit card expense is recorded at the time the sale is recorded.

2. ( ) Businesses with credit customers must maintain a separate account for each customer.

3. ( ) After all entries are posted, the sum of the balances in the Accounts Receivable Ledger should be equal to the balance of the Accounts Receivable account in the General Ledger.

4. ( ) Under the allowance method of accounting for bad debts, accounts receivable are reported on the balance sheet at the amount of cash proceeds expected from their collection.

5. ( ) At the time an adjusting entry to record estimated bad debts expense is made, the credit side of the entry is to Accounts Receivable.

6. ( ) When an account deemed uncollectible is written off against Allowance for Doubtful Accounts, the estimated realizable amount of Accounts Receivable is decreased.

7. ( ) The income statement approach to estimating bad debts is based on the idea that some percentage of credit sales will be uncollectible.

8. ( ) The balance sheet approach to estimating bad debts is based on the idea that some particular percentage of a company's credit sales will become uncollectible.

9. ( ) Aging of accounts receivable requires the examination of each account in the accounts receivable ledger.

10. ( ) A 90-day note, dated August 17, matures on November 16.

11. ( ) Although the direct write-off method of accounting for bad debts usually mismatches revenues and expenses, it may be allowed in cases where bad debt losses are immaterial in relation to total net sales and net income.

12. ( ) A company that pledges its accounts receivable as security for a loan should disclose the fact in the notes to the financial statements.

Problem II

You are given several words, phrases, or numbers to choose from in completing each of the following statements or in answering the following questions. In each case select the one that best completes the statement or answers the question and place its letter in the answer space provided.

_____ 1. Orion Company has decided to write off the account of Jack Irwin against the Allowance for Doubtful Accounts. The $2,100 balance in Irwin's account originated with a credit sale in July of last year. What is the general journal entry to record this write-off?

a.	Allowance for Doubtful Accounts	2,100	
	Accounts Receivable—Jack Irwin......................		2,100
b.	Accounts Receivable...	2,100	
	Allowance for Doubtful Accounts......................		2,100
c.	Bad Debts Expense	2,100	
	Allowance for Doubtful Accounts......................		2,100
d.	Accounts Receivable...	2,100	
	Accounts Receivable—Jack Irwin......................		2,100
e.	Bad Debts Expense	2,100	
	Accounts Receivable		2,100

_____ 2. Hitech Corporation had credit sales of $3,000,000 in 2007. Before recording the December 31, 2007, adjustments, the company's Allowance for Doubtful Accounts had a credit balance of $1,400. A schedule of the December 31, 2007, accounts receivable by age is summarized as follows:

December 31, 2007 Accounts Receivable	Age of Accounts Receivable	Uncollectible Percent Expected
$285,000	Not due	1.5
87,000	1-45 days past due	8.2
34,000	46-90 days past due	37.0
8,000	over 90 days past due	70.0

Calculate the amount that should appear on the December 31, 2007, balance sheet as allowance for doubtful accounts.

a. $28,189.

b. $5,600.

c. $25,314.

d. $30,989.

e. $29,589.

_____ 3. Based on the information given in problem 4, what is the general journal entry to record bad debts expense for 2007?

a. Debit Bad Debts Expense; credit Allowance for Doubtful Accounts.

b. Debit Accounts Receivable; credit Allowance for Doubtful Accounts.

c. Debit Bad Debts Expense; credit Accounts Receivable.

d. Debit Allowance for Doubtful Accounts; credit Bad Debts Expense.

e. Debit Accounts Receivable; credit Bad Debts Expense.

_____ 4.   MBC Company discounts a $25,000 note receivable, with recourse, and receives proceeds of $25,250. MBC's entry to record the transaction would include the following:

a. $25,000 debit to Cash.

b. $250 debit to Interest Expense.

c. $250 credit to Interest Revenue.

d. $25,250 credit to Notes Receivable.

e.   None of the above.

_____ 5.   Westing Company had net sales of $400,000 and $500,000 for 2007 and 2008, respectively. Accounts receivable at December 31, 2007 and 2008, were $45,000 and $55,000. What is Westing's accounts receivable turnover for 2008?

a.   11.1 times.

b.   10.0 times.

c.   20.0 times.

d.   9.0 times.

e.   None of the above.

Problem III

Many of the important ideas and concepts discussed in Chapter 9 are reflected in the following list of key terms. Test your understanding of these terms by matching the appropriate definitions with the terms. Record the number identifying the most appropriate definition in the blank space next to each term.

_____ Accounts receivable
_____ Accounts receivable turnover
_____ Aging of accounts receivable
_____ Allowance for Doubtful Accounts
_____ Allowance method
_____ Bad debts
_____ Direct write-off method
_____ Interest

_____ Maker of a note
_____ Matching principle
_____ Materiality principle
_____ Maturity date of a note
_____ Payee of a note
_____ Principal of a note
_____ Promissory note
_____ Realizable value

1. Measure of both the quality and liquidity of accounts receivable; it indicates how often receivables are received and collected during the period; computed by dividing net sales by average accounts receivable balance.

2. Person/company who signs a note and promises to pay it at maturity.

3. Procedure that (1) estimates and matches bad debts expense with its sales for the period and (2) reports accounts receivable at estimated realizable value.

4. Person/company to whom a note is made payable.

5. Method that records the loss from an uncollectible accounts receivable at the time it is determined to be uncollectible; no attempt is made to estimate uncollectible accounts or bad debt expense.

6. Implies an amount can be ignored if its effect on financial statements is unimportant to users.

7. Accounts of customers who do not pay what they have promised to pay; the amount is an expense of selling on credit; also called uncollectible accounts.

8. Requires expenses to be reported in the same period as the sales they helped produce.

9. Expected proceeds from converting an asset into cash.

10. Contra asset account with a balance approximating uncollectible accounts receivable; also called *allowance for uncollectible accounts*.

11. Date on which the principal and interest on a note are due and payable.

12. Process of classifying accounts receivable by how long they are past due for the purpose of estimating the amount of uncollectible accounts.

13. Amounts due from customers for credit sales.

14. Written promise to pay a specified amount of money either on demand or at a definite future date.

15. Charge for using money (or other assets) until repaid at a future date.

16. Amount that the signer of a note agrees to pay back when it matures, not including interest.

Problem IV

On December 12, Lark Company received from Guy Hall, a customer, $300 in cash and a $1,500, 12%, 60-day note dated December 11 in granting a time extension on Hall's past-due account. On December 31, Lark Company recorded the accrued interest on the note, and Guy Hall paid the note and its interest on the following February 9. Complete the general journal entries to record these transactions.

DATE	ACCOUNT TITLES AND EXPLANATION	P.R.	DEBIT			CREDIT		
Dec. 12								
	Received cash and a note in granting a time extension							
	on a past-due account.							
31								
	To record accrued interest on a note receivable.							
Feb 9								
	Received payment of a note and interest							

Problem V

On March 1 Lark Company accepted a $1,200, 12%, 60-day note dated that day from a customer, Mary Dale, in granting a time extension on the customer's past-due account. When Lark Company presented the note for payment on April 30, it was dishonored, and on December 20 Lark Company wrote off the debt as uncollectible. Present entries to record the dishonor and the write-off against the company's Allowance for Doubtful Accounts.

DATE	ACCOUNT TITLES AND EXPLANATION	P.R.	DEBIT			CREDIT		
Apr 30								
	To charge the account of Mary Dale for her							
	dishonored $1,200, 12%, 60-day note.							
Dec. 20								
	To write off the uncollectible note of Mary Dale.							

Problem VI

Marin Company uses the allowance method in accounting for bad debt losses, and over the past several years it has experienced an average loss equal to one-fourth of 1% of its credit sales. During 2007 the company sold $928,000 of merchandise on credit, including a $98 credit sale to Gus Bell on March 5, 2007. The $98 had not been paid by the year's end.

1. If at the end of 2007 Marin Company, in providing for estimated bad debt losses, assumes history will repeat, it will provide an allowance for 2007 estimated bad debts equal to _____ % of its $928,000 of 2007 charge sales; and the adjusting entry to record the allowance will appear as follows:

DATE	ACCOUNT TITLES AND EXPLANATION	P.R.	DEBIT		CREDIT	
2007						
Dec. 31						
	To record estimated bad debts					

2. The debit of the foregoing entry is to the expense account, _____ _____, which is closed to the _____ account at the end of the accounting period just as any other expense account is closed.

3. The effect of the foregoing adjusting entry on the 2007 income statement of Marin Company is to cause an estimated amount of bad debts expense to be deducted from the $928,000 of revenue from 2007 charge sales. This complies with the accounting principle of _____ _____.

4. The credit of the foregoing adjusting entry is to the contra account _____ _____. On the December 31, 2007, balance sheet the balance of this contra account is subtracted from the balance of the _____ account to show the amount that is expected to be realized from the accounts receivable.

5. On March 31, 2008, the Accounts Receivable controlling account and the Allowance for Doubtful Accounts account of Marin Company had the following balances:

Accounts Receivable		Allowance for Doubtful Accounts	
Mar. 31 65,625			Mar. 31 4,475

A balance sheet which was prepared on March 31, 2008, would show that Marin Company expects to collect $ _____ of its accounts receivable.

6. On April 1, 2008, Marin Company decided the $98 account of Gus Bell (sale made on March 5 of the previous year) was uncollectible and wrote it off as a bad debt. (Complete the entry and post to the above T-accounts the portions affecting the accounts.)

DATE	ACCOUNT TITLES AND EXPLANATION	P.R.	DEBIT		CREDIT	
2008						
Apr. 1						
	To write off the account of Gus Bell					

7. If a balance sheet was prepared immediately after the entry writing off the uncollectible account of Gus Bell was posted, it would show that Marin Company expected to collect $ _____ of its accounts receivable. Consequently, the write-off _____ (did, did not) affect the net balance sheet amount of accounts receivable. Likewise, the entry writing off the account did not record an expense because the expense was anticipated and recorded in the _____ _____ entry made on December 31, 2007, the year of the sale.

Problem VII

Pell Company sells almost exclusively for cash, but it does make a few small charge sales, and it also occasionally has a small bad debt loss which it accounts for by the direct write-off method.

1. Give below the entry made by Pell Company on February 5 to write off the $55 uncollectible account of Joan Bond (the goods were sold during the previous period.)

DATE	ACCOUNT TITLES AND EXPLANATION	P.R.	DEBIT		CREDIT	
Feb. 5						

2. Writing off the foregoing bad debt directly to the Bad Debts Expense account violates the accounting principle of _____.
However, due to the accounting principle _____
the direct write-off is permissible in this case because the company's bad debt losses are very small in relation to its sales.

Problem VIII

A company that ages its accounts receivable and increases its allowance for doubtful accounts to an amount sufficient to provide for estimated bad debts had a $75 debit balance in its Allowance for Doubtful Accounts account on December 31. If on that date it was estimated that $1,800 of its accounts receivable were uncollectible, it should make a year-end adjusting entry crediting $ _____ to its Allowance for Doubtful Accounts account.

Problem IX

Pierce Company allows its customers to use two credit cards: the University National Bank credit card and the Community Credit Card. Based on the information provided below, prepare general journal entries for Pierce Company to record the following credit card transactions:

a) University National Bank charges a 3% service fee for sales on its credit card. As a commercial customer of the bank, Pierce Company receives immediate credit when it makes its daily deposit of sales receipts.

   May 2   Sold merchandise for $525 to customers who used the University National Bank credit card.

DATE	ACCOUNT TITLES AND EXPLANATION	P.R.	DEBIT	CREDIT

b) Community Credit Card Company charges 4% of sales for use of its card. Pierce Company submits accumulated sales receipts to Community Company and is paid within 30 days.

   May 3   Sold merchandise for $675 to customers using the Community Credit Card. Submitted receipts to Community Company for payment

   30   Received amount due from Community Credit Card Company.

DATE	ACCOUNT TITLES AND EXPLANATION	P.R.	DEBIT	CREDIT

Solutions for Chapter 9

Problem I

1. T	7. T
2. T	8. F
3. T	9. T
4. T	10. F
5. F	11. T
6. F	12. T

Problem II

1. A
2. E
3. A
4. C
5. B

Problem III

13	Accounts receivable	2	Maker of a note
1	Accounts receivable turnover	8	Matching principle
12	Aging of accounts receivable	6	Materiality principle
10	Allowance for Doubtful Accounts	11	Maturity date of a note
3	Allowance method	4	Payee of a note
7	Bad debts	16	Principal of a note
5	Direct write-off method	14	Promissory note
15	Interest	9	Realizable value

Problem IV

Dec. 12	Cash...	300	
	Notes Receivable..	1,500	
	Accounts Receivable--Guy Hall...........................		1,800
31	Interest Receivable ($1,500 x .12 x 20/360)	10	
	Interest Revenue...		10
Feb 9	Cash...	1,530	
	Interest Receivable		10
	Interest Revenue...		20
	Notes Receivable...		1,500

Problem V

Apr. 30	Accounts Receivable--Mary Dale	1,224	
	Interest Revenue		24
	Notes Receivable		1,200
Dec. 20	Allowance for Doubtful Accounts	1,224	
	Accounts Receivable--Mary Dale		1,224

Problem VI

1. one fourth of 1%, or .25%

Dec. 31	Bad Debts Expense	2,320	
	Allowance for Doubtful Accounts		2,320

2. Bad Debts Expense, Income Summary

3. matching revenues and expenses

4. Allowance for Doubtful Accounts, Accounts Receivable

5. $61,150

6.
Apr. 1	Allowance for Doubtful Accounts	98	
	Accounts Receivable—Gus Bell		98

Accounts Receivable					Allowance for Doubtful Accounts			
Mar. 31	65,625						Mar. 31	4,475
		Apr. 1	98	Apr. 1	98			

7. $61,150, did not, adjusting.

Problem VII

1.
Feb. 5	Bad Debts Expense	55	
	Accounts Receivable--Joan Bond		55

2. matching revenues and expenses, materiality

Problem VIII

$1,875

Problem IX

a)	May 2	Cash	509.25	
		Credit Card Expense ($525 x 0.03)	15.75	
		Sales		525
b)	May 3	Accounts Receivable--Community Company	675.00	
		Sales		675.00
	30	Cash	648.00	
		Credit Card Expense ($675 x 0.04)	27.00	
		Accounts Receivable--Community Company		675.00

CHAPTER 10
PLANT ASSETS, NATURAL RESOURCES, AND INTANGIBLES

Learning Objective C1:

Describe plant assets and issues in accounting for them.

Summary

Plant assets are tangible assets used in the operations of a company and have a useful life of more than one accounting period. Plant assets are set apart from other tangible assets by two important features: use in operations and useful lives longer than one period. The four main accounting issues with plant assets are: (1) computing their costs, (2) allocating their costs to the periods they benefit, (3) accounting for subsequent expenditures, and (4) recording their disposal.

Learning Objective C2:

Explain depreciation and the factors affecting its computation.

Summary

Depreciation is the process of allocating to expense the cost of a plant asset over the accounting periods that benefit from its use. Depreciation does not measure the decline in a plant asset's market value, or its physical deterioration. Three factors determine depreciation: cost, salvage value, and useful life. Salvage value is an estimate of the asset's value at the end of its benefit period. Useful (service) life is the length of time an asset is productively used.

Learning Objective C3:

Explain depreciation for partial years and changes in estimates.

Summary

Partial-year depreciation is often required because assets are bought and sold throughout the year. Depreciation is revised when changes in estimates such as salvage value and useful life occur. If the useful life of a plant asset changes, for instance, the remaining cost to be depreciated is spread over the remaining (revised) useful life of the asset.

Learning Objective A1:

Compare and analyze alternative depreciation methods.

Summary

The amount of depreciation expense per period is usually different for different methods, yet total depreciation expense over an asset's life is the same for all methods. Each method starts with the same total cost and ends with the same salvage value. The difference is in the pattern of depreciation expense over the asset's life. . Common methods are straight-line, double-declining-balance, and the units-of-production.

Learning Objective A2:

Compute total asset turnover and apply it to analyze a company's use of assets.

Summary

Total asset turnover measures a company's ability to use its assets to generate sales. It is defined as net sales divided by average total assets. While all companies desire a high total asset turnover, it must be interpreted in comparison with that for prior years and its competitors.

Learning Objective P1:

Apply the cost principle to compute the cost of plant assets.

Summary

Plant assets are recorded at cost when purchased. Cost includes all normal and reasonable expenditures necessary to get the asset in place and ready for its intended use. The cost of a lump-sum purchase is allocated among its individual assets.

Learning Objective P2:

Compute and record depreciation using straight-line, units-of-production, and declining-balance methods.

Summary

The straight-line method divides the cost less salvage value by the asset's useful life to determine depreciation expense per period. The units-of-production method divides cost less salvage value by the estimated number of units the asset will produce over its life to determine depreciation per unit. The declining-balance method multiplies the asset's beginning-of-period book value by a factor that is often double the straight-line rate.

Learning Objective P3:

Distinguish between revenue and capital expenditures, and account for them.

Summary

Revenue expenditures expire in the current period and are debited to expense accounts and matched with current revenues. Ordinary repairs are an example of revenue expenditures. Capital expenditures benefit future periods and are debited to asset accounts. Examples of capital expenditures include extraordinary repairs and betterments.

Fundamental Accounting Principles, 18/e

Learning Objective P4:

Account for asset disposal through discarding or selling an asset.

Summary

When a plant asset is discarded, sold or exchanged, its cost and accumulated depreciation are removed from the accounts. Any cash proceeds from discarding or selling an asset are recorded and compared to the asset's book value to determine gain or loss.

Learning Objective P5:

Account for natural resource assets and their depletion.

Summary

The cost of a natural resource is recorded in a noncurrent asset account. Depletion of a natural resource is recorded by allocating its cost to depletion expense using the units-of-production method. Depletion is credited to an Accumulated Depletion account.

Learning Objective P6:

Account for intangible assets.

Summary

An intangible asset is recorded at the cost incurred to purchase it. The cost of an intangible asset is allocated to expense using the straight-line method and is called *amortization*. Goodwill and intangible assets with an indefinite useful life are not amortized—they are annually tested for impairment. Intangible assets include patents, copyrights, leaseholds, goodwill, and trademarks.

Learning Objective P7[A]:

Account for asset exchanges.

Summary

For an asset exchange with commercial substance, a gain or loss is recorded based on the difference between the book value of the asset given up and the market value of the asset received. For an asset exchange without commercial substance, no gain or loss is recorded, and the asset received is recorded based on book value of the asset given up.

Chapter Outline

I. **Plant Assets**—Tangible assets used in a company's operations that have a useful life of more than one accounting period. Consistent with cost principle, recorded at cost. Cost includes all normal and reasonable expenditures necessary to get the asset in place and ready for its intended use.

A. Land

Cost includes purchase price, real estate commissions, title insurance, legal fees, accrued property taxes, legal fees, title insurance fees, accrued property taxes, surveying, clearing, landscaping, and local government assessments (current or future) for streets, sewers, etc. Also includes cost of removal of any existing structures (less proceeds from sale of salvaged material). Land is not depreciated.

B. Land Improvements

Costs that increase the usefulness of the land.

1. Examples: parking lot surfaces, driveways, fences, and lighting systems (all have limited useful lives).

2. Costs are charged to a separate Land Improvement account.

3. Costs are allocated to the periods they benefit (depreciated).

C. Buildings

1. If purchased, cost usually includes its purchase price, brokerage fees, taxes, title fees, attorney costs, and all expenditures to make it ready for its intended use (any necessary repairs or renovations such as wiring, lighting, flooring and wall coverings).

2. If constructed for own use, cost includes materials and labor plus a reasonable amount of indirect overhead cost (heat, lighting, power, and depreciation on machinery used to construct the asset). Cost also includes design fees, building permits, and insurance during construction.

D. Machinery and Equipment

Costs include all normal and necessary expenditures to purchase them and prepare them for their intended use (purchase price, taxes, transportation charges, insurance while in transit, and the installing, assembling and testing of machinery and equipment).

E. Lump-Sum Purchase

A group of plant assets purchased with a single transaction for a lump-sum price. Individual asset cost is determined by allocating the cost of the purchase among the different types of assets acquired based on their *relative market values*.

II.   **Depreciation**—The process of allocating the cost of a plant asset to expense in the accounting periods benefiting from its use. Recorded as a debit to Depreciation Expense and a credit to Accumulated Depreciation.

    A. Factors in Computing Depreciation

        1. Cost—described in section I above.

        2. Salvage value—(*residual value* or *scrap value*) an estimate of the asset's value at the end of its benefit period.

        3. Useful life—(*service life*) length of time the asset is expected to be productively used in a company's operations. Factors affecting useful life include:

            a. *Inadequacy*—the insufficient capacity of plant assets to meet the company's growing productive demands.

            b. *Obsolescence*—refers to a plant asset that is no longer useful in producing goods or services with a competitive advantage because of new inventions and improvements.

    B. Depreciation Methods

        1. Straight-line method—charges the same amount to expense for each period of the asset's useful life. Method used by most companies.
Computation: Cost minus salvage value (equals the *depreciable cost)* divided by the number of accounting periods in the asset's useful life equals the periodic depreciation.

        2. Units-of-production method—charges a varying amount of cost to expense for each period of an asset's useful life depending on its usage. Examples of capacity measurements: miles driven, product outputs, hours used. *Computation:*

            a. Cost minus salvage value divided by the total number of units expected to be produced during assets useful life equals the *depreciation per unit.*

            b. Depreciation per unit is multiplied by number of units consumed in the period equals the period's depreciation.

        3. Declining-balance method—an accelerated depreciation method which yields larger depreciation expenses during the early years of an asset's life and smaller charges in later years. *Computation:* Multiply the asset's beginning of period book value by a depreciation rate (usually twice the straight-line rate) to determine the period's depreciation. If double the straight-line rate is used the method is referred to as *double declining-balance.* (Note that salvage value *is not used* in the calculation.)

      4. Depreciation for tax reporting—differences between financial and tax accounting systems are normal and expected.

         a. Many companies use accelerated depreciation in computing taxable income because it postpones its tax payments by charging higher depreciation expense in the early years and lower amounts in the later years.

         b. Federal income tax law rules for depreciating assets are called the *Modified Accelerated Cost Recovery System (MACRS)*.

         c. MACRS is not acceptable for financial reporting because it allocates costs over an arbitrary period that is less than the asset's useful life.

  C. Partial Year Depreciation

      When an asset is purchased (or disposed of) at a time other than the beginning or end of an accounting period, depreciation is recorded for part of the year.

  D. Revising Depreciation

      If estimated salvage and/or useful life is revised:

      1. Depreciation expense computations are revised by spreading the remaining cost to be depreciated over the revised useful life remaining.

      2. The revision is referred to as a *change in an accounting estimate* and is reflected in current and future financial statements, not prior statements.

  E. Reporting Depreciation

      1. Cost of plant assets and accumulated depreciation are reported on the balance sheet or in its notes.

      2. To satisfy the full-disclosure principle, the depreciation method or methods used must be disclosed in a balance sheet note.

      3. Plant assets are reported at their undepreciated costs (book value, not at market value.

      4. Accumulated depreciation on the balance sheet does not represent funds accumulated to buy new assets when the presently owned assets must be replaced.

III. **Additional Expenditures**—Those made to operate, maintain, repair, or improve plant assets after their initial purchase. To record these expenditures one must decide whether to capitalize (increase and asset) or expense in current period.

    A. Ordinary Repairs—expenditures to keep an asset in normal, good operating condition. They do not materially increase the asset's life or productive capabilities.

        1. Treated as *revenue expenditures* (also called *income statement expenditures*). Recorded as expenses on current period's income statement.

        2. Examples: cleaning, repainting, and lubricating.

    B. Betterments (Improvements) and Extraordinary Repairs— expenditures to make a plant asset more efficient or productive.

        1. *Betterments* often involves adding a component to an asset that does not always extend its useful life.

            a. Examples: adding a wing to a building or changing a machine from manual function to automatic.

            b. Debited to the asset account.

            c. The increase in asset's book value results in need to revise future depreciation.

        2. *Extraordinary repairs* are expenditures that do extend the asset's useful life beyond its original estimate.

            a. Examples: roofing replacement and major overhauls of machinery and equipment.

            b. Treated as capital expenditures (debited to asset account) because they benefit future periods.

Chapter Outline

IV. **Disposals of Plant Assets**—Assets may be *discarded, sold, or exchanged* due to wear and tear, obsolescence, inadequacy, or damage by fire or other accident. <u>General accounting steps</u> in a disposal of a plant asset:

- Record depreciation up to the date of disposal—this also updates Accumulated Depreciation.

- Remove account balances of the disposed asset—including its Accumulated Depreciation.

- Record any cash (and/or other assets) received or paid in the disposal.

- Record any gain or loss resulting from comparing the asset's book value with the market value of any assets received. *Exception:* in the case of an exchange that lacks commercial substance—discussed in Appendix 10[A].

A. Discarding Plant Assets—no longer useful and has no market value
Follow general accounting steps above.

1. If fully depreciated, no loss.

2. If not fully depreciated, record loss equal to the book value.

B. Selling Plant Assets
Follow general accounting steps above.

1. Sale is at a gain if value received exceeds book value.

2. Sale is at a loss if value received is less than book value.

V.   **Natural Resources**—Assets that are physically consumed when used. Examples include timber, mineral deposits, and oil and gas fields. Often called *wasting assets*.

    A. Cost Determination and Depletion

        1. Recorded at cost, which includes all expenditures necessary to acquire the resource and prepare it for its intended use.

        2. *Depletion* is the process of allocating the cost of natural resources to the periods when it is consumed, known as the resource's useful life.

        3. Depletion expense (debit) per period is based on the units extracted. The calculation is similar to units-of-production depreciation. Accumulated depletion is credited in the recording.

        4. Natural resources are reported on the balance sheet at cost less accumulated depletion.

    B. Plant Assets Used in Extracting Resources
When the usefulness of these plant assets is directly related to the depletion of the resource, the plant asset is depreciated in proportion to the depletion of the resource (use units-of-production method and the life of the resource).

VI.   **Intangible Assets**—Certain nonphysical assets (used in operations) that confer on owners long-term rights, privileges, competitive advantages. Examples in B below.

    A. Cost Determination and Amortization

        1. Recorded at cost when *purchased*. If simply developed by the business, relative immaterial costs are expensed.

        2. *Amortization*—process of systematically allocating cost of intangible asset to expense over its estimated useful or economic life. (If it has an indefinite useful life, it should not be amortized but is tested annually for impairment—this test is discussed in advanced course)

            a. Useful or economic life may differ from legal life.

            b. Computed on a straight-line basis (cost divided by useful or economic life)

            c. Amortization period cannot exceed 40 years.

            d. Debit Amortization Expense and credit Accumulated Amortization.

            e. Leasehold improvements are amortized over the life of the lease or the life of the improvements whichever is shorter. Debit *Rent Expense* to amortize.

Chapter Outline   **Notes**

    B. Types of Intangibles

1. *Patent*—an exclusive right granted to its owner to manufacture and sell a patented item or to use a process for 20 years.

2. *Copyright*—the exclusive right to publish and sell a musical, literary, or artistic work during the life of the creator plus 70 years.

3. *Leasehold*—the rights to possess and use leased property granted by the property's owner (lessor) to the lessee in a contract called a lease. Recorded, if there was a cost involved, as an intangible asset by the lessee (or sublessee). As Leaseholds are amortized, the cost is charged to Rent Expense.

4. *Leasehold improvements*—alterations or improvements to leased property, such as partitions, painting, and storefronts. Amortization results in debit to Amortization Expense—Leasehold Improvements.

5. *Franchises and Licenses*—rights that a company or government grants an entity to deliver a product or service under specified conditions.

6. *Trademarks and Trade Names*—symbols, names, phrases, or jingles identified with a company, product, or service.

7. *Goodwill—specific meaning in accounting*: the amount by which the value of a company exceeds the value of its individual assets and liabilities. Implies the company as a whole has certain valuable attributes not measured among its individual assets and liabilities. Goodwill is measured as the excess of cost of an acquired entity over the valuable of net assets acquired. It is not amortized but is tested annually for impairment.

VII. Decision Analysis—Total Asset Turnover

A. A measure of how efficiently a company uses its assets to generate sales.

B. Calculated by dividing net sales by average total assets.

VIII. Exchanging Plant Assets —Appendix 10A

A. Accounting for the exchange depends on whether the transaction has commercial substance. Commercial substance exists if the company's future cash flows change as a result of the transaction.

B. If commercial substance exists, a gain or loss is recorded based on the difference between the book value of the assets given up and the market value of the assets received.

C. If exchange lacks commercial substance, no gain or loss is recorded, and the asset received is recorded based on the book value of the assets given up.

FORMULAS FOR DEPRECIATION METHODS

1. STRAIGHT LINE

$$\frac{FHC^* - \text{Estimated salvage}}{\text{Estimated useful life}} = \frac{\text{Annual}}{\text{Depreciation}}$$

*Full Historical Cost

---

2. UNITS OF PRODUCTION

a) $$\frac{FHC - \text{Estimated salvage}}{\text{Predicted units of production}} = \frac{\text{(Depreciable)}}{\text{Cost per Unit}}$$

b) $$\frac{CPU^* \times \text{units produced in period}}{} = \frac{\text{Depreciation}}{\text{for PERIOD}}$$

(In last year, depreciate to estimated salvage value; never depreciate below this amount.)

**Cost Per Unit

---

3. (DOUBLE) DECLINING BALANCE

Book Value (beginning of period) x RATE* = Depreciation (for that year)

*RATE → The rate used is constant and it is twice what the straight line rate would have been for this asset.
(In the last year, depreciate to estimated salvage value; never depreciate below this amount.)

Problem I

The following statements are either true or false. Place a (T) in the parentheses before each true statement and an (F) before each false statement.

1. ( ) Cost is the basis for recording the acquisition of a plant asset.

2. ( ) The cost of a plant asset constructed by a business for its own use would include depreciation on the machinery used in constructing the asset.

3. ( ) Depreciation is a process of determining the value of assets.

4. ( ) The cost of extraordinary repairs which extend the service life of an asset should be debited to a Repairs Expense account.

5. ( ) The service life of a plant asset can be affected by inadequacy or obsolescence.

6. ( ) Accelerated depreciation methods increase taxable income in the early years of an asset's life.

7. ( ) Straight-line depreciation charges each year of an asset's life with an equal amount of expense.

8. ( ) Double-declining-balance depreciation applies twice the straight-line rate to the beginning-of-the-year book value of an asset to calculate each year's depreciation expense.

9. ( ) Total asset turnover is calculated by dividing average total assets by net sales.

10. ( ) The cost of making an ordinary repair to a machine should be classified as a revenue expenditure.

11. ( ) The credit balance in accumulated depreciation represents funds accumulated to buy new assets when the presently owned assets must be replaced.

12. ( ) If a cost is incurred to modify an existing plant asset for the purpose of making it more efficient or more productive, the cost should be classified as an extraordinary repair.

13. ( ) A betterment is recorded by reducing accumulated depreciation.

14. ( ) Natural resources appear on the balance sheet at cost less accumulated depreciation.

15. ( ) The depletion cost of any mined but unsold natural resources that are held for sale is carried forward on the balance sheet as a current asset.

16. ( ) Trademarks and organization costs are intangible assets and must be amortized over the asset's useful life (not to exceed 40 years).

17. ( ) The amortization entry for the costs of leasehold improvements would debit Rent Expense and credit Accumulated Amortization—Leasehold Improvements..

18. ( ) The cost of all intangible assets must be amortized over 40 years.

Problem II

You are given several words, phrases, or numbers to choose from in completing each of the following statements or in answering the following questions. In each case select the one that best completes the statement or answers the question and place its letter in the answer space provided.

_____ 1. Jocelyn Leland, CPA, paid $165,000 to purchase approximately two acres of land and the building on it to be used as an office. The building was appraised at $84,000 and the land was appraised at $126,000. What amount should be debited to the Land account?

a. $165,000

b. $211,000

c. $126,000

d. $ 66,000

e. $ 99,000

_____ 2. Flintstone Company depreciated a machine that cost $21,600 on a straight-line basis for three years under the assumption it would have a five-year life and a $3,600 trade-in value. At that point, the manager realized that the machine had three years of remaining useful life, after which it would have an estimated $2,160 trade-in value. Determine the amount of depreciation to be charged against the machine during each of the remaining years in its life.

a. $3,240

b. $1,800

c. $2,640

d. $2,880

e. $3,888

_____ 3. Busy Bee Industries installed a machine in its factory at a cost of $84,000 on May 1, 2007. The machine's useful life is estimated at eight years with a $9,000 salvage value. Determine the machine's 2007 depreciation using the double-declining-balance method of depreciation.

a. $14,000

b. $10,500

c. $21,000

d. $12,500

e. $18,750

_____ 4. Spacely's Sprockets purchased a machine on September 1 for $400,000. The machine's useful life was estimated at six years or 500,000 units of product with a $25,000 trade-in value. During Its second year, the machine produced 87,000 units of product. Assuming units-of-production depreciation, calculate the machine's second-year depreciation.

a. $69,600

b. $66,667

c. $65,250

d. $62,500

e. $31,250

_____ 5. A machine that cost $40,000 and had been depreciated $30,000 was traded in on a new machine having an estimated 10-year life and market value of $50,000. In addition to the old machine an additional $37,000 cash was paid. The exchange has commercial substance. What gain or loss should be recorded on the exchange? (Appendix 10^A)

    a. none

    b. $3,000 gain

    c. $10,000 gain

    d. $3,000 loss

    e. $13,000 gain

_____ 6. The Romeo Company exchanged its used bottle-capping machine for a new bottle capping machine. The old machine cost $14,000, and the new one had a cash price or market value of $19,000. Romeo had taken $12,000 depreciation on the old machine and was allowed a $500 trade-in allowance. The company anticipates an increase in future cash flows as a result of this exchange. What gain or loss should be recorded on the exchange? (Appendix 10^A)

    a. None

    b. $ 500 gain

    c. $1,500 loss

    d. $1,500 gain

    e. $4,500 gain

_____ 7. Cherokee Company had a bulldozer destroyed by fire. The bulldozer originally cost $16,000, but insurance paid only $14,200. Accumulated depreciation on this bulldozer was $2,000. The gain or loss from the fire is:

    a. No gain or loss

    b. $ 200 gain

    c. $ 200 loss

    d. $ 1,800 loss

    e. $16,000 loss

_____ 8. Following is selected year-end financial statement information from the Mega Life Company:

	12/31/07	12/31/08
Total assets	$18,500	$20,000
Total liabilities.............	12,750	11,900
Net sales......................	73,000	88,550
Total expenses	48,200	53,150

What is the total asset turnover for 2008?

    a. 4.4

    b. 2.9

    c. 0.2

    d. 4.6

    e. 1.8

_____ 9. Fleet Lines made a $3,000 modification to one of its trucks that made the truck more efficient. The $3,000 should be debited to which account?

    a. Trucks

    b. Accumulated Depreciation, Trucks

    c. Betterments

    d. Extraordinary Repairs

    e. Capital Expenditures

_____ 10. The process of allocating the cost of a patent to expense over time:

    a. Is called depletion.
    b. Is sometimes called depreciation.
    c. Is usually done by the declining-balance method over 50 years.
    d. Is seldom limited to less than 40 years.
    e. Should be accomplished in 17 years or less.

Problem III

Many of the important ideas and concepts discussed in Chapter 10 are reflected in the following list of key terms. Test your understanding of these terms by matching the appropriate definitions with the terms. Record the number identifying the most appropriate definition in the blank space next to each term.

_____ Accelerated depreciation method	_____ Lease
_____ Amortization	_____ Leasehold
_____ Betterment	_____ Leasehold improvements
_____ Book value	_____ Lessee
_____ Capital expenditure	_____ Lessor
_____ Change in an accounting estimate	_____ Modified Accelerated Cost
_____ Copyright	Recovery System (MACRS)
_____ Cost	_____ Natural resources
_____ Declining-balance method	_____ Obsolescence
_____ Depletion	_____ Ordinary repairs
_____ Depreciation	_____ Patent
_____ Extraordinary repairs	_____ Plant assets
_____ Franchises, Licenses	_____ Revenue expenditure
_____ Goodwill	_____ Salvage value
_____ Impairment	_____ Straight-line depreciation
_____ Inadequacy	_____ Total asset turnover
_____ Indefinite useful life	_____ Trademark
_____ Intangible asset	_____ Units-of-production depreciation
_____ Land improvements	_____ Useful (or service) life

1. Depreciation system required by federal income tax law.

2. Estimate of amount to be recovered at the end of an asset's useful life; also called *residual*, or *scrap, value*

3. Condition in which, because of new inventions and improvements, a plant asset can no longer be used to produce goods or services with a competitive advantage.

4. A method that charges a varying amount to depreciation expense for each period of an asset's useful life depending on its usage.

5. Assets that increase the benefits of land, have a limited useful life, and are depreciated.

6. Measure of a company's ability to use its assets to generate sales; calculated by dividing net sales by average total assets.

7. Method that determines depreciation charge for the period by multiplying a depreciation rate (up to twice the straight-line rate) by the asset's book value at the beginning of the period.

8. Process of allocating the cost of an intangible asset to expense over its estimated useful life.

9. Method that allocates an equal portion of the total depreciation for a plant asset (cost minus salvage) to each accounting period in its useful life.

10. Total cost of an asset less its accumulated depreciation (or depletion or amortization).

11. Method that produces larger depreciation charges during the early years of an asset's life and smaller charges in its later years.

12. Length of time an asset will be productively used in the operations of a business.

13. Condition in which the capacity of plant assets is too small to meet the company's productive demands.

14. Expenditure to make a plant asset more efficient or productive; also called *improvement*.

15. Additional costs of plant assets that provide material benefits extending beyond the current period; also called *balance sheet expenditure*.

16. A change in a financial statement amount that results from new information, subsequent developments, better insight, or improved judgment.

17. Expenditure reported on the current income statement as an expense because it does not provide benefits in future periods.

18. Repairs made to keep a plant asset in normal, good operating condition; which are treated as a revenue expenditure.

19. Major repairs that extend the service life of a plant asset beyond prior expectations; treated as a capital expenditure.

20. Right giving the owner the exclusive privilege to publish and sell musical, literary, or artistic work during the life of the creator plus 70 years.

21. All normal and reasonable expenditures necessary to get a plant asset in place and ready for its intended use.

22. Amount by which a company's value exceeds the value of its individual assets and liabilities.

23. Process of allocating the cost of natural resources to periods when they are consumed.

24. Process of allocating the cost of a plant asset to expense in the periods benefiting from its use.

25. Long-term rights, privileges, or competitive advantages that belong to the owner of these nonphysical assets used in operations.

26. Alterations or improvements to leased property such as partitions, painting, and storefronts.

27. Contract specifying the rental of property.

28. Exclusive right granted to its owner to manufacture and sell an item, or to use a process, for 17 years.

29. Rights the lessor grants to the lessee under the terms of a lease.

30. Tangible assets used in a company's operations that have a useful life of more than one period.

31. Party to a lease who secures the right to possess and use the property from another party.

32. Symbol, name, phrase, or jingle identified with a company, product or service.

33. Assets physically consumed when used; examples are timber, mineral deposits, and oil and gas field; also called *wasting assets*.

34. Party to a lease who grants another party the right to possess and use the property.

35. Privileges granted by a company or government to sell a product or service under specified conditions.

36. Diminishment of an assets value.

37. Asset life that is not limited by legal, regulatory, contractual, competitive, economic, or other factors.

Problem IV

Complete the following by filling in the blanks.

1. Land has an unlimited useful life, is not consumed when it is used, and therefore is not subject to _____. Costs that increase the usefulness of the land, such as parking lots or fences, should be classified as _____.

2. There are several factors that affect the useful life of some assets. These factors include:
   a. _____
   b. _____
   c. _____

3. The method of depreciation currently used by most companies for financial accounting purposes is _____.
   The most commonly used accelerated method of depreciation for financial accounting purposes is _____.

4. While MACRS is required for tax purposes, it is not acceptable for financial accounting because it allocates depreciation over an arbitrary recovery period that is _____.

5. An example of revenue expenditure is an _____ repair. Two types of capital expenditures are: (1) _____ repairs and (2) _____.

6. The tax advantage of accelerated depreciation is that _____.

7. Trucks held for sale by a dealer and land held for future expansion are not classified as plant assets because _____.

8. Depreciation allocates and charges the cost of an asset's usefulness to _____.
   Depreciation does not measure the asset's decline in _____ nor its physical _____.

9. The book value of a plant asset is its "value" as shown by the books and computed as follows: _____ minus its _____.

10. To record the disposal of a plant asset, the journal entry or entries related to the disposal should:

a. Record _____ and _____
up to the date of the disposal.

b. Remove the _____ and _____
account balances relating to the disposal.

c. If the disposal is a sale, the entry should record any _____ received and any or _____
or _____ as a result of the sale, which is determined by comparing the _____ of the
asset sold with the _____ received.

Problem V

A machine was purchased for $7,000, terms 2/10, n/60, FOB vendor's factory. The invoice was paid within the discount period along with $175 of freight charges. The machine was installed on a special concrete base by the employees of the company that bought it. The concrete base and special power connections for the machine cost $575, and the wages of the employees during the period in which they installed the machine amounted to $425. The employees accidentally dropped the machine while moving it onto its special base, causing damages to the machine which cost $125 to repair. As a result of all this, the cost of the machine for accounting purposes should be:

$_____

Problem VI

A machine with a cost of $8,000, an estimated eight-year service life, and an $800 salvage value, was purchased on July 1, 2007. It was estimated that the machine would produce 144,000 units of product during its life, and it produced 10,000 units during its first year. The depreciation expense for 2007 was:

1. $_____ calculated on a straight-line basis.

2. $_____ calculated using the units-of-production method.

3. $_____ calculated using the double-declining-balance method.

Problem VII

A machine that cost $45,000 and had been depreciated $20,000 was sold. Present a general journal entry to record the disposal under each of the following unrelated assumptions:

(a) The machine was sold for $20,000.

(b) The machine was sold for $27,000.

(c) The machine was sold for $25,000.

Solutions for Chapter 10

Problem I

1. T	10. T
2. T	11. F
3. F	12. T
4. F	13. F
5. T	14. F
6. F	15. T
7. T	16. T
8. T	17. T
9. F	18. F

Problem II

1. E	6. C
2. D	7. B
3. A	8. D
4. C	9. A
5. B	10. E

Problem III

11	Accelerated depreciation method	27	Lease
8	Amortization	29	Leasehold
14	Betterment	26	Leasehold improvements
10	Book value	31	Lessee
15	Capital expenditure	34	Lessor
16	Change in an accounting estimate	1	Modified Accelerated Cost Recovery System (MACRS)
20	Copyright		
21	Cost	33	Natural resources
7	Declining-balance method	3	Obsolescence
23	Depletion	18	Ordinary repairs
24	Depreciation	28	Patent
19	Extraordinary repairs	30	Plant assets
35	Franchises, Licenses	17	Revenue expenditure
22	Goodwill	2	Salvage value
36	Impairment	9	Straight-line depreciation
13	Inadequacy	6	Total asset turnover
37	Indefinite useful life	32	Trademark
25	Intangible asset	4	Units-of-production depreciation
5	Land improvements	12	Useful (or service) life

Problem IV

1. depreciation; land improvements
2. (a) wear and tear
   (b) inadequacy
   (c) obsolescence
3. straight-line; declining-balance
4. usually much shorter than the estimated service life of an asset
5. ordinary; extraordinary; betterments
6. the payment of income taxes is deferred or postponed to later years
7. they are not being used in the production or sale of other assets or services
8. the accounting periods that benefit from the asset's use; market value; deterioration
9. cost; accumulated depreciation
10. (a) depreciation expense; accumulated depreciation
    (b) asset; accumulated depreciation
    (c) cash , gain, loss, book value, cash (or value received)

Problem V

$7,000 - ($7,000 x 2%) + $175 + $575 + $425 = $8,035

Problem VI

1. ($8,000 - $800)/8 x 6/12 = $450
2. [($8,000 - $800)/144,000] x 10,000 = $500
3. (100%/8) x 2 = 25% double-declining-balance rate

   $8,000 x 25% x 6/12 = $1,000

Problem VII

(a)	Cash	20,000.00	
	Accumulated Depreciation Machinery	20,000.00	
	Loss on Disposal of Machinery	5,000.00	
	Machinery		45,000.00
(b)	Cash	27,000.00	
	Accumulated Depreciation Machinery	20,000.00	
	Gain on Disposal of Machinery		2,000.00
	Machinery		45,000.00
(c)	Cash	25,000.00	
	Accumulated Depreciation Machinery	20,000.00	
	Machinery		45,000.00

CHAPTER 11
CURRENT LIABILITIES AND PAYROLL ACCOUNTING

Learning Objective C1:

Describe current and long-term liabilities and their characteristics.

Summary

Liabilities are probable future payments of assets or services that past transactions or events obligate an entity to make. Current liabilities are due within one year or the operating cycle, whichever is longer. All other liabilities are long-term.

Learning Objective C2:

Identify and describe known current liabilities.

Summary

Known (determinable) current liabilities are set by agreements or laws and are measurable with little uncertainty. They include accounts payable, sales taxes payable, unearned revenues, notes payable, payroll liabilities, and the current portion of long-term debt.

Learning Objective C3:

Explain how to account for contingent liabilities.

Summary

If an uncertain future payment depends on a probable future event and the amount can be reasonably estimated, the payment is recorded as a liability. The uncertain future payment is reported as a contingent liability (in the notes) if *(a)* the future event is reasonably possible but not probable, or *(b)* the event is probable but the amount of the payment cannot be reasonably estimated.

Learning Objective A1:

Compute times interest earned ratio and use it to analyze liabilities.

Summary

Times interest earned is computed by dividing a company's net income before interest expense and income taxes by the amount of interest expense. The times interest earned ratio reflects the company's ability to pay interest obligations.

Learning Objective P1:

Prepare entries to account for short-term notes payable.

Summary

Short-term notes payable are current liabilities; most bear interest. When a short-term note's face value equals the amount borrowed, it identifies a rate of interest to be paid at maturity.

Learning Objective P2:

Compute and record *employee* payroll deductions and liabilities.

Summary

Employee payroll deductions include FICA taxes, income tax, and voluntary deductions such as for pensions and charities. They make up the difference between gross and net pay.

Learning Objective P3:

Compute and record *employer* payroll expenses and liabilities.

Summary

An employer's payroll expenses include employees' gross earnings, any employee benefits, and the payroll taxes levied on the employer. Payroll liabilities include the employees' net pay, withholdings from employee wages , any employer-promised benefits, and the employer's payroll taxes.

Learning Objective P4:

Account for estimated liabilities, including warranties and bonuses.

Summary

Liabilities for health and pension benefits, warranties, bonuses are recorded with estimated amounts. These items are recognized as expenses when incurred and matched with revenues generated.

Learning Objective P5[A] (Appendix 11A):

Identify and describe the details of payroll reports, records, and procedures.

Summary

Employers report FICA taxes and federal income tax withholdings using Form 941. FUTA taxes are reported on Form 940. Earnings and deduction are reported to each employee and the federal government on Form W-2. An employer's payroll records include a payroll register for each pay period, payroll checks and statements of earnings, and individual employee earnings reports.

Fundamental Accounting Principles, 18/e

Chapter Outline

I. **Characteristics of Liabilities**

A. Defining Liabilities
Probable future payments of assets or services that a company is presently obligated to make as a result of past transactions or events. Note three crucial factors:

1. Due to past transaction or event.

2. Present obligation.

3. Future payment of assets or services.

B. Classifying Liabilities

1. Current liabilities (*short-term liabilities*)—Obligations due within one year or the company's operating cycle, whichever is longer.

2. Long-term liabilities—Obligations not expected to be paid within the longer of one year or operating cycle.

C. Uncertainties in Liabilities—requires addressing three important questions that are sometime uncertain at the time liability is incurred:

1. Whom to pay? (Ex. A note "Payable to Bearer")

2. When to pay? (Ex. Unearned revenues—may not know when service will be provided to satisfy)

3. How much to pay? (Ex. Accrued expense that needed to be estimated prior to receipt of bill)

II. **Known (Determinable) Liabilities**—Set by agreements, contracts, or laws and are measurable. Examples of these liabilities in the *current* classification include:

A. Accounts Payable
Amounts owed to suppliers for products or services purchased with credit.

B. Sales Taxes Payable
Amounts the retailer (seller) collects as sales taxes from customers when sales occur, and currently owes to the government until remitted.

C. Unearned Revenues— also known as *deferred revenues, collections in advance and prepayments*.
Amounts received in advance from customers for future products or services.

D. Short-Term Notes Payable
    Written promise to pay a specified amount on a definite future
    date within one year or the company's operating cycle, whichever
    is longer. Can arise from many transactions; two common
    examples:

1. Creditor requires the substitution of an interest-bearing note
    for an overdue account payable that does not bear interest.
    (*Dr* Accounts Payable, *Cr* Notes Payable)

2. Note given to borrow money from bank.

    Ex. Face value equals amount borrowed (*principal*) and at
    maturity a larger amount is repaid. The difference between
    amount borrowed and repaid is the *interest*. The note is
    recorded at and reported at face value.
    (*Dr* Cash, *Cr* Notes Payable)
    In both examples above, interest is recorded as incurred. This
    may be when paid with note or as end-of -period accrued
    interest adjustment.
    (*Dr* Interest Expense and Note Payable, *Cr* Cash) if interest is
    being recorded as note is paid at maturity.
    (*Dr* Interest Expense and *Cr* Interest Payable) if accrued
    interest is being recorded at end-of-period adjustment.

E. Payroll Liabilities

1. Gross pay—total compensation an employee earns. (includes
    wages, salaries, commissions, bonuses). Gross pay amount is
    recorded as Salaries *Expense (Dr)*.

2. Net pay—gross less all deductions; also called *take-home pay*
    Net pay is recorded as Payroll *Payable (Cr)*.

3. Payroll deductions—amounts withheld from an employee's
    gross pay, either involuntary or voluntary; also called
    withholdings. Each is recorded as a separate *liability* (*Cr*).

    a. FICA (Federal Insurance Contributions Act) taxes can be
        separated into two groups—Social Security and Medicare
        taxes. FICA tax is computed as current rate multiplied by
        gross wages *subject to tax*. For year 2006, Social Security
        tax is 6.2% of the *first* $94,200 (maximum of $5,840)
        earned by the employee in the calendar year and Medicare
        tax is 1.45% of *all* wages earned by the employee.

    b. Employee Income tax payable is determined from chart
        based on their gross pay, pay period, marital status and
        number of withholding allowances the employee claims.

      c. Voluntary deductions (charitable contributions, health insurance premiums, **union** dues) result in various payables.
      (Note: *All* the payroll components, gross pay, each deduction and net pay, are recorded in one journal entry.)

    4 Employer Payroll Taxes—payroll taxes in addition to those required of employees. These taxes result in expenses (*Dr*) and current liabilities (*Cr*).

      a. FICA taxes—employers must pay and amount equal to employee contribution.

      b. Unemployment taxes—(state and federal) current tax rate multiplied by wages subject to tax. The total rate is up to 6.2% of the first $7000 earned by each employee. The federal rate can be reduced by a credit of up to 5.4% for taxes paid to a state program.

F. Multi-Period Known Liabilities—known liabilities that extend over many periods. Ex. Unearned Revenues and Notes Payable. Classification is based upon period in which they will be satisfied.

  1. Current Liability—portion that will be fulfilled in next year.

  2. Long- term Liability—portion that will be fulfilled after next year.

III.   **Estimated Liabilities**—Known obligations of uncertain amounts that can be reasonably estimated. Recorded as expenses (*Dr*) and payables (*Cr*).Examples are:

A. Health and Pension Benefits—benefits beyond salaries and wages provided by business. Appropriate proportion accrued at time of each payroll.

B. Vacation Benefits—estimated and recorded by the employer during the weeks the employees are working and earning the vacation time. Appropriate proportion accrued at time of each payroll.

C. Bonus Plans—employee bonuses must be estimated and recorded in year-end adjusting entries.

D. Warranty Liabilities—reported to comply with the *full disclosure* and *matching principles*. Seller reports the expected warranty expense *(Dr)* and liability (*Cr*) in the period when revenue from the sales of the product is reported. When warranty liabilities are settled the liability is removed and the asset used (Ex. Parts Inventory) is reduced.
Note: Estimated liabilities can also be current and long-term (multi-period) and must be classified based upon when they will be satisfied.

IV. **Contingent liabilities**—Contingent liability is a potential liability that depends on a future event arising from a past transaction.

    A. Accounting for Contingent Liabilities—depends on likelihood that a future event will occur and the ability to estimate the future amount. (Accounting motivated by *full-disclosure principle*.) Three categories and appropriate accounting for each:

        1. *Probable* (likely)—record if amount can be reasonably estimated; if cannot be estimated, disclose in footnotes to financial statements.

        2. *Possible* (could occur)—disclose in financial statement notes

        3. *Remote* (unlikely)—omit (do not record or footnote)..

    B. *(Reasonably) Possible* Contingent Liabilities (category 2 above). Examples:

        1. Potential legal claims—recorded in the accounts only if payment for damages is probable *and* the amount can be reasonably estimated. If can't be reasonably estimated or less than probable but *reasonably possible*, disclose in notes.

        2. Debt guarantees (of a debt owed by another company)—require disclosure in financial statement notes if potential liabilities are *reasonably possible*.

        3. Other Contingencies (e.g., environmental damages, possible tax assessments, insurance losses, and government investigations)—require disclosure in notes if potential liabilities are reasonably possible.

    Note: Uncertainties (ex. Natural disasters) are not contingent liabilities because they are future events *not* arising from past transactions.

V. **Decision Analysis—Times Interest Earned Ratio**

    A. Used to describe the risk of covering interest commitments when income varies.

    B. Calculated as *income before interest expense and income taxes* divided by interest expense.

Appendix 11A—Payroll Reports, Records and Procedures

VI. **Payroll Reports**—employers are required to prepare and submit the following reports:

    A. Employer's Quarterly Federal Tax Return (IRS Form 941) Filed within one month after the end of each calendar quarter to report FICA and income withholding taxes owed and remitted.

    B. Annual Federal Unemployment Tax Return (IRS Form 940) Must be mailed on or before January 31 following the end of each tax year to report an employer's FUTA taxes.

C. Wage and Tax Statement (Form W-2)

Must be mailed on or before January 31 following the year covered by the report; employers must give each employee an annual report of the employee's wages subject to FICA and federal income taxes and the amounts of these taxes withheld.

VII. Payroll Records

A. Payroll Register

A record for a pay period that shows the pay period dates and the hours worked, gross pay, deductions, and net pay of each employee; contains all the data needed to record payroll (for each pay period) in the General Journal.

B. Payroll Check

Generally accompanied with a detachable *statement of earnings* showing gross pay, deductions, and net pay.

C. Employee's Earnings Report

A cumulative record of an employee's hours worked, gross pay, deductions, net pay, and certain personal information about the employee; contains the data the employer needs to prepare a Form W-2.

VIII. Payroll Procedures

A. Federal Income Tax Withholdings

Computed using a wage brackct withholding *table* based on gross pay, number of personal exemptions, the employee's tax status, and pay period.

1. Withholding allowance—a number that is used to reduce the amount of federal income tax withheld from an employee's pay, and which corresponds to the personal exemptions the employee is allowed to subtract from annual earnings in calculating taxable income.

2. Form W-4—withholding allowance certificate form. Filed by employee with employer to identify personal exemptions claimed.

B. Payroll Bank Account

A separate payroll bank account used in a company with many employees.

1. One check for total payroll is drawn on the regular bank account or an *electronic funds transfer* for this amount is executed to provide deposit for the payroll bank account.

2. Individual payroll checks are drawn on payroll account.

3. Helps with internal control and reconciling the regular bank account.

Appendix 11B—Income Taxes

IX.   **Income Tax Liabilities**

    A. Corporations (not sole proprietorships or partnerships) are subject to income taxes and must estimate their income tax liability when preparing financial statements. Adjusting entry: *Dr* Income Taxes Expense, *Cr* Income Taxes Payable. Quarterly payments remove (*Dr*) the liability, and credit Cash.

    B. Deferred Income Tax Liabilities
Arise from temporary differences between GAAP and income tax rules. This results in temporary differences between the tax return and the income statement. This difference results in a deferred income tax liability. Adjusting entry: *Dr* Income Taxes Expense, *Cr* Deferred Income Tax Liability.

Problem I

The following statements are either true or false. Place a (T) in the parentheses before each true statement and an (F) before each false statement.

1. ( ) An example of an estimated liability is a warranty.

2. ( ) Contingent liabilities are generally not recognized on the balance sheet.

3. ( ) Interest-bearing short-term notes payable are frequently requested by creditors to substitute for an overdue account payable.

4. ( ) Unearned revenues are classified as current liabilities.

5. ( ) When an interest-bearing short-term notes payable is issued to borrow money, the Interest Expense account is immediately debited.

6. ( ) (Appendix 11B) A corporation would report a deferred income tax liability when reported income tax expense for the year is greater than the amount of tax actually paid.

7. ( ) Federal unemployment taxes are withheld from employees' wages at the rate of 1.45% on the first $87,000 earned.

8. ( ) Social Security taxes are levied equally on the employee and the employer.

9. ( ) Employee benefit costs represent expenses to the employer in addition to the direct costs of salaries and wages.

10. ( ) Each time a payroll is recorded, a separate journal entry usually is made to record the employer's FICA and state and federal unemployment taxes.

11. ( ) Since federal income taxes withheld from an employee's wages are expenses of the employee, not the employer, they should not be treated as liabilities of the employer.

12. ( ) Since Jon Company has very little employee turnover, the company has received a very favorable merit rating. As a result, Jon Company should expect to pay substantially smaller amounts of FICA taxes than normal.

13. ( ) Select Company's income before interest is $292,400 and interest expense is $86,000. Select's times interest earned is 3.4 times.

14. ( ) (Appendix 11A) Employer's FICA taxes are reported annually on a Form 940.

15. ( ) (Appendix 11A) If an employer's total FUTA taxes for the year are $100 or less, the amount due may be remitted annually rather than quarterly.

16. ( ) (Appendix 11A) As the number of withholding allowances claimed increases, the amount of income tax to be withheld increases.

17. ( ) (Appendix 11A) A special payroll bank account is used to replenish the regular bank account after all the employees are paid.

Problem II

You are given several words, phrases, or numbers to choose from in completing each of the following statements or in answering the following questions. In each case select the one that best completes the statement or answers the question and place its letter in the answer space provided.

_____ 1. On November 1, 2007, Profitable Company borrowed $50,000 by giving a 90-day, 12% note payable. The company has an annual, calendar-year accounting period and does not make reversing entries. What amount should be debited to Interest Expense on January 30, 2007?

   a. $6,000

   b. $1,500

   c. $1,000

   d. $ 500

   e. $ 0

For the next three questions, use the following information as to earnings and deductions taken from a company's payroll records for the pay period ended November 15:

Employee's Name	Earnings to End of Previous Week	Gross Pay This Week	Federal Income Taxes	Medical Insurance Deducted
Rita Hawn	$25,700	$ 800	$155.00	$ 35.50
Dolores Hopkins	930	800	134.00	35.50
Robert Allen.....................................	86,900	1,000	193.00	42.00
Calvin Ingram	18,400	740	128.00	42.00
		$3,340	$610.00	$155.00

_____ 2. Employees' FICA taxes are withheld at an assumed rate of 6.2% on the first $87,000 earned for Social Security and 1.45% of all wages earned for Medicare. The journal entry to accrue the payroll should include a:

   a. Debit to Accrued Payroll Payable for $3,340.

   b. Debit to FICA Taxes Payable—Medicare for $48.43.

   c. Debit to Payroll Taxes Expense for $765.

   d. Credit to FICA Taxes Payable—Social Security for $151.28.

   e. Credit to Accrued Payroll Payable for $2,575.

_____ 3. Assume a state unemployment tax rate of 5.4% on the first $7,000 paid each employee and a federal unemployment tax rate of 0.8% on the first $7,000 paid each employee. The journal entry to record the employer's payroll taxes resulting from the payroll should include a debit to Payroll Taxes Expense for:

   a. $249.31

   b. $277.91

   c. $293.23

   d. $349.03

   e. The entry does not include a debit to Payroll Taxes Expense.

_____ 4. The amount of the net pay is:

   a. $3340.00

   b. $2575.00

   c. $2375.29

   d. $4205.00

   e. $4304.71

Problem III

Many of the important ideas and concepts that are discussed in Chapter 11 are reflected in the following list of key terms. Test your understanding of these terms by matching the appropriate definitions with the terms. Record the number identifying the most appropriate definition in the blank space next to each term.

_____ Contingent liability
_____ Current liability
_____ Current portion of long-term debt
_____ Deferred income tax liability
_____ Employee benefits
_____ Employee earnings report
_____ Estimated liability
_____ Federal depository bank
_____ FICA taxes
_____ Form 940
_____ Form 941
_____ Form W-2
_____ Form W- 4
_____ FUTA taxes

_____ Gross pay
_____ Known liability
_____ Long-term liability
_____ Merit rating
_____ Net pay
_____ Payroll bank account
_____ Payroll deductions
_____ Payroll register
_____ Short-term note payable
_____ SUTA taxes
_____ Times interest earned ratio
_____ Wage bracket withholding table
_____ Warranty

1. Corporation income taxes that are deferred until future years because of temporary differences between GAAP and tax rules.

2. Obligation of an uncertain amount that can be reasonably estimated.

3. Potential liability that depends on a future event arising from a past transaction.

4. Withholding allowance certificate, filed with the employer, identifying the number of withholding allowances claimed.

5. Table of the amounts of income tax withheld from employee's wages..

6. Obligations due within a year or the company's operating cycle whichever is longer; paid using current assets or by creating other current liabilities.

7. Portion of long-term debt due within one year or the operating cycle, which ever is longer.

8. Yearly report by an employer to each employee showing the employee's wages subject to FICA and federal income taxes along with the amounts of taxes withheld.

9. Taxes assessed on both employers and employees under the Federal Insurance Contributions Act (FICA); these taxes fund Social Security and Medicare programs.

10. Ratio of income before interest expense (and any income taxes) divided by interest expense; reflects risk of interest commitments when income varies.

11. Agreement that obligates the seller to repair or replace a product or service when it fails to perform properly within a specified period.

12. IRS form used to report an employer's federal unemployment taxes (FUTA) on an annual filing basis.

13. Rating assigned to an employer by a state based on the employer's past record regarding unemployment.

14. Additional compensation paid to or on behalf of employees, such as premiums for medical, dental, life, and disability insurance and contributions to pension plans, and vacation pay.

15. Payroll taxes on employers assessed by the federal government to support the federal unemployment insurance program.

16. State payroll taxes on employers to support unemployment programs.

17. Total compensation earned by an employee.

18. Current obligation in the form of a written promissory note.

19. Obligations of a company with little uncertainty; set by agreements, contracts or laws; also called *definitely determinable liabilities*.

20. Amounts withheld from an employee's gross pay; also called *withholdings*.

21. Obligations not requiring payment within one year or the operating cycle, whichever is longer.

22. Gross pay less all deductions; also called *take home pay*.

23. Record of an employee's gross pay, deductions, net pay, and year-to-date information.

24. Bank account used solely for paying employees, each pay period an amount equal to the total employees' net pay is deposited in it and the employees' payroll checks are drawn on that account.

25. IRS form filed to report FICA taxes owed and remitted.

26. Record for a pay period that shows the pay period dates, regular and overtime worked, gross pay, net pay, and deductions.

27. Bank authorized to accept deposits of amounts payable to the federal government.

Problem IV

Complete the following by filling in the blanks.

1. A debt guarantee is an example of a _____ liability.

2. Promissory notes are _____ , meaning they can be transferred from party to party by endorsement.

3. Short-term notes payable are issued for many reasons. Two common reasons are:
    (1)_____ (2)_____.

4. The _____ principle requires accrued but unpaid interest to be recorded in an _____ entry at the end of an accounting period.

5. The _____ pay minus the total payroll _____ equals the amount of the net pay.

6. Good employer merit ratings give employers a reduction in their state unemployment tax rates as a reward for_____.

7. The two components of FICA taxes are _____ and _____.

8. Employers pay FICA taxes _____ to those withheld from employees.

9. (Appendix 11A) According to law, a _____ showing wages earned and taxes withheld must be given by the employer to each employee within one month after the year-end.

10. (Appendix 11A) The amount to be withheld from an employee's wages for federal income taxes is determined by (a)_____ and (b)_____.

11. (Appendix 11A) According to the wage bracket withholding table of Exhibit 11A.6 in your text, $ _____ should be withheld from the wages of an employee for federal income taxes if the employee has two exemptions and earned $680 in a week.

12. (Appendix 11A) According to the Federal Insurance Contributions Act, an employer must file an Employer's Quarterly Federal Tax Return (Form_____) within one month after the end of each _____.

13. (Appendix 11A) The _____ contains all the data needed to prepare the general journal entry to record payroll.

14. (Appendix 11A) An employee's time worked, gross earnings, deductions, and net pay for a full year are summarized in a _____.

Problem V

Glitz Company estimates that future costs to satisfy its product warranty obligation amount to 3% of sales. In January, the company sold merchandise for $50,000 cash and paid $1,200 to repair products returned for warranty work. Present the journal entries related to the product warranty.

DATE	ACCOUNT TITLES AND EXPLANATION	P.R.	DEBIT	CREDIT

Problem VI

A company whose accounting periods end each December 31 borrowed $10,000 by signing a $10,000, 12% interest-bearing, 60 day note on December 16, 2007. Complete the following entries involving this note.

DATE	ACCOUNT TITLES AND EXPLANATION	P.R.	DEBIT	CREDIT
2007				
Dec. 16				
	Borrowed cash with a 60 day, 12% note.			
31				
	To record interest on note payable.			
2008				
Feb. 14				
	To pay note with interest			

Problem VII

The following information as to earnings and deductions for the pay period ended November 15 was taken from a company's payroll records:

Employee's Name	Earnings to End of Previous Week	Gross Pay This Week	Federal Income Taxes	Medical Insurance Deducted
Rita Hawn	$25,700	$ 800	$155.00	$ 35.50
Dolores Hopkins	930	800	134.00	35.50
Robert Allen.....................................	94,100	1,000	193.00	42.00
Calvin Ingram	18,400	740	128.00	42.00
		$3,340	$610.00	$155.00

Required:

1. Calculate the employees' FICA taxes withheld assuming a rate of 6.2% on the first $94,200 earned for Social Security and 1.45% of all wages earned for Medicare, and prepare a journal entry to accrue the payroll under the assumption that all of the employees work in the office.
2. Prepare a journal entry to record the employer's payroll taxes resulting from the payroll. Assume a state unemployment tax rate of 5.4% on the first $7,000 paid each employee and a federal unemployment tax rate of 0.8% on the first $7,000 paid each employee.

DATE	ACCOUNT TITLES AND EXPLANATION	P.R.	DEBIT	CREDIT

Problem VIII (Appendix 11A)

The Payroll Register of Whiteman Sales for the <u>first week</u> of the year follows. The deductions and net pay of the first three employees have been calculated and entered.

1. Complete the payroll information opposite the name of the last employee, Fred Clarke. Use an assumed 8% FICA tax rate (Medicare and Social Security rates have been combined and rounded for ease of calculation in this problem). In addition to FICA taxes, Mr. Clarke should have $111 of federal income taxes, $20 of medical insurance, and no union dues withheld from his wages, which are chargeable to office salaries. The overtime premium rate is 50%.

PAYROLL REGISTER

EMPLOYEE'S NAME	CLOCK CARD NUMBER	DAILY TIME							TOTAL HOURS	O.T. HOURS	REG. PAY RATE		EARNINGS							
		M	T	W	T	F	S	S					REGULAR PAY		O.T. PREMIUM PAY		GROSS PAY			
Delbert Landau	12	8	8	8	7	4	0	0	35		11	00	385	00			385	00	1
Maria Garza	9	8	8	8	5	4	0	0	35		12	00	396	00			396	00	2
Ralph Webster	15	8	8	7	8	4	0	0	35		13	00	455	00			455	00	3
Fred Clarke	4	8	8	8	8	8	4	0	44	4	14	00							4
																			5

Week ending January 8, 2007

	DEDUCTIONS									PAYMENT				DISTRIBUTION					
	FICA TAXES		FEDERAL INCOME TAXES		MEDICAL INSURANCE		UNION DUES		TOTAL DEDUC-TIONS		NET PAY		CHECK NUMBER	SALES SALARIES		OFFICE SALARIES		DELIVERY WAGES	
1	30	80	65	00	20	00	10	00	125	80	259	20						385	00
2	31	68	63	00	20	00	10	00	124	68	271	32		396	00				
3	36	40	68	00	20	00	10	00	134	40	320	60		455	00				
4																			
5																			

Fundamental Accounting Principles, 18/e

2. Complete the Payroll Register by totaling its columns, and give the general journal entry to record its information.

DATE	ACCOUNT TITLES AND EXPLANATION	P.R.	DEBIT	CREDIT

Whiteman Sales uses a special payroll bank account in paying its employees. Each payday, after the general journal entry recording the information of its Payroll Register is posted, a single check for the total of the employees' net pay is drawn and deposited in the payroll bank account. This transfers funds equal to the payroll total from the regular bank account to the payroll bank account. Then special payroll checks are written on the payroll bank account and given to the employees. For the January 8 payroll, four payroll checks beginning with payroll Check No. 102 were drawn and delivered to the employees. Record this information in the Payroll Register.

3. Make the entry to record the transfer of cash to the payroll bank account for the January 8 payroll.

DATE	ACCOUNT TITLES AND EXPLANATION	P.R.	DEBIT	CREDIT

4. Make the general journal entry to record the payroll taxes levied on Whiteman Sales as a result of the payroll entered in its January 8 Payroll Register. The company has a merit rating that reduces its state employment tax rate to 1% of the first $7,000 paid each employee. (Assume the federal unemployment tax rate is 0.8%.)

DATE	ACCOUNT TITLES AND EXPLANATION	P.R.	DEBIT	CREDIT

Solutions for Chapter 11

Problem I

1.	T	9.	T
2.	T	10.	T
3.	T	11.	F
4.	T	12.	F
5.	F	13.	T
6.	T	14.	F
7.	F	15.	T
8.	T	16.	F
		17.	F

Problem II

1. D
2. D
3. A
4. C

Problem III

3	Contingent liability		17	Gross pay
6	Current liability		19	Known liability
7	Current portion of long-term debt		21	Long-term liability
1	Deferred income tax liability		13	Merit rating
14	Employee benefits		22	Net pay
23	Employee earnings report		24	Payroll bank account
2	Estimated liability		20	Payroll deductions
27	Federal depository bank		26	Payroll register
9	FICA taxes		18	Short-term note payable
12	Form 940		16	SUTA taxes
25	Form 941		10	Times interest earned
8	Form W-2		5	Wage bracket withholding table
4	Form W-4		11	Warranty
15	FUTA taxes			

Problem IV

1. contingent
2. negotiable
3. (1) to borrow money (2) to get a time extension on an account payable that is due
4. matching, adjusting
5. gross, deductions
6. providing stable employment for employees
7. Social Security taxes, Medicare taxes
8. Equal
9. Form W-2 (Wage and Tax Statement)
10. (a) the amount of his or her wages,
    (b) the number of his or her withholding allowances
11. $68
12. 941, calendar quarter
13. Payroll Register
14. Employee's Individual Earnings Record

Problem V

Jan. --	Warranty Expense ($50,000 x 0.03)	1,500.00	
	Estimated Warranty Liability...		1,500.00
--	Estimated Warranty Liability...	1,200.00	
	Cash		1,200.00

Problem VI

2007			
Dec. 16	Cash	10,000.00	
	Notes Payable..		10,000.00
31	Interest Expense..	50.00	
	Interest Payable...		50.00
2008			
Feb. 14	Interest Expense..	150.00	
	Interest Payable...	50.00	
	Notes Payable	10,000.00	
	Cash		10,200.00

Problem VII

Nov. 15	Office Salaries Expense	3,340.00	
	FICA Taxes Payable		199.71
	Employees' Federal Income Taxes Payable		610.00
	Employces' Hospital Insurance Payable		155.00
	Accrued Payroll Payable...		2,375.29

($800 + $800 + $100 + $740) x .062 = $151.28
$3,340 x .0145 = $48.43
$151.28 + $48.43 = $199.71

15	Payroll Taxes Expense...	249.31	
	FICA Taxes Payable		199.71
	State Unemployment Taxes Payable...............................		43.20
	Federal Unemployment Taxes Payable............................		6.40

$800 x 0.054 = $43.20
$800 x 0.008 = $6.40

Problem VIII (Appendix 11A)

1.

EMPLOYEE'S NAME	CLOCK CARD NUMBER	DAILY TIME							TOTAL HOURS	O.T. HOURS	REG. PAY RATE		REGULAR PAY		O.T. PREMIUM PAY		GROSS PAY		
		M	T	W	T	F	S	S											
Delbert Landau	12	8	8	8	7	4	0	0	35		11	00	385	00			385	00	1
Maria Garza	9	8	8	8	5	4	0	0	35		12	00	396	00			396	00	2
Ralph Webster	15	8	8	7	8	4	0	0	35		13	00	455	00			455	00	3
Fred Clarke	4	8	8	8	8	8	4	0	44	4	14	00	560	00	84	00	644	00	4
													1,796	00	84	00	1,880	00	5

Week ending January 8, 2007

	DEDUCTIONS									PAYMENT				DISTRIBUTION					
	FICA TAXES		FEDERAL INCOME TAXES		HOSPITAL INSURANCE		UNION DUES		TOTAL DEDUC-TIONS		NET PAY		CHECK NUMBER	SALES SALARIES		OFFICE SALARIES		DELIVERY WAGES	
1	150	40	65	00	20	00	10	00	245	40	139	60	102					385	00
2	31	68	63	00	20	00	10	00	124	68	271	32	103	396	00				
3	36	40	68	00	20	00	10	00	134	40	320	60	104	455	00				
4	51	52	111	00	20	00			182	52	461	48	105			644	00		
5	270	00	307	00	80	00	30	00	687	00	1193	00		851	00	644	00	385	00

2. Jan. 8 Sales Salaries Expense.. 851.00
   Office Salaries Expense 644.00
   Delivery Wages Expense 385.00
       FICA Taxes Payable 270.00
       Employees' Federal Income Taxes Payable 307.00
       Employees' Medical Insurance Payable........................... 80.00
       Employees' Union Dues Payable 30.00
       Accrued Payroll Payable.. 1,193.00

3. Jan. 8 Accrued Payroll Payable.. 1,193.00
       Cash 1,193.00

4. Jan. 8 Payroll Taxes Expense.. 184.24
       FICA Taxes Payable 270.00
       State Unemployment Taxes Payable 18.80
       Federal Unemployment Taxes Payable 15.04

270   Fundamental Accounting Principles, 18/e

CHAPTER 12
ACCOUNTING FOR PARTNERSHIPS

Learning Objective C1:

Identify characteristics of partnerships and similar organizations.

Summary

Partnerships are voluntary associations, involve partnership agreements, have limited life, are not subject to income tax, include mutual agency, and have unlimited liability. Organizations that combine selected characteristics of partnerships and corporations include limited partnerships, limited liability partnerships, "S" corporations, and limited liability companies.

Learning Objective A1:

Compute partner returns on equity and use it to evaluate partnership performance.

Summary

Partner return on equity provides each partner an assessment of his or her return on equity invested in the partnership.

Learning Objective P1:

Prepare entries for partnership formation.

Summary

A partner's initial investment is recorded at the market value of the assets contributed to the partnership.

Learning Objective P2:

Allocate and record income and loss among partners.

Summary

A partnership agreement should specify how to allocate partnership income or loss among partners. Allocation can be based on a stated ratio, capital balances, or salary and interest allowances to compensate partners for differences in their service and capital contributions.

Learning Objective P3:

Account for the admission and withdrawal of partners.

Summary

When a new partner buys a partnership interest directly from one or more existing partners, the amount of cash paid from one partner to another does not affect the partnership total recorded equity. When a new partner purchases equity by investing additional assets in the partnership, the new partner's investment can yield a bonus to either existing partners or to the new partner. The entry to record a withdrawal can involve payment from either (1) the existing partners' personal assets or (2) from partnership assets. The latter can yield a bonus to either the withdrawing or remaining partners.

Learning Objective P4:

Prepare entries for partnership liquidation.

Summary

When a partnership is liquidated, losses and gains from selling partnership assets are allocated to the partners according to their income-and-loss-sharing ratio. If a partner's capital account has a deficiency that the partner cannot pay, the other partners share the deficit in their relative income-and-loss-sharing ratio.

I. **Partnership Form of Organization**—An unincorporated association of two or more people to pursue a business for profit as co-owners.

   A. Characteristics of Partnerships

      1. Voluntary association.

      2. Partnership contract (called *articles of copartnership*)—should be in writing but may be expressed orally.

      3. Limited life—death, bankruptcy, or expiration of the contract period automatically ends a partnership.

      4. Taxation—not subject to tax on income—partners report their share of income on personal income tax return.

      5. Mutual agency—each partner is an agent of the partnership and can enter into and bind it to any contract within the normal scope of its business.

      6. Unlimited liability—each general partner is responsible for payment of all the debts of the partnership if the other partners are unable to pay a share.

      7. Co-ownership of property—assets are owned jointly by all partners but claims on partnership assets are based on their capital account and the partnership contract.

   B. Organizations with Partnership Characteristics

      1. Limited Partnership (LP or Ltd.) has two classes of partners, general (at least one) and limited. The general partners assume unlimited liability for the debts of the partnership. The limited partners assume no personal liability beyond their invested amounts and cannot take active role in managing the company.

      2. Limited Liability Partnership (LLP) is designed to protect innocent partners from malpractice or negligence claims resulting from the acts of another partner. Generally, all partners are personally liability for other partnership debts.

      3. "S" Corporation has 75 or fewer stockholders, is treated as a partnership for income tax purposes but otherwise is accounted for as a "C" corporation.

      4. Limited Liability Company (LLC or LC) owners are called members, are protected with the limited liability feature of corporations and can assume an active management role. The LLC has a limited life and is typically classified as a partnership for tax purposes.

   B. Choosing a Business Form

      Factors to be considered include: taxes, liability risk, tax and fiscal year-end, ownership structure, estate planning, business risks, and earnings and property distributions.

II.   **Basic Partnership Accounting**—Same as accounting for a proprietorship except for transactions directly affecting partners' equity. Use separate capital and withdrawal accounts for each partner. Allocates net income or loss to partners according to the partnership agreement.

    A.   Organizing a Partnership
Each partner's investment is recorded at an agreed upon value, normally the market value of the assets and liabilities at their date of contribution.

    B.   Dividing Income and Loss
1. Any agreed upon method of dividing income or loss is allowed. If there is no agreement, the net income or loss is divided equally.

2. Common methods of dividing partnership earnings use:

    a.   Stated ratio.

    b.   Allocation on capital balances.

    c.   Allocation on service, capital, and stated ratio—salary and interest allowances, and a fixed ratio are specified—when income exceed allowances, the remainder is allocated to individual partners using a fixed ratio and added to their individual planned allowance. But when allowances exceed the income, the negative amount or shortage is allocated using the ratio and applied *against* each partner's total allowance.

3. Salaries to partners and interest on partners' investments are not partnership expenses; they are allocations of net income.

4. Partners may agree to salary and interest allowances to reward unequal contributions of services or capital.

    C.   Partnership Financial Statements
Similar to a proprietorship except:
1. The statement of partners' equity usually shows changes for each partner's capital account, including the allocation of income.

2. The balance sheet generally lists a separate capital account for each partner.

III. **Admission and Withdrawal of Partners**

    A. Admission of a Partner—two means:

        1. Purchase of partnership interest.

           a. The purchase is a personal transaction between one or more current partners and the new partner.

           b. Purchaser does not become a partner until accepted by the current partners.

           c. Involves a reallocation of current partners' capital to reflect the transaction.

        2. Investing assets in a partnership.

           a. The transaction is between the new partner and the partnership. Invested assets become partnership property.

           b. New partner's equity recorded for assets invested may be equal to, less than, or greater than investment.

           c. When the recorded new partner's equity differs from investment, there is a bonus to new or old partner's equity.

           d. Bonuses to old partners are allocated based on their income and loss sharing agreement.

    B. Withdrawal of a Partner—two means:

        1. Withdrawing partner sells his or her interest to another person who pays cash or other assets to the withdrawing partner.

        2. Cash or other assets of the partnership can be distributed to the withdrawing partner in settlement of his or her interest.

           a. Withdrawing partner may accept assets equal to, less than, or greater than his/her equity.

           b. When the withdrawing partner's equity differs from assets withdrawn, there is a bonus to remaining or withdrawing partner's equity.

           c. Bonuses to remaining partners are allocated based on their income and loss sharing agreement.

    C. Death of a Partner

        1. Dissolves a partnership.

        2. Deceased partner's estate is entitled to receive his or her equity. Contract usually calls for closing of the books and determining current value of assets and liabilities to update equity.

        3. Settlement of the deceased partner's equity can involve selling the equity to remaining partners or to an outsider, or it can involve withdrawing assets.

IV.   **Liquidation of a Partnership**

    A. Involves four steps:

       1. Noncash assets are sold for cash and a gain or loss on liquidation is recorded.

       2. Allocate gain or loss on liquidation is to partners using their income-and-loss ratio.

       3. Pay or settle liabilities.

       4. Distribute any remaining cash to partners based on their capital balances.

    B. Allocating gains or losses on liquidation may result in:

       1. No capital deficiencies—all partners' have a zero or credit balance in their capital accounts equivalent to final distribution of cash.

       2. Capital deficiencies—when at least one partner has a debit balance in his/her capital account.

          a. Partners with a capital deficiency must, if possible, cover the deficit by paying cash into the partnership.

          b. When a partner is unable to pay the deficiency, the remaining partners with credit balances absorb the unpaid deficit according to their income-and-loss ratio. Inability to cover deficiency does not relieve partner of liability.

V.   **Decision Analysis—Partner Return on Equity**

    A. Evaluates partnership success compared with other opportunities.

    B. Computed separately for each partner.

    C. Computed by dividing partner's share of net income by that partner's average partner equity.

Problem I

The following statements are either true or false. Place a (T) in the parentheses before each true statement and an (F) before each false statement.

1. ( ) Partnership accounting is exactly like that of a single proprietorship except for transactions affecting the partners' equities.

2. ( ) Although a partner does not work for either a salary or interest, to be fair in the distribution of partnership earnings, it is often necessary to provide allowances for services and investments.

3. ( ) In the liquidation of a partnership, after selling all assets and paying all debts, the partners share any remaining cash equally.

4. ( ) When a partner withdraws from a partnership, that partner always withdraws assets equal to his equity.

5. ( ) Partners return on equity is computed by dividing a partner's average investment by that partner's share of net income.

Problem II

You are given several words, phrases, or numbers to choose from in completing each of the following statements or in answering the following questions. In each case select the one that best completes the statement or answers the question and place its letter in the answer space provided.

_____ 1. Reggie and Veronica began a partnership by investing $28,000 and $20,000, respectively, and during its first year the partnership earned a $42,000 net income. What would be the share of each partner in the net income if the partners had agreed to share by giving a $16,400 per year salary allowance to Reggie and an $18,000 per year salary allowance to Veronica, plus 10% interest on their beginning-of-year investments, and the remainder equally?

    a. Reggies' share, $20,600; Veronica's share, $21,400.
    b. Reggies' share, $22,200; Veronica's share, $19,800.
    c. Reggies' share, $21,400; Veronica's share, $20,600.
    a. Reggies' share, $24,500; Veronica's share, $17,500.
    b. Reggies' share, $21,000; Veronica's share, $21,000.

_____ 2. Red and White operate a partnership in which they have agreed to share profits and losses in a ratio of 3:2 respectively. They have agreed to accept Blue as a partner, offering him a 25% share for an $80,000 investment. Prior to his investment the combined equity of Red and White totals $120,000. The admission of Blue as a partner will result in

    a. a bonus of $30,000 to Blue.
    b. a bonus of $18,000 to Red and $12,000 to White.
    c. a bonus of $30,000 each to Red and Blue.
    d. a bonus of 15,000 each to Red and Blue.
    e. no bonus for any of the parties.

Problem III

Many of the important ideas and concepts discussed in Chapter 12 are reflected in the following list of key terms. Test your understanding of these terms by matching the appropriate definitions with the terms. Record the number identifying the most appropriate definition in the blank space next to each term.

_____ C corporation
_____ General partner
_____ General partnership
_____ Limited liability company (LLC)
_____ Limited liability partnership (LLP)
_____ Limited partners
_____ Limited partnership

_____ Mutual agency
_____ Partner return on equity
_____ Partnership
_____ Partnership contract
_____ Partnership liquidation
_____ S Corporation
_____ Statement of partners' equity
_____ Unlimited liability

1. Partners who have no personal liability for partnership debts beyond the amounts they have invested in the partnership.

2. Partnership in which all partners have mutual agency and unlimited liability for partnership debts.

3. A partnership that has two classes of partners, limited partners and general partners.

4. Partner who assumes unlimited liability for the debts of the partnership; the general partner in a limited partnership is responsible for its management.

5. Legal relationship among partners whereby each partner is an agent of the partnership and is able to bind the partnership to contracts within the scope of the partnership's business.

6. Agreement among partners that sets terms under which the affairs of the partnership are conducted.

7. Legal relationship among general partners that makes each of them responsible for partnership debts if the other partners are unable to pay their shares.

8. Unincorporated association of two or more persons to pursue a business for profit as co-owners.

9. Corporation that does not qualify for and elect to be treated as a partnership for income tax purposes and therefore is subject to income taxes.

10. Partnership in which partner is not personally liable for malpractice or negligence unless that partner is responsible for providing the service that resulted in the claim.

11. Dissolution of a business partnership by (1) selling noncash assets and allocating the gain or loss according to partners' income-and-loss ratio, (2) paying liabilities, and (3) distributing any remaining cash according to partners' capital balances.

12. Corporation that meets special tax qualifications so as to be treated as a partnership for income tax purposes.

13. Financial statement that shows the total capital balances at the beginning of the period, any additional investment by partners, the income or loss of the period, the partners' withdrawals, and the ending capital balances; also called *statement of partners' capital*.

14. Form of organization that combines corporation and limited partnership features; provides limited liability to its members (owners), and allows members to actively participate in management.

15. Partner net income divided by average partner equity.

Problem IV

Complete the following by filling in the blanks.

1. A _____ (limited, general) partnership has two classes of partners.

2. Blake and Dillon are partners who have always shared incomes and losses equally. Hester has sued the partners on a partnership debt and obtained a $12,000 judgment. The partnership and Dillon have no assets; consequently, Hester is attempting to collect the entire $12,000 from Blake. Blake has sufficient assets to pay the judgment but refuses, claiming she is liable for only one-half of the $12,000. Hester _____ (can, cannot) collect the entire $12,000 from Blake because _____.

3. Since a partnership is a voluntary association, an individual _____ (can, cannot) be forced against his will to become a partner; and since a partnership is based on a contract, its life is _____.

4. Partners work for partnership _____ and not for a salary. Furthermore, when a partnership agreement calls for an interest and/or salary allowance, these allowances are only used to calculate the allocation of _____.

5. The phrase mutual agency, when applied to a partnership, means _____
    _____
    _____.

6. The four steps in the liquidation of a partnership are:
    _____
    _____
    _____
    _____.

7. If the allocation of loss from sale of the assets results in a deficit balance in a partner's capital account, that partner is responsible for making up the negative amount. If the partner fails to make up the negative then the other partners _____
    _____.

Problem V

Flip and Flop began a partnership by investing $14,000 and $10,000, respectively, and during its first year the partnership earned a $21,000 net income. Complete the tabulation below to show, under the several assumptions, the share of each partner in the $21,000 net income.

		Flip's Share	Flop's Share
1.	The partners failed to agree as to the method of sharing............	_____	_____
2.	The partners had agreed to share in their beginning-of-year investment ratio	_____	_____
3.	The partners had agreed to share by giving an $8,200 per year salary allowance to Flip and a $9,000 per year salary allowance to Flop, plus 10% interest on their beginning-of-year investments, and the remainder equally........	_____	_____

Solutions for Chapter 12

Problem I

1. T
2. T
3. F
4. F
5. F

Problem II

1. A
2. B

Problem III

9	C corporation	5	Mutual agency
4	General partner	15	Partner return on equity
2	General partnership	8	Partnership
14	Limited liability company (LLC)	6	Partnership contract
10	Limited liability partnership	11	Partnership liquidation
1	Limited partners	12	S Corporation
3	Limited partnership	13	Statement of partners' equity
		7	Unlimited liability

Problem IV

1. limited
2. can, each partner has unlimited liability for the debts of the partnership
3. cannot, limited
4. profits, or earnings, profits or earnings (net income also correct)
5. each partner is an agent of the partnership and can bind it to contracts
6. (1) Noncash assets are sold for cash and a gain or loss on liquidation is recorded; (2) gain or loss on liquidation is allocated to partners using their income-and-loss ratio; (3) liabilities are paid; and (4) remaining cash is distributed to partners based on their capital balances.
7. must absorb the negative amount according to their ratio for sharing income or loss.

Problem V

1. $10,500, $10,500
2. $12,250, $8,750
3. $10,300, $10,700

APPENDIX B
TIME VALUE OF MONEY

Learning Objective C1:

Describe the earning of interest and the concepts of present and future values.

Summary

Interest is the payment by a borrower to the owner of an asset for its use. Present and future value computations are a way for us to estimate the interest component of holding assets or liabilities over a period of time.

Learning Objective P1:

Apply present value concepts to a single amount by using interest tables.

Summary

The present value of a single amount received at a future date is the amount that can be invested now at the specified interest rate to yield that future value.

Learning Objective P2:

Apply future value concepts to a single amount by using interest tables.

Summary

The future value of a single amount invested at a specified rate of interest is the amount that would accumulate by the future date.

Learning Objective P3:

Apply present value concepts to an annuity by using interest tables.

Summary

The present value of an annuity is the amount that can be invested now at the specified interest rate to yield that series of equal periodic payments.

Learning Objective P4:

Apply future value concepts to an annuity by using interest tables.

Summary

The future value of an annuity invested at a specified rate of interest is the amount that would accumulate by the date of the final payment.

Appendix Outline

I. **Present Value and Future Value Concepts**

   A. As time passes, certain assets and liabilities that are held grow.

   B. Growth is due to interest.

   C. Present and future value computations are a way for us to measure or estimate the interest component of holding assets or liabilities over time.

II. **Present Value of a Single Amount**

   A. The present value of a single amount received at a future date is the amount that can be invested now at the specified interest rate to yield that future value.

   B. A table of present values for a single amount shows the present values of $1 for a variety of interest rates and a variety of time periods that will pass before the $1 is received.

II. **Future Value of a Single Amount**

   A. The future value of a single amount invested at a specified rate of interest is the amount that would accumulate by the future date.

   B. A table of future values of a single amount shows the future values of $1 invested now at a variety of interest rates for a variety of time periods.

III. **Present Value of an Annuity**

   A. An *ordinary annuity* is defined as equal end-of-period payments at equal intervals.

   B. The present value of an annuity is the amount that can be invested now at the specified interest rate to yield that series of equal periodic payments.

   C. A table of present values for an annuity shows the present values of annuities where the amount of each payment is $1 for different numbers of periods and a variety of interest rates.

IV. **Future Value of an Annuity**

   A. The future value of an annuity invested at a specified rate of interest is the amount that would accumulate by the date of the final payment.

   B. A table of future values for an annuity shows the future values of annuities where the amount of each payment is $1 for different numbers of periods and a variety of interest rates.

Problem I

The following statements are either true or false. Place a (T) in the parentheses before each true statement and an (F) before each false statement.

1. (   ) In discounting, the number of periods must be expressed in terms of 6-month periods if interest is compounded semiannually.

2. (   ) One way to calculate the present value of an annuity is to find the present value of each payment and add them together.

3. (   ) A table for the future values of 1 can be used to solve all problems that can be solved using a table for the present values of 1.

4. (   ) Erlich Enterprises should be willing to pay $100,000 for an investment that will return $20,000 annually for 8 years if the company requires a 12% return. (Use the tables to get your answer.)

Problem II

You are given several words, phrases, or numbers to choose from in completing each of the following statements or in answering the following questions. In each case select the one that best completes the statement or answers the question and place its letter in the answer space provided. Use the tables in your text as necessary to answer the questions.

_____ 1. Ralph Norton has $300 deducted from his monthly paycheck and deposited in a retirement fund that earns an annual interest rate of 12%. If Norton follows this plan for 1 year, how much will be accumulated in the account on the date of the last deposit? (Round to the nearest whole dollar.)

    a. $3,600.
    b. $4,032.
    c. $3,805.
    d. $7,240.
    e. $4,056.

_____ 2. Maxine Hansen is setting up a fund for a future business. She makes an initial investment of $15,000 and plans to make semiannual contributions of $2,500 to the fund. The fund is expected to earn an annual interest rate of 8%, compounded semiannually. How much will be in the fund after five years?

    a. $52,218.
    b. $36,706.
    c. $68,600.
    d. $45,332.
    e. $51,373.

_____ 3. Tricorp Company is considering an investment that is expected to return $320,000 after four years. If Tricorp demands a 15% return, what is the most that it will be willing to pay for this investment?

    a. $320,000.
    b. $177,696.
    c. $182,976.
    d. $ 45,216.
    e. $278,272.

_____ 4. Tom Snap can invest $6.05 for 17 years, after which he will be paid $10. What annual rate of interest will he earn?

    a. 15%.

    b. 9%.

    c. 7%.

    d. 5%.

    e. 3%.

Problem III

Complete the following by filling in the blanks. Use the tables in Appendix C to find the answers.

1. Leila Turner expects to invest $0.83 at a 7% annual rate of interest and receive $2 at the end of the investment. Turner must wait _____ years before she receives payment.

2. Jim Ables expects to invest $5 for 35 years and receive $102.07 at the end of that time. He will earn interest at a rate of _____% on this investment.

Solutions for Appendix B

Problem I

1. T
2. T
3. T
4. F

Problem II

1. C
2. A
3. C
4. E

Problem III

1. Table E-1 show that when the interest rate = 7% and the present value of 1 = 0.4150 ($0.83/$2), the number of periods = 13.

2. Table E-2 shows that when the number of periods = 35 and the future value of 1 = 20.4140 ($102.07/$5), the interest rate = 9%.